the world's best
street
food

where to find it
& how to make it

Melbourne * London * Oakland

BARTOSZ HADYNIAK / ISTOCKPHOTO.C

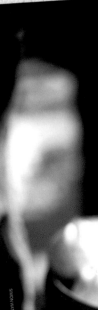

SIMON WATSON | GETTY C

* Sweet *

*

Contents

*

* Introduction *

By Tom Parker Bowles

You never forget the first time. Mine took place, nearly 20 years back, on an insalubrious backstreet in Bangkok's Patpong. The experience was brief, and fairly inglorious, but remains seared in my soul forever. One taste was all it took. The stall was little more than a pushcart with a bright yellow awning. A tattered advert for Carnation milk hung precariously from the side while the owner, a small woman in a Coca-Cola cap, gossiped incessantly with a friend perched on a wobbly plastic stool. Workspace was severely limited, as a huge wooden pestle and mortar dominated the display. Neatly arranged around it, like small satellites circling the sun, were metal bowls filled with ingredients of every hue.

As a street-food virgin, I wasn't exactly sure where to start. A friend more experienced in the ways of the road had told me about *som tam*. 'Just look for the stall with the fat, shiny green fruit. And someone pounding the hell out of their mortar.' So I giggled nervously and pointed at the plump papaya. The lady stopped her chat and smiled back. 'You want farang hot? Or Thai hot?' she asked as she threw a handful of green beans into the dark wooden depths. 'Umm, Thai hot,' I muttered, puffing out my chest. 'OK,' she answered, adding what seemed like a suicidal amount of scud chillies, along with a few cloves of garlic. She pounded and mixed

with a technique well honed by experience. I was mesmerised. Dried shrimp and peanuts were dropped in. Pound, pound, mix, mix, mix. Then palm sugar and tomatoes. Pound, pound, mix, mix. And lime juice and fish sauce. Pound, pound, mix. Then a mass of green papaya, cut into the thinnest of strands. One final mix, and it was dumped onto a polystyrene tray and handed over.

I took a bite. The first taste was sharp and fresh, then salty, from the chewy dried shrimp. Sweetness came next, underscoring and smoothing every discordant note. Tomatoes jostled with peanuts and crisp green beans as they swirled around my mouth. An involuntary smile spread across my face. This was food like I'd never tasted before, big, ballsy and beautifully balanced, the sort of thing to restore one's faith in life, love, the universe...then the chillies hit. Hard. So hard that my eyes flooded with tears, my tongue seemed to swell and I lost the power of speech. Even thinking hurt. It took a full five minutes for the pain to subside, replaced by that heady endorphin warmth sent in by the body to battle the pain. I looked up. Both ladies were crying. But tears of laughter rather than agony. 'You like?' asked one, between fits of hysterics. 'Yes,' I managed to mutter. 'Hell yes.'

Since then, street food has become my obsession. Some travel to drink in the culture, others to lap up the sun. I travel to eat, preferably on the street. Because this is where you'll find the real soul of a cuisine, somewhere among the taco carts and noodle stalls and baskets of herbs. Michelin stars hold little interest, with the rarest of exceptions. And the tourist restaurants, with their bland, dreary, 'safe' menus fill me with gloom. No, my first stop is always the street. The scent of wood fires and burning fat, the glare of artificial lights, the natural hubbub of regalement, and proper good cheer. No foams, or smears or strangely shaped plates. No egos, or supercilious sommeliers or dining rooms with all the atmosphere of a morgue. Just food to make the taste buds sing.

Some of the finest things to ever have passed my lips have been eaten standing up, or sitting at the most rickety of roadside tables, surrounded by diesel fumes, cigarette smoke and noise. There was that noodle soup in Luang Prabang, the buffalo broth looking like melted amber, with a depth I can only dream of re-creating. Or those *tacos al pastor* from the hole in the wall in Mexico City – thin shavings of pork doner kebab, mixed with hot sauce, and fresh salsa, and lime. Then wrapped in a steaming taco. *Takoyaki* (balls of octopus-spiked batter), eaten in the freezing Tokyo night, their outsides crisp, their innards just

the right side of molten. *Baozi* (Chinese steamed buns) in Shanghai, oyster cakes in Bangkok and *panelle* (chickpea-flour fritters), all soft, salty crunch, sold on a Palermo street corner. I could go on and on and on. Street food is the most democratic grub in the world, a place where politician eats alongside peasant, and flavours are unashamedly bold. I like the fact that countries with a strong street-food culture – Mexico, Thailand, China, Malaysia and Vietnam, to name but a few – take it very seriously indeed. Everyone has their own view as to what makes the finest tamales, samosas, stinky tofu, laksa or spring rolls.

That's not to say that everything cooked up on the sidewalk is edible gold. Far from it. There's a lot of tired, dirty, grease-soaked muck about. However, armed with this tome, you'll march straight past the second-rate pretenders. Local recommendations are worth their weight in spice, and always look for queues. High turnover not only means they must be getting something right, but that the food's cooked fresh too, as there isn't time for it to sit around. Lack of native language is unimportant. Communication of pleasure and delight is universal. A smile, or vigorous rubbing of the gut. You get to see far more of an alien culture from behind glowing charcoal or a wok than through any number of guidebooks. Find a busy stall, watch what the locals are ordering and when you arrive at the front, just smile and point. The only phrase you really need is 'thank you'. And don't be afraid. Most street-food sellers are delighted when a foreigner appreciates their work. This is a book dedicated to some of the greatest eating in the world. Clasp it to your chest and hit the streets. Gastronomic bliss awaits.

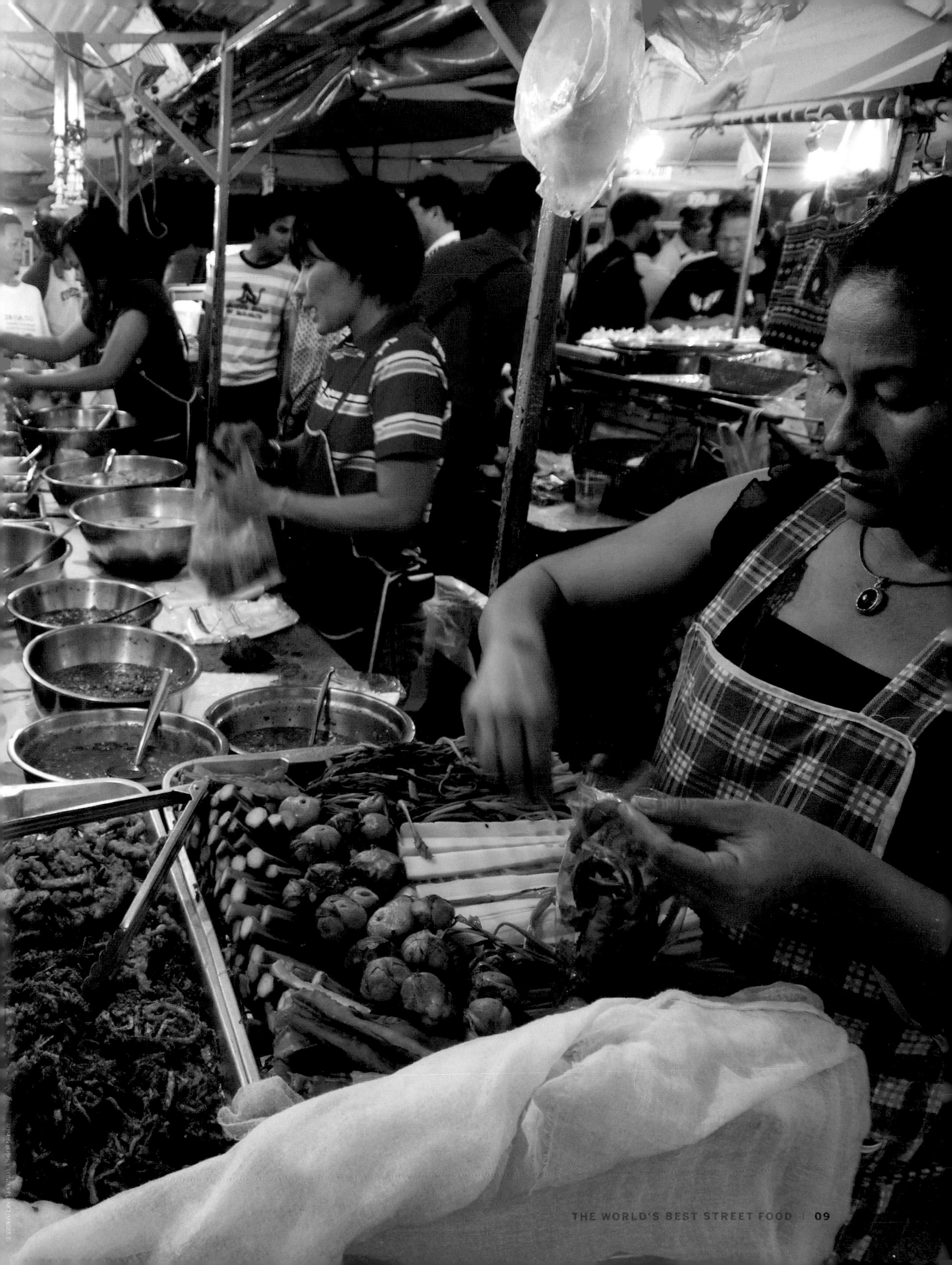

THE WORLD'S BEST STREET FOOD

* Savoury *

Legend

Recipe

(E) **Easy** - A very basic recipe, eg, putting together a sandwich or tossing salad ingredients.

(M) **Medium** - Suitable for the average home cook.

(C) **Complex** - Several parts to make, or lots of ingredients to prepare, or a specific technique involved that may take some practice.

Utensils

 Hands

 Knife * Fork * Spoon

Chopsticks

Drinks

Spicy   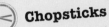 **Vegetarian**

Note Definitions for words in blue in the recipes can be found in the glosssary on page 214.

* Acarajé *

SALVADOR, BAHIA, BRAZIL

A tantalising taste of Africa in the New World, these shrimp-stuffed black-eyed pea fritters are Brazil's most beloved street food.

What is It?

Acarajé begins with black-eyed peas, soaked in water, hulled and mashed into a paste. The resulting batter is then dropped by the ladleful into a sizzling vat of *dendê* – the highly scented, reddish palm oil characteristic of traditional Bahian cooking – and finally enhanced with a variety of other spicy and savoury accompaniments.

Origin

Acarajé was originally brought to Brazil by Yoruba-speaking slaves from West Africa, where bean fritters known as *akará* were (and continue to be) a staple of the local diet. In the New World, *acarajé* evolved into a sacred food, strongly associated with the Afro-Brazilian religion Candomblé and figuring prominently in ritual meals offered to Lansã, goddess of fire, wind, thunder and lightning. Women from the religious sisterhood of Lansã became the first – and for many decades, the only – *acarajé* vendors, their presence in the streets already well documented in the 19th century.

Tasting

Acarajé is sold on street corners throughout Bahia, but especially in the capital city, Salvador. The best and most traditional carts are still operated by *baianas de acarajé,* women clad in the white hooped skirts, blouses and headscarves associated with Candomblé priestesses. *Baianas* typically sit behind a tray displaying their wares, stirring the *acarajé* batter with a giant wooden spoon and frying as needed throughout the day.

Hot from the fryer, each fritter is sliced open. Then comes the fun part – choosing from the various fillings on display: spicy *malagueta* pepper sauce, dried shrimp, *vatapá* (a paste made from ground peanuts and/or cashews, coconut milk, palm oil and shrimp), *salada* (chopped tomatoes, onions and coriander) and occasionally *carurú* (a shrimp-and-okra stew). Be adventurous and pile on a little of everything. Crispy, smooth, pungent and spicy, bursting with earthy and exotic flavours, it's a combination of tastes and textures you won't encounter anywhere else on earth.

Finding It

Acarajé is never far away in Salvador; start your search near the Pelourinho, the city's historical centre. Expect to pay R$3 (US$2).

* THE CHEFS * Bahia's traditional *acarajé* vendors, the *baianas de acarajé*, are a venerable cultural icon. They've been immortalised in song, celebrated in Carnaval processions, and even honoured with a special day on Brazil's national calendar: 25 November, the Dia Nacional da Baiana de Acarajé.

* By Gregor Clark *

Recipe Acarajé

Difficult to replicate at home, these fritters are a true labour of love with the time-intensive soaking and hulling of the beans – but are well worth the effort. Deep-frying these black-eyed pea patties in *dendê* oil will give them their characteristic red hue but if you do not have a Brazilian grocer handy, vegetable or canola oil is an acceptable substitute. Improvise on the *malagueta* pepper sauce filling with hot Tabasco and chopped green tomatoes.

YOU'LL NEED

400g (14oz) dried black-eyed peas

1 onion, roughly chopped

1 tsp salt

dendê oil for deep frying

dried shrimp, hot pepper sauce and chopped green tomatoes to serve

METHOD

1. Soak the peas overnight in plenty of cold water.

2. Skin the peas by rubbing and breaking them up or by quickly pulsing in a food processor, resoaking in water and letting the loosened skins come up to the surface.

3. Discard the skins and drain the peas.

4. Using a food processor, puree the peas with the onion and salt into a smooth mixture.

5. Divide the mixture into equal size balls and flatten each ball into the shape of a hamburger patty.

6. Heat the oil in a deep-fryer or heavy-bottomed saucepan.

7. Fry each patty until it becomes golden brown in colour on both sides.

8. Slit each patty horizontally and fill the *acarajé* sandwich with dried shrimp, pepper sauce and green tomatoes.

9. Serve immediately.

MAKES APPROXIMATELY 10–12 PATTIES

* Arancino *

SICILY, ITALY

A deep-fried fistful of flavour, the _arancino_ (or _arancina_ if you're from Palermo) – a plump, golden croquette of rice, meat and melted cheese – is the king of Sicilian street food.

What is It?

Arancini are made with rice, saffron, a smidgen of _ragù_ (meat sauce), peas and a few cubes of cheese. The ingredients are rolled into a ball, coated with breadcrumbs and fried until they're a golden orange colour – hence the name _arancino_ or 'little orange'. They are typically served in takeaways and cafes as a snack or appetiser.

Finding It

Try Pasticceria Alba in Palermo or Spinella in Catania. Expect to pay about €2.80 (US$4).

Tasting

Although they're a Sicilian icon, _arancini_ combine flavours from the whole of Italy: saffron-tinted risotto from Milan, _ragù_ from Bologna and cheese from southern Italy. They're served across the country, but for the full-on _arancino_ experience, join the locals in a Sicilian cafe and eat yours standing at the bar. Here they'll be piled up like cannonballs before a battle and handed out with practised dexterity by well-drilled bar staff. Eating one is a deliciously messy operation. Once you've bitten through the crisp, crunchy coating into the soft insides, you'll have to contend with fallout from seeping rice, escaping peas, and strings of gluey melted cheese. But don't worry. This is Sicily, where people revel in food and even simple bar snacks are enjoyed with operatic gusto.

Origin

The _arancino_ has its origins in the Arabic cuisine that Sicily's 9th- and 10th-century Saracen rulers brought with them from North Africa. However, it wasn't until the 13th century that chefs started coating rice balls with breadcrumbs and frying them. The idea was to conserve the rice and provide King Federico II with a portable snack for his long hunting trips. _Ragù_ was a later modification, added after the Spanish introduced the tomato into Italy in the 16th century.

* VARIATIONS * _Arancini_ come in various shapes and sizes: in Palermo, they're usually round; in Messina and Catania they're often pear-shaped. Fillings also vary, combining all sorts of ingredients, including mozzarella, ham, spinach, eggplant and seafood. There's even a sweet _arancino_ that's traditionally served in Palermo on the feast day of Santa Lucia (13 December).

* By Duncan Garwood *

Recipe Arancino

YOU'LL NEED

Rice Mix

500g (1lb) arborio rice

salt

1 sachet saffron powder (0.1g)

3 egg yolks

100g (¼lb) grated pecorino or parmesan cheese

30g (1oz) butter

Ragù Filling

½ onion, finely chopped

1 tbs butter

olive oil

150g (5oz) mince (beef, pork or a mixture of both)

½ cup red wine

2 tbs tomato paste

salt

pepper

80g (2½oz) peas (fresh or frozen)

Assembly & Frying

100g (¼lb) *provola, caciocavallo* or mozzarella cheese

2 eggs, beaten

breadcrumbs

peanut or olive oil

METHOD

1. Cook the rice in lightly salted boiling water.

2. Mix the saffron powder with the egg yolks, and add to the drained rice.

3. Stir in the grated pecorino (or parmesan) cheese and butter.

4. Spread the rice mix out on a large plate to cool for up to two hours.

5. Fry the onion in butter and a couple of tablespoons of olive oil until softened.

6. Add the mince, and cook for a few minutes.

7. Add the red wine.

8. Dilute the tomato paste in a glass of water; add to the mince when the wine has virtually evaporated.

9. Add salt and pepper to taste and cook on a moderate heat for about 20 minutes.

10. While the *ragù* is simmering, cook the peas in water and a tablespoon of olive oil for about 10 minutes, then add them to the mince.

11. Cut the *provola* (or *caciocavallo* or mozzarella) cheese into small cubes.

12. Take enough rice mix to form a flattened patty on your hand. Make an indentation in the middle and fill it with a spoonful of *ragù* and two or three cubes of cheese. Place a second patty of rice mix on top of the first and shape into a ball.

13. Coat the ball with beaten egg and breadcrumbs.

14. Fry the ball in oil heated to about 180°C (350°F). When it's a rich orange-gold colour, remove, and drain of oil.

15. Repeat for each ball.

16. Serve *arancini* hot or at room temperature.

MAKES UP TO 15 *ARANCINI*

* Balık Ekmek *

TURKEY

A fish sandwich to fill your fist (and stomach), *balık ekmek* combines the best of Turkey: fresh fish, sweet tomatoes, olive oil, the tang of lemons, and camaraderie between cook and consumer.

What is It?

A fried fish fillet inserted in half a crusty Turkish loaf with roughly chopped lettuce, onion and fresh tomato, then laced with a generous squeeze of lemon juice. Wrapped in butcher's paper, it's best eaten straight from the grill. There's nothing gourmet about *balık ekmek,* but that's the fun of it. It's oily, lemony, net-fresh fish – an experience hard to beat.

Origin

A seaside equivalent of the ubiquitous Turkish kebab, *balık ekmek* evolved when entrepreneurial fishermen in Istanbul decided to cut out the middle man and sell direct to the hungry masses. Setting up grills right on their boats near the Galata Bridge, they fried fish while rolling with the swell of the Bosphorus, and served it up to porters, merchant sailors, commuters and stevedores who waited on the quayside.

Finding It

Beside the Galata Bridge in Istanbul, fish is cooked in bulk by fellows in embroidered waistcoats then the whole thing put together with a flourish; crowds are eager, turnover is swift. You'll find it in other Turkish seaside towns during the holiday season. Expect to pay 5TL (US$2.80).

Tasting

Start slowly – the fish is piping hot, and quite oily – and take care not to get a mouthful of butcher's paper. Tuck into the light, spongy, white bread, which beautifully soaks up hot pan juices, lemon juice and fish oils. Once you get a taste of sweet mackerel offset with the tartness of citrus, you'll want to wolf it down. Crisp lettuce and onions lend the experience crunch and freshness, and the ruby tomatoes of a Turkish summer give it a sweetness that rounds out the salty, smokiness of it all. It's beyond finger-lickin', it's wipe-your-chin-with-the-back-of-your-hand good!

* TIPS * **If you dare, you might wash your *balık ekmek* down with a glass of vinegary *salgam* (pickle syrup). That's what hard-core Istanbullus do; salty yoghurt *ayran,* or a glass of *çay* (tea), is less, ahem, challenging.**

* By Will Gourlay *

Recipe Balık Ekmek

YOU'LL NEED

Turkish pide bread

mackerel (or similar oily fish), filleted

olive oil

lettuce, roughly chopped

parsley, roughly chopped

white onion, roughly chopped

tomato, sliced

lemon, quartered

sumac

chilli powder

sweet paprika

salt

METHOD

1. Slice pide bread lengthwise to 'butterfly' it.

2. Fry the mackerel fillets on a hot grill with a good splash of olive oil, three or four minutes each side.

3. When the fish is almost ready, rub the opened-out pide on the grill to absorb some oil and fishy flavour.

4. Place fried fish in the pide, add a handful of lettuce, parsley and onion, and a few slices of tomato.

5. Squeeze lemon over fish and salad.

6. Sprinkle with sumac, chilli powder, paprika and salt to taste.

* Bamboo Rice *

TAIWAN

Is 'Think globally, act locally' your motto? You can't get any more local than this delicious, dense, highly nutritious meal-in-bamboo made entirely from locally grown, gathered and hunted ingredients.

What is It?

Zhutong fan (bamboo rice) is made by stuffing thick stalks of bamboo with a mixture of glutinous rice, vegetables and wild boar meat. The stalk is then sealed (usually with tinfoil and a rubber band) and steamed over hot coals. The result is a filling and flavourful snack that's perfect for toting along on treks through mountains and jungles, or, if you're less ambitious, for just sitting on the side of the road.

Tasting

A 30-minute bus ride from Taipei's southernmost MRT station brings you to a world far removed from the urban landscape of Taipei to the riverside mountain town of Wulai. In addition to boasting some of northern Taiwan's finest hiking and hot springs, it's here on Wulai's cobblestone-paved main drag where you'll find *zhutong fan* stalls springing up in the winter months, when the bamboo is mature.

Though no one will fault you for enjoying your *zhutong fan* on the street, for a more genuine experience why not take a couple of stalks (and maybe a bottle of millet wine, another local speciality) on a bit of a trek? Hike along the river (steaming in spots – it's geothermal) until you find a spot that feels right. Crack open a bamboo stalk and peel off the outer layer like a banana skin. Then enjoy the sticky, savoury rice – held together by the onion-skin-like inner membrane and emanating the delicate fragrance of bamboo – in the time-honoured manner of the people who created the dish.

Finding It

Wulai in Taipei County and other areas with large tribal populations along Taiwan's east coast are the best places to find this dish; it's also available in Xishuangbana (Yunnan, China). It will cost around 50 to 60 Taiwan dollars (US$1.65 to $US2).

Origin

Zhutong fan owes its existence to the nutritional needs of tribal hunter-gatherers. After all, what better way to carry a full, filling and nutritionally sound meal of glutinous rice, boar meat and locally harvested vegetables than inside an easily tucked-away (in belt, quiver or loincloth) bamboo stalk?

* **VARIATIONS** * Though *zhutong fan* is typically made with pork, some tribal chefs cater to vegetarians, substituting chunks of wild mushroom for boar meat. To indicate that you're a vegetarian, say '*Wo jiu chi sude*', which, literally translated, means 'I only eat pure'.

By Joshua Samuel Brown

Recipe Taiwanese
Bamboo Cup Sticky Rice

As the particular kind of bamboo used in this street snack is only available in limited locations for a short period of the year, we've provided an alternative but similar recipe that can be much more easily produced at home. Using cups made from bamboo stalks will impart the flavour of the bamboo to the rice, but if you can't find these, use eight small pudding basins or rice bowls instead, greased with a little oil.

YOU'LL NEED

4 cups sticky rice

8–10 dried shiitake mushrooms

½ tbs dried shrimp

a little cooking oil

230g (½lb) minced pork

3 tbs thick soy sauce

2–3 shallots, chopped

boiling water

optional garnish: sweet chilli sauce, coriander leaves (cilantro)

METHOD

1. Wash the rice thoroughly and drain.

2. Reconstitute the dried mushrooms and shrimp in hot tap water for 10 minutes and then chop into pieces.

3. Stir-fry the pork with the cooking oil in a hot wok until brown. Drain excess oil.

4. Stir in the mushrooms, shrimp, soy sauce and shallots.

5. Divide the pork mixture between the bamboo cups or greased pudding bowls and press down firmly with a spoon.

6. Add rice, again packing down with a spoon, until each cup is about two-thirds full.

7. Add boiling water to just cover the rice in each cup.

8. Place the cups in a bamboo steamer. Alternatively you can place the cups directly in a large pot with about 5cm (2in) of water in the bottom, and cover with a lid.

9. Steam at a high heat for 30–35 minutes. Leave in the steamer an additional 10 minutes with the heat off before serving.

10. To serve, you can either turn the rice out onto a plate, or leave it in the cups. It's great on its own or topped with a little sweet chilli sauce and coriander leaves.

SERVES 8

* Banh Mi *

VIETNAM

A little-known culinary secret is that the world's best sandwich isn't found in Rome, Copenhagen or even New York City, but rather, on the streets of Vietnam.

What is It?

The sandwich known as *banh mi* begins with a light baguette that has been grilled over coals. After a smear of mayonnaise and a dollop of pâté are added, the crispy shell is filled with a mixture of meat, crunchy pickled vegetables and fresh herbs. *Banh mi* is then typically seasoned with a few drops of soy sauce and a spicy chilli condiment.

Finding It

If you're in Hoi An, head to Phuong, a legendary *banh mi* stall where a sandwich costs 15,000 dong (about US$0.75).

Tasting

Banh mi is the epitome of street food; the sandwiches are sold almost exclusively from informal stalls and vendors across Vietnam. If there's any seating at all at a *banh mi* stand, it usually takes the form of tiny plastic stools, and the sandwiches are generally served to go, wrapped snugly in recycled paper. Pâté? Meatballs or grilled pork? Chilli? Mayonnaise? Diners are asked to choose their meats, as well as their preferred toppings and condiments. If you're feeling indecisive, you can go for *banh mi dac biet* ('special' *banh mi* that runs the gamut of Vietnamese-style charcuterie, from head cheese to steamed sausage). Regardless, the result is crispy, meaty, rich and spicy – a collection of the best of Southeast Asian cuisine in a distinctly Western package.

Origin

Banh mi is an early example of fusion food. The dish's primary ingredients – baguette, mayonnaise and a type of pork-liver pâté – show an obvious link with the French, who introduced these foods to the Vietnamese under their tenure as colonial rulers during the early 20th century. Other ingredients, including *xa xiu*, the barbecued pork better known as *char siu*, have Chinese origins, while the herbs and seasonings are distinctively Southeast Asian. The sandwich is now popular around the world, and in 2011 the word 'banh mi' was added to the *Oxford English Dictionary*.

* **VARIATIONS** * If your *banh mi* craving extends to breakfast, you're not alone: *banh mi trung – banh mi* served with egg – is a popular way to start the day. The egg, which is scrambled or fried, can be served in the buttered baguette, or on the side.

* By Austin Bush *

Recipe Banh Mi

It won't be easy to find a true Vietnamese baguette. While a French one will make a fine substitute, try to look for a light roll that's crusty on the outside and soft on the inside. An authentic *banh mi* will also have tinned liver spread and Vietnamese-style ham, which you can find at Asian supermarkets.

YOU'LL NEED

1 long crusty bread stick, halved then sliced lengthways

whole-egg mayonnaise

1 tin liver spread or coarse liver pâté

4 slices cooked pork belly, sliced thinly

4 slices *cha lua* (Vietnamese-style ham) or mortadella

4 slices cucumber

Maggi Seasoning or light soy sauce, to taste

2 red chillies, chopped

a handful of coriander leaves (cilantro)

Carrot & Daikon Pickle

1 tsp salt

125g (4.4oz) sugar

1 medium carrot, julienned

1 daikon, julienned

1 cup white wine vinegar

1 cup water

METHOD

1. Make the pickle at least an hour before using by sprinkling the salt and 2 tsp of the sugar on the carrot and daikon in a bowl.

2. Extract as much liquid as possible by pressing on the vegetables gently.

3. Rinse with cold water and press again to extract as much water as possible.

4. In a small saucepan, gently heat the remaining sugar, vinegar and and water until the sugar dissolves.

5. Pour the vinegar mixture over the vegetables and set aside for at least an hour.

6. To assemble the *banh mi*, spread some mayonnaise on the top half of the bread stick, and the liver spread on the bottom half.

7. Layer two slices each of the pork belly, ham and cucumber. Season with Maggi Seasoning or light soy.

8. Drain the julienned carrot and daikon from the vinegar mixture and add to the sandwich.

9. Add the chillies and coriander leaves and serve immediately.

MAKES 2 SANDWICHES

* Baozi *

CHINA

This billowy, pillowy steamed or baked bun, filled with anything from slow-cooked meat and fragrant pork broth to garish custard and sweet lotus-seed paste, is hawked from the side of the road.

What is It?

Baozi is the ubiquitous Chinese steamed bun, although it can be baked or fried. There are as many fillings as there are opinions on this bite-sized snack. As common on the street as it is in dim sum shops, *baozi* is mainly eaten at breakfast and mid-morning – never, traditionally, at night.

Tasting

All over China, from dawn until after lunch, roadside pots bubble, steaming a million of these buns in small bamboo baskets. Dipped in ginger vinegar, or a splash of soy sauce, they're stodge of the finest kind. Freshness is everything, though, as they tend to sag as they cool, so try to eat within a minute or two. And beware: the broth is often piping hot. Make a small nick, and carefully suck out the juice, before wolfing down the rest.

Origin

Legend has it that the dish was created by Zhuge Liang, the great military strategist and inventor of the Three Kingdoms period (AD 220–280). While in the deep south of China his soldiers were struck down by the plague. Zhuge Liang made the buns to look like human heads and used them as both sustenance and a sacrifice to the gods, and thus cured their sickness. Mighty buns indeed.

Finding It

Xisi Baozi Restaurant, a Beijing institution, serves six types of *baozi*. It costs 18 to 26 yuan (US$3 to US$4) for a decent serving.

* VARIATIONS *

Best known, perhaps, is the Cantonese *char siu bau*, those great cumulus clouds filled with slow-cooked and sticky pork. There are specialities up and down the country, but on the whole, the northern style is salty while the southern is slightly sweet. *Meigancai*, a speciality of the south, contains dry pickled vegetables. *Goubuli* hail from Tianjin in the north and are filled with meat. In Shanghai, dumpling-like *xiaolongbao* have a stronger dough, since they generally hold more broth and are served in soup.

* By Tom Parker Bowles *

Recipe Baozi

YOU'LL NEED

Filling

250g (½lb) minced pork
(medium-lean)

3 scallions (spring onions), chopped

3 shiitake mushrooms, chopped

2 tbs ginger, finely chopped

2–3 garlic cloves, finely chopped

2 tbs dark soy sauce

1 tbs oyster sauce

1 tbs rice wine or sherry

1 tsp sugar

½ tsp sesame oil

Dough

3 tbs melted lard

¾ cup hot water

400g (14oz) plain (all-purpose) flour

1½ tsp baking powder

2 tsp instant dry yeast

4 tbs sugar

1 tsp salt

¼ cup cold water

Baking

1 tbs sesame oil

baking parchment cut into 16 squares
of 7.5cm (3in) each

METHOD

1. Mix all filling ingredients into a bowl. Set aside for one hour minimum.

2. Mix lard in with half of the hot water. Then mix together all dry ingredients for dough.

3. Pour 90% of the dry ingredients mix into the lard/water mixture, stirring vigorously with a tablespoon. Continue adding hot water until dough begins to form, then add cold water. Knead mixture for seven to eight minutes into a smooth, stiff dough. Add water as needed if too stiff to shape.

4. Allow the dough to sit and ferment until it has doubled in volume (at least 30 minutes). Then knead for a few minutes to degas.

5. Cut the dough into 16 sections. Roll each section into a small ball. Flatten and shape each ball into a thin disc approximately 11cm (4.5in) in diameter. Aim to keep dough thin around the edges.

6. Spoon roughly 1 tbs of filling into each disc's centre. Crimp edges together around the filling.

7. Brush sesame oil onto a square of baking parchment, then set the crimped bun onto it.

8. Allow the bun to rise again on a covered plate or tray for a further 20 minutes before placing in a steamer to cook for 15 minutes.

9. Once pork is thoroughly cooked through, serve hot.

MAKES 8–10 LARGE BUNS

* Bhelpuri *

MUMBAI, INDIA

A fiery constellation of vegetables, pulses, spices and chutney, *bhelpuri* is a perfect mirror for the melting-pot city that created it. It's salad, Jim, but not as you know it.

What is It?

People describe *bhelpuri* as a salad, but put any idea of tomato, cucumber and lettuce out of your mind. This fiery Indian *chaat* (savoury snack) is built on a tantalising base of crispy *sev* (fried chickpea-flour noodles), puffed rice and tamarind chutney, and layers of flavour are added in the form of tomato, onion, coriander leaves, green chilli, potato, lemon juice and spices. Eat it standing up at street stands – everyone does.

Origin

The first written recipe for *bhelpuri* is attributed to an English army cook called William Harold, who was dispatched to the streets of colonial Bombay to bring back a list of ingredients for this delicious snack so it could be added to the menu in the officers' mess. However, Indians trace the origins of this spicy treat back to the Maratha leader Chhatrapati Shivaji Maharaj, who demanded a snack that could be prepared and consumed on the way to battle.

Tasting

Bhelpuri will put your taste buds through their paces. First comes the crunch, from the rice puffs and crispy *sev* noodles. Next comes the tang – thanks to the tamarind chutney. Then comes the chilli hit, riding on a wave of masala spices, followed by lingering sweet, salt and sour aftertastes. The setting makes all the difference – this snack is best consumed on Mumbai's Chowpatty Beach, as a precursor to an evening promenade along Marine Dr, or opening-night seats for the latest Bollywood blockbuster. Many sit-down restaurants serve their own interpretations, but the best *bhelpuri* comes from street stalls and hawker stands, served on paper plates and prepared on the spot to keep all the ingredients firm and fragrant (if left to sit, the noodles lose their crispiness and the *chaat* its punch). Traditionally, *bhelpuri* is scooped from plate to mouth with the fingers of the right hand, but most vendors will provide a plastic spoon or fork if you ask.

Finding It

Surrounded by fortune-tellers, hustlers and hand-cranked Ferris wheels, the hawker stalls on Chowpatty Beach serve staggering volumes of *bhelpuri* to the crowds who gather nightly. You'll pay ₹10 to ₹30 (US$0.22 to US$0.70).

* TIPS * If you plan to make *bhelpuri* at home, the first step is to stock up on puffed rice and *sev* noodles. Indian supermarkets sell these *chaat* essentials, but premade Bombay mix is a convenient, if not entirely authentic, alternative. Chutneys are best made at home – tamarind chutney, made from dates, tamarind, chilli, sugar, salt and spices, will last for a month in the fridge, six months in the freezer.

· By Joe Bindloss ·

Recipe Bhelpuri

YOU'LL NEED

Tamarind Chutney

¼ cup fresh or dried tamarind

½ cup deseeded dates

½ cup jaggery (or soft brown sugar)

½ tsp ground cumin seed

¼ tsp ground dried chilli

¼ tsp salt

Mint Chutney

1 cup coriander leaves (cilantro)

½ cup mint leaves

3 green chillies, deseeded

1 tbs lime juice

salt to taste
water

Bhelpuri

½ cup boiled potato, finely chopped

½ cup tomato, finely chopped

½ cup red onion, finely chopped

3 green chillies, deseeded and chopped

¼ cup coriander leaves (cilantro), finely chopped

¼ cup tamarind chutney

¼ cup mint chutney

1 tbs grated ginger

1 tbs garam masala powder

salt to taste

¾ cup sev

1 cup puffed rice

1 lemon, cut into quarters, for juice

METHOD

Tamarind Chutney

Remove the seeds from your tamarind, and mash the flesh into a pulp with ½ cup of water. Squeeze the mixture through a sieve to create ½ cup tamarind water; add to a pan with the remaining ingredients, bring to the boil, then simmer for about 10 minutes. Allow the mixture to cool, then pass through a blender to create a smooth paste. Chill before serving.

Mint Chutney

Finely chop the coriander leaves, mint and chillies, then blend into a fine paste with the lime juice, salt and a little water.

Bhelpuri

1. In a large bowl, mix together the vegetables, chillies, most of the coriander leaves (reserve some for use as a garnish), chutneys and spices.

2. Add the *sev* and puffed rice to the mix, stir and serve immediately with a squeeze of lemon juice and a sprinkle of coriander leaves.

* Bo Bia *

VIETNAM

As delicate as morning dew, this Vietnamese roll wrapped in translucent rice paper is a mighty mouthful.

What is It?

Rice paper wrapped around a mixture of red Chinese sausage, dried shrimp, jicama, pickled carrot and radish, peanuts, lettuce, noodles and basil, *bo bia* is usually served with *tuong,* a tart, mildly spicy bean-paste sauce. Stalls selling *boa bia* tend to appear on Saigon streets in the late afternoon.

Tasting

Look out for the mobile carts on the streets of Saigon towards dinnertime. Freshness is key: not just of the wrappers (which tend to dry up if left too long), but the ingredients too. They're kept in a glass cabinet atop the cart, and each *bo bia* is made to order. If the rolls are sitting there, ready-made, move on or ask if they can be made in front of you.

Biting in, you get the sweet chew of the sausage, the dry, saltier hit of the shrimp, and the soft heft of the noodles, as well as crunch from jicama (part of the radish family) and pickled vegetables. All of these ingredients provide a riot of tastes and textures, and the dipping sauce, *tuong,* adds mild, tart heat. A pair makes a snack, a quartet a dinner to remember.

Origin

Bo bia is the Vietnamese version of *popiah,* a Hokkien-style spring roll found in Singapore and Malaysia. In Vietnam, the traditional wheat wrappers have been replaced with the lighter rice-paper ones, and you'll find herbs exclusive to Vietnam. The concept travelled to Vietnam (as well as Thailand, Malaysia and Singapore) when emigrants left the Fujian province of China and settled elsewhere.

Finding It

Nguyen Du St, in Saigon, is a good place to start, but you'll find *bo bia* all over town. Or try 2B Su Thien Chieu St, District 3, in Ho Chi Minh City. Expect to pay 5000 Vietnamese dong (US$0.25) each.

---

* VARIATIONS * *Gui cuon*, a rice-paper wrapper stuffed full with pork or shrimp, noodles, herbs and chopped vegetables, is *bo bia's* better-known cousin.

Recipe Bo Bia

YOU'LL NEED

light cooking oil

2 cups grated carrots

2 cups julienned jicama

1 tsp salt

fish sauce

6 eggs

5 Chinese sausage links

½ cup dried shrimp

4 cloves garlic, finely chopped

1 pack round rice paper

1 head leafy lettuce, washed
and de-ribbed

Dipping Sauce

1 cup hoisin sauce

up to ¼ cup warm water (to thin the
sauce to desired consistency)

¼ cup smooth peanut butter

1 tbs rice vinegar

1–3 minced Thai chillies, or more
depending on desired spiciness

30g (1oz) dry roasted peanuts, chopped

METHOD

Vegetable Slaw

Heat a small amount of cooking oil in a large pot. Saute the carrots, jicama, salt and fish sauce (to taste) over medium heat until the jicama and carrots have softened, but are still crunchy – about 15 minutes. Set aside.

Egg Ribbons

1. Beat the eggs in a large bowl until they are well combined.

2. Preheat a lightly oiled frying pan over a medium heat, then coat the bottom of the pan with a third of the egg mixture. Once it sets, flip it and cook the other side for a minute or so. Repeat twice more.

3. Allow the omelettes to cool, then roll them up and thinly slice the roll into ribbons.

Chinese Sausages

Add half a cup of water to a small frying pan with the sausages. Cover and bring to the boil, then allow to steam for about 10 minutes. Slice the cooled sausages on an angle as thinly as you can.

Dried Shrimp

Saute the dried shrimp and garlic in a lightly oiled pan over medium heat for about five minutes or until the garlic is golden and the shrimp are crisp. Set aside.

Wrapping

1. Place a piece of rice paper on a clean, flat surface. Wet your hand with water and apply a coat of water over the paper.

2. Place a lettuce leaf on the lower half of the rice paper. Add a good pinch of the slaw, some egg ribbons, shrimp, and about 5 slices of the sausage, evenly dotted across the paper over about 7cm (3in).

3. Fold the sides of the paper in towards the centre, then from the bottom, roll the paper up over the fillings as tightly as you can, until you're left with a perfect roll.

4. Repeat to make about 24 rolls. Best eaten soon after making.

Dipping Sauce

Mix all the ingredients except the peanuts together till smooth and the consistency is right for dipping. Top with the chopped peanuts.

* Breakfast Burrito *

NEW MEXICO, USA

In the American west, street food becomes pick-up-truck food, epitomised by the breakfast burrito: filling, inexpensive and easy to eat with one hand – while you steer with the other.

What is It?

The breakfast burrito is a rancher's or ski bum's morning meal, rendered portable by its tender flour-tortilla wrapper. Rolled up inside is what you'd find on any diner plate: scrambled eggs, home fries or hash-brown potatoes, and bacon or sausage. What makes it a New Mexican classic is diced, roasted green chilli, the state's speciality that's wake-you-up hot.

Finding It

Abe's Cantina y Cocina in Arroyo Seco, just north of Taos, doles out breakfast burritos every morning for US$4.25.

Tasting

Wrapped in foil and warm to the touch, the breakfast burrito is an enigma. There's no way to gauge the quality until you bite in. But not too fast – you can't get greedy and unwrap more than an inch or so at a time, or you'll wind up with your breakfast in your lap. A quality specimen, ideally served in a dim, family-run corner store, on a back road to a great hiking trail or a ski area, has truly crispy potatoes and a generous amount of green chilli and chewy pieces of bacon, structure so that each bite contains a bit of everything. Fortunately, a good breakfast burrito is neither large nor expensive – and even a not-great version can hit the spot, when eaten in a truck with the heater on full blast and the winter chill safely outside.

Origin

Tia Sophia's, a classic diner in Santa Fe, claims to have invented the breakfast burrito in the 1970s. But its version, which dominates the southern half of the state, is a plated dish, bloated to fill a heavy porcelain platter and smothered in red or green chilli sauce – delicious, but hardly portable. It's not clear who first made the smaller, tidier hand-held version, before Taco Bell and McDonald's started serving it nationwide in the 1980s. But New Mexicans know these versions are imposters, as they lack the essential chunks of green chilli.

* VARIATIONS * Some restaurants offer, in addition to bacon and sausage, *carne adovada* (another classic New Mexican dish of pork chunks stewed in red chilli) or cinnamon-laced Mexican chorizo. These are nice extra-local touches, though some argue that these flavours interfere with the green-chilli kick.

* By Zora O'Neill *

Recipe Breakfast Burrito

Given the number of pans required, this is a better recipe to make for a group. If wrapping up your burritos to go, make them no more than an hour in advance of eating, as the tortillas can get soggy.

YOU'LL NEED

8 strips bacon

2 potatoes, grated

salt

pepper

1–2 tbs vegetable oil

1 tsp butter

8 eggs, lightly beaten

½ cup (or more) roasted, peeled and chopped New Mexico green chillies

4 flour tortillas

METHOD

1. Cook bacon until done to your preference; set aside to cool, then tear into 2.5cm (1in) pieces. Wipe any burned pieces out of the skillet (frying pan) and pour off grease (or leave it in if you wish – it adds good flavour to the potatoes).

2. Make hash browns. Set heavy-bottomed skillet on medium heat. Squeeze out extra liquid from grated potatoes, then toss with salt and pepper. Add 1 tbs vegetable oil to skillet, then arrange potatoes in an even layer. Fry on medium heat until browned on the bottom, then flip and cook till crispy (you may need to flip repeatedly to avoid burning; you may also need additional oil). Remove from heat and set aside on paper towel to absorb excess oil. Cut or tear into 5cm (2in) pieces.

3. Prepare the eggs. Wipe skillet clean of any potato bits, then heat butter on medium-low heat until bubbling. Add a pinch of salt to the beaten egg and pour into the skillet. Stir slowly until cooked to your liking. Remove from skillet and set aside.

4. Set up your assembly line: bacon, hash browns, scrambled eggs and green chilli. Have one large plate for working on, and four more for serving (or foil to wrap up the burritos).

5. Wipe skillet clean and place over high heat. Heat tortilla in skillet until slightly puffed and dotted with brown spots – you'll want to flip it several times. Place tortilla on plate and lay out a quarter of the scrambled eggs horizontally in the centre. Add a quarter of the hash browns, then chilli and bacon, taking care to spread the ingredients evenly. Roll up the burrito, starting with the bottom third folded up over the eggs, then each end folded over, then rolling the remainder tightly away from you. Serve as is or wrap in foil.

MAKES 4 BURRITOS

* Brik *

TUNISIA

A simple and savoury pastry packet, the *brik* is a study of compatible contrasts: crispy and soft, fresh and salty, mild and tangy. It's a mouthful of all that's Mediterranean.

What is It?

The *brik* is a deep-fried, triangular 'turnover' generally filled with a whole egg, tuna, onion, harissa and parsley. Other stuffings include minced (ground) meat, potato, anchovies and capers. The casing is a thin semolina-based pastry sheet called *malsouka,* often described as a cross between filo pastry and egg/spring roll wrapping. The *brik* is a quick snack enjoyed year-round and at any time of day.

Origin

The origins of the Tunisian *brik* can be traced to the Turkish *börek* (from which its name is also derived), an ancient invention that migrated to Anatolia with the people from central Asian Turkistan hundreds of years ago. Today, according to Tunisian tradition, if a young man spills any yolk of a special *brik* prepared by his prospective wife's mother, he may not be allowed to wed. In Tunisia, the *brik* is customarily the food used to break the Ramadan fast.

Finding It

Briks are sold everywhere for about 1 dinar (US$0.75). Chez Mohsen in La Goulette is called and considered 'the king of the brik'.

Tasting

The most common, inexpensive and delicious street treat in Tunisia, the *brik* is practically a daily necessity for any traveller on a budget, anyone who likes to chat with locals, and, frankly, anyone with taste buds. Part of the delight of eating a *brik* is lining up with everyone else at a street cart or hole-in-the-wall market stall in the middle of a buzzing souk, admiring the slick movements of the *brik* maker and then savouring the airy and soft, crisp and crusty textures and fresh Mediterranean flavours. Watch how deftly practised *brik* eaters keep the soft yolk from spilling!

* TIPS * When it comes to eating a *brik*, Tunisians are quite particular. There appears to be two camps: those who start by eating the soft eggy middle (don't let it run or fall) and those who save the egg for last. Pick your tactic and stick with it, but always use your fingers.

* By Ethan Gelber *

Recipe Brik

YOU'LL NEED

170g (6oz) tinned tuna

2 tbs parsley, chopped

2 tbs grated parmesan

salt

pepper

1 small onion, finely chopped (optional)

4 outer shells (*malsouka* or substitute egg/spring roll wrappers)

4 eggs

olive oil

lemon

harissa (optional)

METHOD

1. Combine the tuna, parsley and parmesan with salt and pepper to taste. Add lightly sauteed onion if desired. Divide this mix into four equal parts.

2. Add one portion of the mix to the centre of each of four outer shells. Break an egg over the top of each one, making sure it stays in place (it helps to make a small well in the mix to hold the egg).

3. Fold the wrappers (which should be square) in half along the diagonal to make a triangular shape. Slide them into a pan of hot olive oil (about half an inch deep). Fry for a couple of minutes until golden brown on one side and then flip. Do the same to the other side.

4. Set *briks* aside to drain. Then sprinkle with lemon juice and serve hot.

MAKES 4

TIP Have harissa on hand for extra spice, or the harissa may be added to the mix before it gets cooked.

* Bsarra *

FEZ, MOROCCO

Classic Moroccan cuisine isn't about rushing (think slowly simmering *tajines*) but *bsarra* twists this concept to make the perfect street food: bowls of filling soup for workers on the go.

What is It?

Bsarra is a thick soup made from broad beans (fava beans). These are slowly cooked with garlic, and served with plenty of olive oil, a good pinch of spice and a hunk of fresh *khobz* (Moroccan bread). It's never made at home, but cooked up in great cauldrons every morning to be eaten on the way to work.

Finding It

Head to Talaa Kebira street, near Bab Bou Jeloud in the Fez medina. A bowl of *bsarra* costs around 5 dirham (US$0.60).

Tasting

Bsarra shops tend to be classic hole-in-the-wall places: open-fronted with a big soup vat in the front, and enough space behind for half a dozen people to squeeze around a bench. Rough bowls and battered spoons are the order of the day. The lake of olive oil that invariably accompanies the soup might look excessive, but it deepens the taste of the soup and gives it a smooth texture that lifts into something special. Be equally generous with the shakers of cumin and paprika, and add salt to taste. Some people prefer to dip their bread, while others tear the loaf into the soup to soak up the flavour. Either way, we'd recommend leaving at least a crust to clean the bowl with at the end. Wash the lot down with a glass of sweet and scalding mint tea and you're set for a day exploring the Moroccan souks.

Origin

Moroccans don't give much credence to the saying that breakfast is the most important meal of the day: a glass of sweet tea and a piece of bread often suffices. But workers often need something more substantial, and *bsarra* is a dish to fill the hole. Soup shops open early in the morning to cater to demand, and are washing up their pots by lunchtime – *bsarra* tends to run out by the time that the call to midday prayers rings through the medina.

* VARIATIONS * In Morocco, *bsarra* is particularly associated with Fez, but variations on the dish can be found across North Africa. In Tunisia, the beans are usually substituted with chickpeas, while Egyptian *bsarra* is often reduced down until it's more a thick paste than a soup so it can be used as a dip.

Recipe Bsarra

YOU'LL NEED

500g (1lb) dried skinless broad beans (fava beans), soaked overnight

4 cups water

8 garlic cloves, crushed

1 tsp salt

olive oil

cumin

paprika

METHOD

1. Soak the broad beans in water overnight, then drain and rinse.

2. Bring the 4 cups water to the boil and add the beans, crushed garlic and salt. Simmer for at least 30 minutes, until the beans are well cooked.

3. Blend in a food processor.

4. Serve with a generous drizzle of olive oil and sprinkle of cumin and paprika.

* Bún Cha *

HANOI, VIETNAM

Bún cha's fragrant combo of grilled pork, fresh herbs and vermicelli noodles is now found across Vietnam, but the best flavours are still in the simple street food kitchens of Hanoi.

What is It?

A sprawling serving of *bún cha* is a deceptively simple dish. Smoky pork – either marinated or minced and combined with garlic and shallots – blends with tender rice noodles and a fragrant herb-laden broth. The overflowing plate of fresh mint, coriander and lettuce on every table provides more zingy goodness. A side order of crunchy *nem cua be* (crab spring rolls) is recommended for the ultimate Hanoi lunch.

Finding It

Try *bún cha* at Bun Cha Nem Cua Be Dac Kim, in Hanoi's Old Quarter. Expect to pay around 40,000 Vietnamese dong (US$2).

Tasting

To find *bún cha,* sharpen your sense of smell and look for the mini-clouds of fragrant smoke drifting through the labyrinth of Hanoi's Old Quarter. The most humble of *bún cha* places is just a simple charcoal grill and a few kid-size pieces of furniture. Pull up a tiny blue plastic chair and bite into the smoky and caramelised pork, carefully grilled on the outside, but moist and delicate to the taste. *Bún cha* is also the ultimate DIY meal; just stir in more sweetly fragrant broth, slivers of green pawpaw, or fresh herbs, chilli and garlic for a tasty customised combination of pork and vermicelli noodles. Don't forget to save a few handfuls of herbs to go with the crab spring rolls.

Origin

In the middle of Hanoi's rapidly modernising cityscape, the preparation of *bún cha* is continuing as it has done for centuries. A single multitasking vendor often does it all, hunched over a simple charcoal grill, methodically fanning the embers to obtain the optimum amount of heat. Fuelled by unctuous fat dripping onto hot coals, lots of billowing smoke is essential to maximise the pork's fragrant marinade, and heaped plates of fresh herbs are traditionally sourced from the nearby village of Lang.

* TIPS * In Hanoi, *bún cha* is traditionally a lunchtime-only meal, and from around 10.30am to 2.30pm, hungry diners crowd into impossibly compact eateries, at sidewalk level or up rickety staircases to balconies overlooking the Old Quarter's compelling chaos. Look forward to sharing a table with a few friendly locals, and complete the experience with a plastic cup of crisp and hoppy *bia hoi* (freshly brewed Hanoi beer).

* By Brett Atkinson *

Recipe Bún Cha

A handful of *shiso* leaves (also known as *perilla* leaves), if you can find them, will add extra oomph to this delightfully herby dish.

YOU'LL NEED

500g (1lb) pork belly, sliced thinly

4 tbs fish sauce

2 tbs spring onions, chopped

2 tbs Chinese chives, chopped

4 tsp soy sauce

4 red Asian shallots, chopped

4 cloves garlic, crushed

500g (1lb) thin rice noodles, prepared as per packet directions

200g (7oz) beanshoots, trimmed

1 head of lettuce, shredded

large handful fresh Thai basil leaves

large handful fresh Vietnamese mint leaves

large handful fresh coriander leaves (cilantro)

Dressing

2 tbs fish sauce

2 tbs white wine vinegar

2 tbs sugar

½ cup water

1 red chilli, chopped

2 garlic cloves, crushed

1 tbs lime juice

METHOD

1. Combine the fish sauce, spring onions, chives, soy sauce, shallots and garlic in a shallow bowl.

2. Add the pork and marinate in the fridge for at least two hours or preferably overnight.

3. Combine all the dressing ingredients and bring them to a boil in a saucepan over medium heat. Set aside.

4. Grill the pork over medium-high heat for a few minutes on each side.

5. Assemble the salad on individual plates with a handful each of noodles, beanshoots, lettuce, herbs and pork. Pour over some dressing and serve.

SERVES 4

* Burek *

BOSNIA & HERCEGOVINA

Crisp yet moist, hearty yet subtly spiced, *burek* is *the* Balkan street food. It's savoury and filling and will fuel you through a day of exploring mountain villages or market towns.

What is It?

Filo pastry is filled with aromatic minced (ground) meat – or spinach (*zeljanica*) – and onion, cheese and herbs (*sirnici*), then rolled, glossed with either butter or olive oil and baked till golden. *Burek* can be eaten at any hour: for breakfast accompanied by black tea, or after a busy night in the bars of Sarajevo's Baščaršija district.

Tasting

Though *burek* can be eaten either hot or cold, it's best straight from the oven. The pastry will be nicely flaky on the outside – yielding a pleasing 'crunch' as you bite into it – but on the inside, where it is moistened by the contents, it should be tender, with the consistency of perfectly cooked pasta. The contents should be moist, but not gooey, offsetting the crisp outer layers. Brushed with butter or olive oil, the whole affair is slightly greasy. In Bosnia it is cooked in great spirals in round baking trays. Choose which variety you want, and the baker will slice it with a pizza cutter and wrap it in butcher's paper for you.

Origin

Found in different forms across the Balkans and beyond, *burek* originates in Turkey (where it is known as *börek*). The name comes from the Turkish *burmak* (literally 'to twist'). As the Turkish Ottoman Empire expanded from the 14th to the 18th centuries, this tasty pastry moved with it, assuming different ingredients, forms and additives.

Finding It

In Sarajevo, *pekaras* (bakeries) at either end of Pigeon Sq sell *burek* by weight. Expect to pay around 3MK to 5MK (US$2 to US$3.50) for a good serve.

* VARIATIONS * In Turkey, *sigara böregi*, generally containing white *peynir* cheese, is rolled into slim 'cigarettes' and deep-fried. Greek *galaktoboureko* is a sweet *burek* containing custard and dusted with sugar. The Tatars of the Crimea make half-moon-shaped *çig börek*, which is fried in a pan.

* By Will Gourlay *

Recipe Burek

YOU'LL NEED

3 onions, diced

750g (26oz) minced (ground) beef (or lamb)

1 tbs sweet paprika

1 tbs allspice

½ tsp cinnamon

4 sheets filo pastry

¼ cup melted butter (or olive oil)

1 beaten egg (optional)

METHOD

1. Heat oven to around 200°C (400°F).

2. Fry onions until soft and almost caramelised.

3. Add mince and fry until browned and slightly crumbly (drain off excess moisture or fat).

4. Remove pan from heat, add paprika, allspice and cinnamon, stir through and allow the meat mixture to cool.

5. Place a single sheet of filo pastry on bench, and brush lightly with melted butter (or olive oil).

6. Spread a quarter of the meat mixture along one edge of the filo pastry.

7. Roll the pastry sheet up to form a long tube enclosing the meat mixture, then twist the tube into a 'snail shell' spiral. Repeat three more times with the remaining ingredients.

8. Brush with more butter or oil (or egg if desired) and place in oven.

9. Bake for 20–30 minutes or until golden.

Alternatively, use a filling of crumbled fetta cheese, parsley and dill, or spinach sauteed with diced onion and dill.

SERVES 4

* Cevapcici *

CROATIA

Laced with garlic and coupled with raw onions, *cevapcici* are spicy, no-nonsense, meaty fare that will fill your tummy and keep vampires away (and probably romantic prospects as well).

What is It?

Grilled, garlicky, skinless sausages, about the length of your finger, made from a blend of minced beef and pork (or lamb in Bosnia and Turkey), *ćevapčići* are served with flat *somun* or pita bread, and traditionally accompanied by diced onions or other accoutrements such as *ajvar* (red pepper and aubergine relish) or yoghurt.

Origin

Ćevapčići arrived in the Balkans with the Ottoman Turks in the 15th century and gradually spread through southeastern Europe. It was a hearty and simple meal – minced meat, bread and onions – that could sustain farmers, soldiers and wanderers through the day. Versions of the dish are now found from Slovenia to Romania, as well as in Turkey. The name is a derivation of the Persian *kebab,* with the Slavic diminutive *-čići* tacked on the end.

Tasting

Ćevapčići are more than just an eating experience: there's the sound – the sizzle of the hotplate – and the scent – the aroma of charcoal embers and the tang of frying meat. You won't need a knife to get started, just a fork – or your hand if you're wrapping each individual *ćevapčić* in bread. The piquancy of the garlic will be released with the first bite, and you'll experience a gentle snap at each mouthful: the meat is firm but tender, chewy but not gristly. Dip each *ćevapčić* into *ajvar* or yoghurt to experience the melding of flavours; intersperse this with forkfuls of diced onion.

Finding It

You'll find *ćevapčići* at any eatery across the Balkans, always sold in multiples of five. In Zagreb, you'll find them on the steps leading to the Dolac produce market for 25KN (US$5).

* VARIATIONS * The Turkish equivalent, *köfte*, is made with minced lamb and served with yoghurt or *kaymak* (clotted cream), or may be cooked on a skewer and flavoured with powdered chilli. The Czech Republic, Slovakia and Austria have a Habsburg take on the dish, serving it with mustard and french fries.

* By Will Gourlay *

Recipe Cevapcici

YOU'LL NEED

250g (½ lb) each of minced beef and pork (substitute lamb for pork, if desired)

diced garlic (amount to taste)

1 egg, beaten

½ tsp bicarb soda (baking soda)

¼ cup of hot (not boiling) water

½ tbs sweet paprika

pinch cayenne pepper or ground red chilli (optional)

pita or other flatbread

white onion, diced

ajvar (optional)

sour cream or yoghurt (optional)

METHOD

1. Place all ingredients except bread, onion and optional accompaniments into a large mixing bowl.

2. Using your hands, mix all ingredients together, ensuring that beef and pork mince blend thoroughly and that garlic and paprika are distributed evenly.

3. Refrigerate for two hours (or longer) to allow garlic and paprika to infuse mixture.

4. Remove bowl from fridge, then take a handful of mixture and fashion it into a short 'sausage' that will fit into your palm. Repeat until all mixture is used.

5. Cook *ćevapčići* on grill preheated to medium hot, turning once and allowing about three to four minutes each side, or until a rich golden brown.

6. Serve with flatbread and diced onion, and with *ajvar*, sour cream or yoghurt if desired.

* Ceviche de Corvina *

PACIFIC COAST, PERU

Combining the marinated fish and chilli peppers that the Inca would have known, zesty Spanish-introduced citrus and a revolutionary makeover from a Peruvian-Japanese chef, Peru's national dish is the ultimate fusion cuisine.

What is It?

Corvina, a Pacific sea bass, is marinated in lime juice (and thus 'cooked' by the citrus acid) along with onion, chilli peppers and garlic. It's served with sweet potato and corn-on-the-cob chunks. Hey presto: ceviche Peru-style. Adapted by many nations, rivalled by none.

Origin

The Inca marinated fish to cook them, but used *chicha*, a fermented corn drink, rather than citrus. Spanish conquistadors brought the limes that became bona fide ceviche marinade. Corvina, prevalent on Peru's coast, became traditionally used. Japanese-Peruvian chef Dario Matsufuji shook up a century-old recipe and reduced marinating time from hours to minutes in the 1970s, which enhanced the taste and became the preparation method to emulate.

Tasting

The sharp, light kick of the lime, the crunch of red onions and the fiery red-yellow of speciality Peruvian chilli pepper *ají limo* mingle with the taste of soft white corvina as it breaks into chunks in your mouth. Then your palate grasps the sweet potato and the clumps of corn that counterbalance the feisty, citrusy fish with an earthiness that reminds you what a unique thing *ceviche de corvina* is in a country where most street snacks are heavy and carbohydrate-dominated. If you're hungry and hot in coastal Peru, this is what you need with your beer. Unlike many street foods, presentation of *ceviche de corvina* is also key. The onion-and-chilli-pepper garnish, along with a dash of coriander, sits on top of the fish, encircled by the sweet potato, corn clumps and occasional hunks of avocado. Proper ceviche is an assault on the eyes as well as the taste buds.

Finding It

Start with the best in Lima at *cebicherias* (ceviche eateries) such as Barranco's Canta Rana. Expect to pay 10/25 Peruvian *nuevo sol* (US$3/8) at a vendor/midrange *cebicheria*.

* VARIATIONS * Ceviche pops up across Latin America and a close relation graces Japanese menus, but Peru is the ceviche granddaddy, with even a national holiday in honour of the lime-dowsed fish. Ecuador concocts a soupier take on *ceviche de corvina* with tomatoes and salted popcorn. Within Peru, Lima folk use sole over corvina, Trujillo further north has shark ceviche and in the Amazon the river fish dorade makes a delicious version of the dish.

* **By Luke Waterson** *

Recipe Ceviche de Corvina

YOU'LL NEED

1 red onion, thinly sliced

500–675g (1–1½lb) sea bass fillets, skinned and chopped into large, bite-sized pieces

pinch of red chilli flakes

1 clove garlic, peeled and grated

juice of 5 limes

500g (1lb) sweet potatoes

1 corn on the cob, chopped into 5cm (2in) pieces

5 tbs olive oil

3 tsp rice vinegar

¼ tsp caster sugar

½ *ají limo* (use normal red chilli pepper if unavailable), seeded and chopped

grated rind of 1 lime

2 small avocados, peeled, stoned and sliced

3 tbs chopped coriander leaves (cilantro)

salt

ground black pepper

METHOD

1. Lay half of the red onions in a large glass bowl with the fish on top. Sprinkle on chilli flakes and the grated garlic clove, then cover with the lime juice.

2. Cover the bowl and chill. Debate varies on the time. Professional ceviche makers in Peru now use the quick marinade which, when preparing large quantities, helps keep the fish fresh, but this is an acquired art and a two-hour marinade is recommended for home cooks. During the chilling/marinating process, spoon the lime juice over the fish again once or twice.

3. Meanwhile, boil sweet potatoes and corn on the cob for 25–30 minutes. Drain and place to one side.

4. Whisk together the oil, rice vinegar and caster sugar until smooth. Then whisk in the chopped *ají limo*/chilli pepper and grated lime rind.

5. When the fish is done, drain and discard the lime juice.

6. Add the fish to the oil/rice vinegar/caster sugar and mix well. Add the diced sweet potato and avocado and mix again.

7. Add the final half of the red onion along with the coriander leaves and the corn-on-the-cob pieces and season to taste with salt and ground black pepper. Serve immediately.

SERVES 6 AS A STARTER

* Chivito al Pan *

URUGUAY

This overloaded steak sandwich – Uruguay's humble yet flamboyant national speciality – offers one of the cheapest, tastiest and most accessible ways to sample the country's famous beef.

What is It?

A fully fledged cholesterol bomb, the *chivito* starts with two pieces of bread slathered with mayonnaise, then gets piled high with layers of grilled steak, ham, bacon, fried or boiled egg and mozzarella cheese. A few token vegetables get thrown in for good measure: lettuce, tomatoes and grilled red peppers come standard, while some places also add pickles, olives, mushrooms or hearts of palm.

Origin

The *chivito* dates back to a dark night in Punta del Este, circa 1950, when a woman stopped in at Antonio Carbonaro's restaurant asking for *chivito* (grilled goat). Señor Carbonaro, finding himself utterly goat-less, improvised a sandwich of steak, ham and a few other goodies. The resulting combination was so tasty that he added it to the menu, and within a couple of years was selling enough *chivitos* to single-handedly keep two butcher shops in business. While none of the sandwich's subsequent variations has ever involved goat, the *chivito* name endures, an incongruous nod to its unlikely origins.

Tasting

You'll find *chivitos* everywhere in Uruguay, from the humblest streetside stall to well-established restaurants. For the best experience, choose a spot where you can observe the chef at work, listen to the sizzle of grilling meat and watch as the cheese is melted on top, the bread toasted directly alongside, the juicy bits of tomato and leafy lettuce tucked into place, and the crowning shake of salt added.

Stretch your fingers before you start – you'll need two hands and lots of napkins! A fully piled *chivito* can rise to ludicrous proportions, often as tall as it is wide. Most places slice it into two halves and valiantly attempt to hold it together with toothpicks; even so, the first giant-sized bite can be a real challenge. Don't worry about the mess – as any Uruguayan can tell you, a good *chivito* is meant to be juicy!

Finding It

Head for Montevideo's Mercado del Puerto, a vast labyrinth of food stalls in a wrought-iron waterfront marketplace. Expect to pay UR$150 (US$8).

* VARIATIONS * While the classic *chivito* comes in sandwich form (*chivito al pan*), restaurants throughout Uruguay also serve a variation called *chivito al plato* – the same ingredients as you'd find on the sandwich, spread out on a platter big enough to feed two, accompanied by a hefty portion of fried potatoes.

* By Gregor Clark *

Recipe **Chivito al Pan**

This recipe is for the basic, traditional *chivito* sandwich but feel free to improvise and add as many extras as you can handle, such as pickles, olives, mushrooms, and pickled or grilled red peppers.

YOU'LL NEED

1 bap or bread roll, sliced in two lengthways

1 tbs mayonnaise

2 slices bacon

1 fillet steak

1 slice ham

1 slice mozzarella cheese

1 egg, boiled and sliced thinly

2 slices tomato

lettuce leaves

METHOD

1. Spread the mayonnaise on both slices of the bap or bread roll.

2. In a lightly oiled pan, fry the bacon slices until crisp. Set aside the cooked bacon.

3. In the same pan, cook the fillet steak as preferred. Just after turning the steak, place the ham and cheese on top and cook until the steak is ready and the cheese melted.

4. To assemble the *chivito*, place the steak, ham and cheese on the bottom slice of bread and then add the bacon, egg, tomato and lettuce. Top with the other slice of bread and serve with plenty of napkins.

SERVES 1 (OR 2 LIGHTER EATERS!)

* Chole Batura *

DELHI, INDIA

Some things are meant to go together: love and marriage, a horse and carriage, and *chole* (tangy, spicy chickpeas) and *batura* (hot, light, puffed-out fried bread).

What is It?

Delhi is famous for its Dilli-ka-Chaat (slang for Delhi street food; *chaat* means 'to lick'). *Chole batura* may not originate from here, but it's an iconic Delhi snack nevertheless. The *chole* is a slick of lightly fierce chickpeas, cooked in ghee (clarified butter), with ginger, cumin, coriander, garam masala and mouth-tingling red chilli. The *batura* is a balloon of hot bread, the ideal complement to and implement for scooping up the moreish chickpea mess.

Origin

Chole batura is from the Punjab, where it's particularly popular as a hearty breakfast. It became a Delhi staple when migrants flooded into the city from what is now Pakistan after Partition in 1947. Eating the rich-in-protein *chole* on the move is made easy via the *batura.* One of Delhi's best outlets was founded by the owner's grandfather, who arrived here from the Punjab more than 60 years ago with his recipe; he and his descendants have sold the dish from a small shop in Paharganj ever since.

Tasting

In Old Delhi, street food rules. Amid a medieval-seeming confusion of streets, stallholders sit behind bubbling cauldrons practising alchemy, at places that specialise in one dish only. Famous food-on-the-run addresses are remarkable for their nondescript surroundings and for the crowds of people that ebb and flow, emerging grasping a fresh, perfect concoction. To taste Delhi's best *chole batura,* first breathe in the aroma of spicy *chole,* the scents of mingling tamarind, chilli, ginger and coriander. Pay the original owner's grandson and then collect your snack from the servers. It's intensely satisfying to deflate the bread and then use it to wipe up the punchy, tingling taste of the chickpeas. The bread alone is a masterpiece: as light as air, a grand puff that is warm to the touch, soft, yet tantalisingly crispy. Alongside it is the *chole,* dark and scented, its lightly fierce spice a foil of perfection.

Finding It

Delhi's Sita Ram Diwan Chand is opposite Imperial Cinema in Paharganj. A portion of *chole batura* here costs around ₹30 (US$1).

* VARIATIONS * The main variations of *chole batura* are to be found in the type of bread, which includes *aloo batura* (filled with potato) and *paneer batura* (stuffed with cottage cheese). At Sita Ram Diwan Chand in Delhi's Paharganj, the *batura* is flecked with strips of paneer, and studded with dots of coriander and pomegranate seeds. Seasonal pickles, such as carrot, may be served up on the side to add to the tanginess. *Chole* is also sometimes called *chana.*

* By Abigail Hole *

Recipe Chole Batura

YOU'LL NEED

Chole

1 ½ cups chickpeas (canned or soaked overnight)

2 tbs ghee or cooking oil

1 onion, finely chopped

1cm ginger, very finely chopped

2 cloves garlic, very finely chopped

1 tsp red chilli powder

pinch salt

1 tsp ground coriander seeds

¼ tsp turmeric powder

¼ tsp garam masala

2 tomatoes, blanched, peeled and chopped

1 tbs tamarind paste

half a glass of hot water

Batura

2 cups plain (all-purpose) flour

1 tbs oil

½ tsp salt

2 tbs yoghurt

1 tsp yeast in 2 tbs warm water with a little ginger (ground or fresh)

METHOD

Chole

1. Drain the chickpeas.

2. Heat oil and fry the chopped onion until pinkish in colour.

3. Add the ginger and garlic and fry for two minutes.

4. Add tomatoes and continue frying.

5. Add chilli, salt, coriander seeds, turmeric and garam masala, then fry for two minutes.

6. Add the chickpeas, tamarind paste and hot water. Let simmer for about 10 minutes, then serve.

Batura

1. Knead the flour with the other ingredients until smooth. Grease a bowl for the dough, then cover and leave for six hours. When it has risen, knead it again.

2. Make small dough balls and roll out thinly.

3. Heat oil until very hot and then carefully put in a disc of dough to deep-fry. Use a slotted spoon to press the dough down in the centre of the oil and it should puff out. Remove and eat with *chole*. If it's oily, the oil wasn't hot enough!

* Choripán *

ARGENTINA

A killer combination of chorizo (Spanish-style sausage) and *pan francés* (French bread), *choripán* is the classic sandwich of Argentinian *futból* (soccer) matches, roadside *puestos* (grill carts) and family *asados* (barbecues).

What is It?

Preparing a perfect *'chori'* is a matter of pride among many Argentinian men. After being grilled on the *parrilla* (grill), the sausage is sliced lengthwise, placed in a crusty roll or a chunk of baguette, and topped with savoury, freshly prepared condiments such as *chimichurri* (a sauce made with chopped parsley, garlic, onions, tomatoes, olive oil and herbs).

Origin

Though the origins of the *choripán* weren't officially recorded, the sandwich has been widely attributed to the gauchos who roamed the nation's expansive landscape several generations ago. Far away in the wide open grasslands of Patagonia and in the pampas surrounding Buenos Aires, these Argentinian cowboys grilled meat over an open fire; they were probably the first to grill chorizo and pair it with bread. The sandwich gained popularity in the cities at family *asados,* street carts and sporting events – particularly at raucous *futból* matches, where fans wolf down their *chori* at half-time.

Tasting

Follow the thick plumes of smoke – and the mouth-watering aroma of sizzling meat – to a *puesto de choripán,* an open-air food cart found at parks and street festivals. The rustic *parrilla,* manned by a no-nonsense *asador* (grillman), will be carefully laid with chorizo and slabs of steak and pork – and probably surrounded by local guys chowing down on oversized sandwiches while listening to *futból* coverage on a plastic transistor radio. Hand over your pesos to the *asador,* then move over to the condiments, where you can top your *chori* with spoonfuls of homemade *chimichurri.* Biting into the sandwich, you'll experience a satisfying explosion of flavours and textures: the crispy grilled surface of the chorizo, the juicy pink pork inside, the tangy *chimichurri,* the heat of the fresh garlic, red chilli pepper and onion. The sauce drips down your wrist and arm as the radio sportscaster bellows 'goooool...goooool...' (goal) and the locals around you start celebrating or fighting – depending on who's playing.

Finding It

Buenos Aires' Costanera has an outdoorsy local ambience and a wide selection of *puestos de choripán.* This classic sandwich costs 5 to 10 pesos (US$1.50 to US$2.50) anywhere in the country.

* TIPS * Do as the locals do and order up '*un chori y una coca*' (a *chori* and Coca-Cola). You'll also see groups of friends washing down their *choripán* with icy Quilmes beer, available for sale at many food carts. For the full experience, savour your *chori* at a plastic table on the sidewalk, at a *futból* game or, if you can score an invitation, at a family *asado.*

* By Bridget Gleeson *

Recipe Choripán

YOU'LL NEED

6 chorizos

1 bunch parsley, chopped

several cloves of garlic (to taste), minced

⅓ cup olive oil

1 small tomato, chopped

1 tbs red onion, chopped (optional)

2 tbs red wine vinegar

crushed red pepper flakes (to taste)

juice of ½ lemon or lime (optional)

salt

pepper

6 crusty French rolls or one baguette

METHOD

1. Place chorizos on grill over medium-high heat.

2. Meanwhile, prepare the *chimichurri* by combining parsley, garlic, olive oil, tomato, red onion, red wine vinegar, crushed red pepper flakes and lemon or lime juice in a small bowl. Season with salt and pepper, and add more olive oil, lemon juice or crushed red pepper if desired. It's also possible to combine the ingredients in a food processor, but be sure not to overly process the mixture – the *chimichurri* should have a slightly chunky texture.

3. Rotate chorizos on grill, turning over to grill evenly on each side.

4. Slice rolls, or cut the baguette into six smaller pieces, then slice.

5. When chorizos are cooked through and somewhat crisp along the edges, remove from grill.

6. Slice chorizos lengthwise, and place each one, face up, on a roll. Spoon *chimichurri* over the chorizo, then close the sandwich. Serve immediately.

SERVES 6 AS AN APPETISER, 3–4 AS A MAIN

NOTE Feel free to be creative with the *chimichurri* proportions, omitting or adding ingredients where desired – Argentinians serve many variations on the sauce.

* Cicchetti *

VENICE, ITALY

The Venetian answer to tapas, these varied, bite-sized morsels are found in tiny bars all over the city. *Cicchetti* are the perfect salve to an afternoon getting lost among the canals and crowds of Venice.

What is It?

Cicchetti (chee-*ket*-tee) comprise a range of different foods, some served hot and some cold. The term derives from the Latin word '*ciccus*,' meaning 'very small', and the smallish bites can include everything from olives and halved hard-boiled eggs to diminutive servings of seafood, meat or vegetables placed atop an open slice of bread. *Cicchetti* are traditionally served in *bàcari,* the many bars that line the canals of Venice.

Origin

The centuries-old custom of enjoying *cicchetti* is unique to Venice, the magical lagoon that Thomas Mann described as 'half fairy-tale, half tourist trap'. During the 15th century, Venice was not only the most powerful and wealthiest city in Europe – it was also considered by many to be the capital of fine dining, attracting the world's most talented chefs. Venice's influence (and merchants) brought a diversity of foods to the many *bàcari* that had long lined Venice's *calli* (side streets) and *campi* (plazas), and the worker's tradition of downing a small sandwich with a glass of wine has continued today.

Tasting

To order, just approach the counter and point at whichever food looks the most interesting. If the place is crowded, you'll be asked to pay as you order, so it's best to order several dishes at once. Fish is a Venetian staple, so you'll often find fried shrimp or calamari, as well as other specialities such as fresh oysters, razor clams, *baccala mantecato* (cod whipped with olive oil) and *sarde in saor* (sardines marinated in vinegar with onions) – commonly served with polenta cakes. Other goodies include *polpette* (a fried veal-and-potato meatball), *arancini* (tiny rice balls), zucchini blossoms and baby octopus. To locate an authentic *cicchetti* bar, venture off Venice's crowded streets and keep an eye out for an unassuming storefront with Venetians spilling out into the streets. Venetians typically *andar per ombre* (head out for *cicchetti*) during the late morning or afternoon.

Finding It

Near Rialto market, the dimly lit Cantina do Mori is Venice's oldest *cicchetti* bar, dating from 1462. *Cicchetti* cost from €1.50 (US$2) each.

* TIPS * *Cicchetti* are best washed down with a glass of local wine known as an *ombra* (literally 'shadow'). The house keg wine will be the cheapest, but spring for a glass of Brunello red from Tuscany: 2004 and 2006 were both excellent years. Alternatively, try the quintessentially Venetian spritz, made with Aperol, prosecco and soda. Before paying your bill, ask for a *fragolino* (sweet wine), which often arrives with a tiny biscotti to dip in.

* By Roger Norum & Strouchan Martins *

Recipe **Mushroom Crostini**

YOU'LL NEED

1 baguette, sliced

1 cup mushrooms (dry porcini, fresh shiitake and cremini)

2 tbs extra virgin olive oil

½ onion, minced

1 clove garlic, minced

salt

pepper

1 tbs fresh flat-leaf Italian parsley, roughly chopped

1 tsp lemon zest

grated parmesan cheese, to taste (optional)

1 tbs heavy whipping cream (optional)

METHOD

1. Preheat oven to 190°C (375°F). Place baguette slices onto a baking sheet. Toast.

2. Soak the porcini in lukewarm water, then chop the mushrooms together. You can also cube the mushrooms instead of slicing them, if you prefer something more delicate.

3. In a saute pan over medium heat, add olive oil, then saute onion and garlic until softened. Add mushrooms, with salt and pepper to taste. Throw in parsley. Cook for approximately 10 minutes until mushrooms have softened, stirring as necessary. If pan begins to dry out, add more olive oil.

4. Add lemon zest. Stir (alternatively, you can use a food processor for a more refined spread). Add parmesan cheese. Remove from heat.

5. Place a spoonful or two of the mushroom mix onto each toasted baguette. If desired, add a shot of cream, then some grated parmesan cheese for added bite. Serve immediately.

MAKES 15 SLICES

* Cocktel de Camarón *

MEXICO

No dreary country-club appetiser here: this Mexican shrimp cocktail is a spicy, sweet-sour treat that capitalises on the freshest seafood. Slurp it with a spoon, with saltine crackers on the side.

What is It?

The exact composition of *cocktel* (sometimes spelled *coctel*) *de camarón* varies, but the fundamentals of this seaside lunchtime treat are plump, chilled shrimp floating in a tangy tomato sauce, with plenty of heat from fresh chilli, and a sweet top note. Some recipes are chunky with raw onion, and others add avocado. Another essential: a curvy parfait glass, to add the requisite fancy flair.

Origin

The states edging the Gulf of Mexico have a booming shrimp industry. (One town, Ciudad del Carmen, even has a giant bronze prawn in the middle of a roundabout.) And Mexican cuisine has a fine tradition of tweaking foreign food to fit local tastes. So it's only natural that when shrimp cocktail was all the rage in the United States in the early 20th century, Mexican chefs put their extra-spicy spin on it. The shrimp is freshest in Veracruz, Tabasco and Campeche, but can be found all over the country, with subtle variations.

Tasting

Sea breezes make everything taste better, and *cocktel de camarón* is no exception. Ideally, you'll enjoy it within view of Mexico's pale green gulf waters, perched on a plastic chair with your feet in the sand – even if you've just hopped out to patronise a rickety roadside stand. Whether your tall parfait glass is filled in a proper kitchen or from a foam cooler, it should be packed to the brim with orange-pink shrimp, swimming in a deep-red sauce, flecked with white onion and bits of green coriander leaves (cilantro). The sauce is bright and sharp, with a hint of citrus. Along with the lapping of waves on the shore, a *cocktel* session is marked by the crinkle of cellophane wrappers: saltine crackers make a fine foil to the intense sauce – and they help if you get a bite spiked with killer-hot *habañero* chilli, a popular sweat-inducing addition in the Yucatán Peninsula.

Finding It

Seafront kiosks on the north side of Campeche, across from the baseball stadium, serve flawless *cocktel de camarón* for M$75 (US$6.30).

* SECRET INGREDIENTS * Fresh juice of limes or, in the Yucatán, bitter oranges, is typically used to give a *cocktel* a sharp, sour edge. But many *cockteleros* swear by a splash of (food snobs, brace yourselves) orange soda. And that tomato base for the mystery sauce: yes, it's pretty much guaranteed to be ketchup.

* By Zora O'Neill *

Recipe Cocktel de Camarón

This recipe is based on a traditional one from the shrimping town of Champotón, Campeche, where the highway is lined with *cockteleros* catering to long-distance truckers. Avocado isn't typical of the region, but it's found in *cockteles* in other parts of Mexico. Clam juice isn't necessary, but a good way to boost the flavour of frozen shrimp.

YOU'LL NEED

ice

2 cups water or clam juice

700g (1½lb) small shrimp

1 cup ketchup

¼ cup olive oil

juice of 4–6 limes

2 tbs Worcestershire sauce

½ teaspoon freshly ground black pepper

salt to taste

½ cup finely chopped coriander leaves (cilantro), loosely packed

½ cup diced white onion

1 habañero chilli, finely chopped (optional)

1 ripe but firm avocado, diced (optional)

Mexican-style vinegar-based hot sauce

lime wedges

saltine crackers

METHOD

1. Fill a medium bowl with ice.

2. Heat water or clam juice to boiling, then add shrimp and cook until just pink (less than one minute). Quickly scoop shrimp out and place in bowl with ice. Reserve cooking liquid. When shrimp are cool enough to handle, peel them and discard shells. Refrigerate shrimp till chilled.

3. To make the cocktail sauce, combine ketchup, olive oil, lime juice, Worcestershire sauce and pepper, then mix in 1 cup of the shrimp-cooking liquid. Taste and add salt and/or more lime juice and cooking liquid if desired – the mix should be a good balance of salty, sweet and tangy.

4. Mix in coriander leaves, onion and chilli (if using), then gently fold in avocado, taking care not to mash the pieces.

5. Divide cooked shrimp into four parfait glasses (or other clear glasses). Top with cocktail sauce and stir gently to combine.

6. Serve with hot sauce, lime wedges and saltine crackers.

SERVES 4 AS A GENEROUS APPETISER

* Conch *

BAHAMAS

In the Bahamas, the giant sea snail known as the conch is more than a food – it's a symbol of the island nation's resourcefulness, humility and oneness with the ocean.

What is It?

A type of marine mollusc with a large, lovely cone-shaped shell, conch is fished from the shallows and brought live to market, then extracted through a hole in the shell. Its tough flesh is white and rubbery, comparable with calamari. Popular conch dishes include cracked conch (battered and fried), conch salad (chopped and tossed with onions, tomatoes and lime juice), conch fritters (deep-fried balls of minced conch and batter) and conch chowder.

Origin

The native Arawak people of the Bahamas were eating conch long before the arrival of Columbus. When Europeans began showing up on the islands in the 1500s, they quickly caught on to conch's usefulness as a quick, high-protein meal. Conch is a deeply rooted part of Bahamian culture – old Bahamian silver dollars are graced with conch imagery, conch shells are a standard home construction material, and 'Conchy Joe' is a common (though potentially insulting) term for white or mixed-race Bahamians. Many of today's common conch dishes such as fritters and conch salad have remained virtually the same for centuries.

Tasting

Though conch is served nearly everywhere in the Bahamas, from the humblest of home kitchens to the chicest of celeb-packed sushi bars, we prefer to munch the mollusc like the locals do, at a 'fish fry' or 'conch shack'. A fish fry is a sort of outdoor food court, often at the edge of town, which comes to life on nights and weekends with the crackling of hot oil and the beat of Bahamian goombay music. A conch shack is a roadside or beachfront stall, open daily, serving all manner of conch to travellers and hungry workers alike. At either place, belly up to the bar and ask the chef what his or her speciality is – some cooks fry legendary conch fritters, while others are known for their zippy conch salad. You can't go wrong with cracked conch, fried to golden brown crispness and served with a creamy orange dipping sauce. It's great, but greasy – wash it down with an icy-cold local Kalik beer. Perfection.

Finding It

At Arawak Cay Fish Fry in Nassau, you can get a plate of cracked conch for 10 Bahamian dollars (US$10).

* TIPS * While conch fritters and conch salad are generally sold alone as a snack, cracked or roasted conch is a full meal, and is usually served with two Bahamian side dishes. Choose from peas n' rice (red beans and rice), mac 'n' cheese (the Bahamian version is extra creamy), plantains, greens or potato salad.

Recipe Conch Salad

YOU'LL NEED

450g (1lb) conch meat, diced to into small chunks

1 green pepper, diced

1 white onion, diced

½ cucumber, diced

1 cup ripe tomato, diced

2 celery stalks, diced

1 jalapeño chilli, diced (optional)

2 garlic cloves, finely chopped

¼ cup lime juice

¼ cup white vinegar

¼ cup orange juice

salt to taste

pepper to taste

METHOD

Toss all ingredients together in a large bowl and allow to sit overnight before serving, allowing flavours to mingle.

* Cornish Pasty *

CORNWALL, ENGLAND

Curvaceous (and controversial) pastry parcels, bulging with hearty goodness, these edible lunch boxes of chunky meat and vegies, wrapped in a golden crust, have fed the poor and peckish for centuries.

What is It?

In 2011 the EU granted the Cornish pasty protected status, declaring it a food of regional importance. Only pasties slow-baked in Cornwall can bear the name; the ingredients (which go in raw) must be chunked potato, swede, onion and at least 12.5% beef; the pastry must be crimped to the side, not on top.

Origin

Pasties have been munched since medieval times, and by the 1530s Henry VIII's third wife, Jane Seymour, was reputedly rather partial to them. But it was the poor folk of Cornwall who made pasties their own: by the end of the 18th century, few miners or farmers would go to work without their pastry-encased lunch. The ingredients were cheap, the product portable and the crimped ridge lifesaving: a disposable grip for miners working amid high levels of arsenic. Today, travellers – five million of whom flock to Cornwall each year – tend to eat the lot.

Tasting

You can taste the heritage of the Cornish pasty: it's not fancy food, it's fuel. The dense filling – lightly seasoned, best hot – is robust and sustaining. Scents of warm baking, cosy as grandma's kitchen, waft from many a Cornish shop. Indeed, buying a pasty is an unceremonious affair: you're as likely to find a good one in the village post office as in any artisan deli.

Biting into a good pasty, pastry melty but firm, slithers of onion caressing tender hunks of beef skirt, is like leaning back into a battered sofa – warm, soft, deliciously comforting. Though there's no fish involved (it's thought bad luck to put fish in a pasty), the best place to eat them is by the sea. Hike some of Cornwall's 500km of coast – a roller coaster of clifftops and coves – and never will a pasty have been more deserved, or taste better.

Finding It

Ann's Famous Pasty Shop – a garage-cum-bakery tucked away in Lizard, Cornwall, England's southernmost point – sells pasties for £2.85 (US$4.60).

* **VARIATIONS** * Hop over the Cornish border into Devon and you'll find equivalent pasty passion. Indeed, Devonians claim that the pasty originates from their county. Traditionally Devon pasties are crimped on top, Cornish ones to the side. In all honesty, both taste good. But it didn't go down well when the 2009 British Pie Awards' top Cornish pasty prize was awarded to Chunk of Devon...

* By Sarah Baxter *

Recipe Cornish Pasty

YOU'LL NEED

Dough

450g (1lb) strong white flour

110g (4oz) lard

100g (3½oz) margarine

¾ cup (175mL) water

Filling

250g (8¾oz) swede, sliced

200g (7oz) onion, sliced

400g (14oz) beef skirt, chunked

600g (1¼lb) potatoes, sliced

black pepper

salt

METHOD

1. Preheat oven to 220°C (430°F).

2. Rub a quarter of the lard into the flour. Add remaining lard and the margarine, and stir (with a knife). Add water; stir till absorbed.

3. Knead the dough, then refrigerate for 30 minutes.

4. Quarter pastry (recipe makes four); on a floured surface, roll each piece into a circle, about 22cm (9in) across.

5. Lay uncooked swede and onion across each circle's middle; season.

6. Layer on raw meat; season.

7. Add most of the potato; season. Top with the rest of the potato – do not salt.

8. Lightly water one side of pastry; fold wet side over the other and gently press together. Crimp edges to tuck in contents.

9. Make a cut in the top; brush top with milk.

10. Bake pasties for 40–50 minutes, checking halfway through; if browning quickly, turn oven down to 160°C (320°F).

11. Slice before eating, to release steam.

SERVES 4

* Currywurst *

GERMANY

Currywurst transforms sausage, chopped and doused in a spicy tomato sauce, into night-time nirvana. As you would expect with a German snack, it's the ultimate beer food.

What is It?

Currywurst consists of a decent fried or boiled sausage, chopped and drowned in a spicy tomato-based slick. There are as many different variations as there are sausages in Germany. Some favour a sauce with a good hint of Indian curry, while other prefer pure chilli heat. One *Currywurst* fanatic might like a mustardy sauce, another opts for one rich with lemongrass and Thai spices. Then there's the choice of chips, white bread or wholegrain roll. There are songs dedicated to the food, and even a museum has been opened in honour of this Berlin mainstay.

Origin

In 1949 when Berlin lay in ruins, an enterprising housewife by the name of Herta Heuwer got hold of some English curry power from British soldiers. They, in exchange, got a few bottles of the local hooch. With this rare ingredient (all food was still in short supply), she created a tomato-based curry sauce and slathered it all over chopped sausage. Her stall sat on the outskirts of what was soon to become the red-light district, and the food, cheap and filling, became hugely popular with local builders and labourers. The *Currywurst* was such a success that Heuwer soon opened a small restaurant. Before long, the city was awash with imitators.

Tasting

It's been a long night. And that last stein of local brew, which seemed such a good idea at the time, has tipped the scales from very merry to downright drunk. As you stumble home, the street all a blur, you make out a welcoming beacon of red neon light. The queues are long and rowdy, though there's no hint of aggression. You shuffle forward, and with each step, your whole being is overcome with the scent of sausage, spice and delight. Within minutes, you've mumbled your order and proceeded to lean against a bright red Coca-Cola table. In the cardboard carton before you are two sausages, chopped up and smothered in a mildly spicy tomato sauce. You stagger home happy, then return the next day to see what tastes like when sober. It's every bit as good.

Finding It

Currywurst 36, at Mehringdamm 36 in Berlin, might be a tourist mecca, but the *Currywurst* is damned good. Expect to pay €2 to €3.50 (US$2.70 to US$4.75) throughout Berlin.

* **VARIATIONS** * Germany is wurst crazy and you'll find every variety of sausage under the sun – boiled, smoked, skinned, straight, curved and fat – in bars and restaurants everywhere. Before reunification sausages for *Currywurst* were fried with the skin on in glitzy West Germany, while the rather more austere East had them boiled, without the skin. As to variations, no two *Currywurst* are the same. Find your favourite and stick with it.

* By Tom Parker Bowles *

Recipe Currywurst

YOU'LL NEED

2 tbs vegetable oil

1 onion, finely diced

2 tbs curry powder

1 tbs hot paprika

2 cups canned tomatoes

½ cup white sugar

¼ cup red wine vinegar

salt and pepper to taste

5 mild sausages of your choice

METHOD

1. Heat the oil in a pan over a medium heat and add onion, cooking until soft.

2. Add curry powder and paprika and cook for one minute, then, using your hands, break up the canned tomatoes and add to the mix.

3. Stir in sugar, vinegar, and salt and pepper to taste. Bring to a boil then reduce to a simmer. Cook until thickened, stirring occasionally. This should take about 25 minutes.

4. Remove from heat and whizz the sauce in a blender until silky smooth, then strain it through a sieve to remove any pulpiness.

5. Grill sausages until thoroughly cooked through and nicely browned on the outside. Remove from the heat and slice into 2cm (1in) rounds.

6. Divide sausage chunks into 5 bowls and top with a hearty dollop of sauce (rewarmed if necessary). Serve with toothpicks.

SERVES 5

* Elote *

MEXICO

A fresh ear of corn is charred to just-blackened perfection over glowing coals, or simply boiled, then anointed with lime, powdered chilli, butter, cream or cheese.

What is It?

Elote is a meaty, not-so-sweet corn on the cob, with great fat kernels that burst in the mouth. The smoky, pit-roasted ears are a staple across Mexico, and it's a dish that is customised, like so many others, to the eater's personal taste.

Origin

Maize is the very heart of Mexican food, and this is the plant in its most basic form. There's little doubt that early man, and certainly the Aztecs, Incas and the rest of the pre-Columbian indigenous civilisations, feasted upon whole cobs of corn, although the butter, cheese and mayonnaise are relatively modern embellishments.

Tasting

In Mexico, you're never far from corn roasting over coals. The charred, sweetish kernels are fat and hot, redolent of the fire. To eat the cob you can use a stick, or grasp it by the undressed husk. Chilli and lime, that ever-dependable Mexican duo, are all that's needed to complete the feast... And perhaps a splodge of mayonnaise and a handful of grated cheese. Up north, you'll find *elote* boiled, and topped with cream, cheese and chilli powder. This is food to be eaten at a slow amble, an elegant appetiser as you wander through the market, looking for the next course.

¡Deliciosos! ELOTES HERVIDOS, ASADOS y ESQUITES = Atendemos Eventos =

Finding It

There is no one place where you'll find the best *elote.* Go to any town, city or village in Mexico and it's impossible to miss. You'll pay about 8 Mexican pesos (US$0.60).

* **VARIATIONS** * In Toluca and Mexico City, you might find *elote* fried with chilli and *epazote* (a common Mexican spice). And in Yucatán, they're pit-roasted in vast sacks, deeply infused with smoke.

Recipe Elote

YOU'LL NEED

4 corn cobs, shucked

2 tsp fresh lime juice

3 tbs mayonnaise

2 tbs finely grated parmesan cheese

½ tsp chilli powder

¼ tsp ground red pepper

¼ tsp ground cumin

pinch salt

METHOD

This one is too easy. Simply grill (broil) or barbecue your corn cobs until they're toasty and tender, making sure they cook evenly on all sides. This should take 10–15 minutes. Meanwhile, combine the lime juice and mayonnaise in one bowl, and all the other ingredients in another. When the corn is done, spread the lime mayo on it and then douse with the spicy cheese mix and devour immediately.

SERVES 4

* Felafel *

ISRAEL

Felafel is fast food without all the fuss. Simple and affordable, this chickpea ball has been filling bellies in the Middle East for centuries and has rolled all over the world.

What is It?

The classic felafel is a deep-fried ball made from ground chickpeas, garlic, coriander and other spices. In Israel felafel can be eaten at any hour of the day or night. Felafel can be served on its own but most popularly comes with heaps of fresh salad in a sturdy pita bread. Hummus is optional, but without it, a felafel somehow feels, well, naked.

Origin

The origin of felafel, like everything else in the Middle East, is the cause for much heated discussion. Arabic, Jewish, Indian, Greek or Turkish – its roots are unclear. Despite the felafel's similarities with chickpea dishes in India, the most common theory is that it was eaten by the early Coptic Christians during Lent in Egypt and journeyed across Arabia, where it was a popular way for Muslims to break the fast at Ramadan. Adopted by Mizrahi Jews living in Arab countries as it suited the kosher diet, the felafel finally found its home in Israel in a pita and became the national dish.

Tasting

A felafel is a quick snack usually found on some busy street corner, but it's also something to be savoured with each bite. The experience begins in the queue – if you're lucky, the cook will give you a baking-hot ball straight from the pan. When ordering, there are important decisions to make, such as whether to add chips, onions, chopped parsley or chilli sauce. Pouring tahini on top is recommended, but not too much in case the bread becomes soggy. It's easy to make a mess while munching on this masterpiece of refreshing salad, tangy pickled cucumbers and smooth, creamy hummus. But the best thing about felafel is that it expands – halfway through you can add more salad fillings. Eventually, all good things come to an end, and at the bottom of the pita you'll find those last fried balls, the foundation of any felafel.

Finding It

Everyone in Israel will tell you they know the best felafel stand. But Gabai, in Bograshov St, Tel Aviv, is the felafel expert. A *manna* (portion in pita) costs NIS 16 (US$4.09).

* VARIATIONS * Popular with vegetarians, felafel (and felafel burgers) can today be found in cities and music festivals worldwide, coming in all shapes and sizes. Within Israel, the Tel Aviv felafel is often crispy and juicy, while in Jerusalem's Old City, Palestinians sell dry, fluffy felafel balls without any of the trimmings. In Egypt the traditional felafel is made from fava beans and you can even order a 'McFelafel' – with fries, of course.

* By Dan Savery Raz *

Recipe Felafel

YOU'LL NEED

400g (14oz) dried chickpeas (soaked overnight)

4 cups water

5 garlic cloves, minced

½ small onion

½ cup coriander leaves (cilantro), chopped

⅓ cup parsley, chopped

1 tsp paprika

1–2 tsp ground cumin

1 cup breadcrumbs

2 tbs flour

2 tsp bicarb soda (baking soda)

1 egg

2 tsp salt

2 tsp fresh ground pepper

vegetable oil for deep-frying

1 cup of flour for dipping

4 pita breads

hummus, pesto or chilli sauce (optional)

salad vegetables

tahini (sesame paste)

METHOD

1. Cook the soaked chickpeas in 4 cups water for 30 minutes, drain and put in a food processor (or mash) with the garlic, onion, coriander leaves, parsley and spices. Grind the mixture until you get a rough, juicy consistency; add a little water if needed and more coriander leaves for greener felafel.

2. Pour the mixture into a big bowl. Add the breadcrumbs, flour, bicarb soda, egg, salt and pepper. Stir the mixture well and leave to stand for 30 minutes.

3. Roll the mixture into about 16 small balls and flatten into patties.

4. Heat about 8cm (3in) of vegetable oil in a saucepan. Dip the felafel balls into flour and deep-fry about five at a time until crispy brown (if the felafel crumbles, add more flour to the mixture). When cooked, put the felafel on a paper towel to drain.

5. Stuff four or five felafels into each pita bread with hummus, salad, tahina or even pesto, and serve hot.

SERVES 4

* Fuul Mudammas *

EGYPT

Egypt's breakfast of champions is the country's national dish. Served up as a sandwich filler, this spice-fest of a stew keeps the 80-million-strong population on the move throughout the day.

What is It?

Forget waking up to cornflakes or muesli. This broad bean (fava bean) dish is a high-energy, supremely nutritious kick-start to your day. Slow-cooked, until easily mashed, the broad beans are mixed with tomatoes, onion, garlic and lemon juice, spiced with cumin and cayenne pepper, and drizzled with olive oil. Spooned into a fresh pita pocket, it's the perfect breakfast on the run.

Origin

The fava bean used for *fuul mudammas* (often simply called *fuul*) is known in Arabic as *fuul-hammam* due to a quirky medieval business monopoly on production. Having stoked the great fires for Cairo's Princess Public Baths all day, the *hammam* attendants came up with a great idea: they'd use the leftover embers to slow-cook great vats of *fuul* overnight to be ready for the breakfast rush. Their ingenious plan proved a hit, and every morning they had all of Cairo clamouring at their door.

Finding It

Seek out Muhammad Ali's *fuul* cart, beside Qasr Beshtak, just off Sharia Al-Muizz li-Din Allah, in Islamic Cairo. Expect to pay 1.25EGP (US$0.20).

Tasting

Wafts of garlic hang over the street. Some of the swelling crowd are clutching empty containers ready to be filled. Squeeze your way up to the front, where the vendor is working up a sweat and the customers are yelling with impatience. You're handed a simple pita sandwich, spread with a generous dollop of *fuul* and garnished with fresh, crunchy salad.

The first bite reveals the soft, comforting texture of beans and olive oil. As you chew, the tart zing of lemon, the peppery taste of cumin and the powerful punch of garlic come into play. It's hearty and wholesome, and surprisingly filling. Your pita is finished. You look back at the crowd and nod at their intelligence. Next time you're bringing a pot to fill as well.

* **VARIATIONS** * **Endlessly adaptable, *fuul* comes in many guises. *Fuul Iskandariya*, which hails from the coastal city of Alexandria, combines an extra-peppery *fuul* mix with a hot and spicy tomato-salsa-like sauce. For a naughty version of this nutritious snack, look out for *fuul bi samna*, which totally trips up the healthy contents of this dish by adding lashings of clarified butter.**

Recipe Fuul Mudammas

YOU'LL NEED

2 cups of dried broad beans (fava beans) – the small, round kind (or cheat by using 4 cups canned cooked beans)

7 cups of water

1 onion, finely diced

3–4 garlic cloves, finely chopped

1 tomato, finely chopped

⅛ cup squeezed lemon juice

½ tsp cumin

½ tsp chilli powder

pinch of turmeric

pinch of cayenne pepper

pinch of cinnamon

salt

pepper

olive oil to taste

pita bread

hard-boiled eggs (optional)

fetta (optional)

parsley

tomatoes

cucumber

METHOD

Broad Beans

Note: you can skip this step by using canned beans.

1. Soak the dried fava beans in cold water for 24 hours (make sure they are completely covered by the water), then drain and rinse.

2. In a large pot bring 7 cups of water to the boil.

3. Add the fava beans to the pot and boil for 10–15 minutes, making sure to skim any foam off the top.

4. Reduce heat, cover pot and leave to simmer for eight hours.

5. After simmering for eight hours, check for dryness. If too dry, add boiling water to the pot.

6. Cover and cook on a low heat for another two hours.

Fuul

1. In a large frying pan, saute the diced onion until translucent.

2. Add garlic and fry on a low heat for two to three minutes.

3. Add the chopped tomato to the pan and fry for approximately another five minutes (until the tomato is at the stage where it is starting to come apart).

4. Transfer the frying-pan mix to the pot of beans.

5. Stir in the lemon juice, all the spices and seasonings and olive oil.

6. On a low heat, leave to cook for 15–20 minutes.

7. Using a potato masher, mash mixture together to a consistency of your liking (or for a less chunky version put it in a blender until smooth).

8. Serve in bowls (drizzled with extra olive oil) with pita bread, hard-boiled eggs, chunks of fetta, and a simple salad of parsley, tomatoes and cucumber for an authentic Egyptian breakfast.

SERVES 4

NOTE Swap and change seasoning measurements to suit your tastes.

* Gordita *

MEXICO

Gordita means 'little fat one', a term of affection, which is the emotion you'll feel upon biting into these fat masa (maize flour dough) cakes puffed up with heat and stuffed with all manner of wonderful ingredients.

What is It?

Gorditas are hand-held heaven, a puffy symphony to Mexican good taste. At some food stalls, cooks will heat a thick slab of masa on a dry griddle until puffed, then stuff it; at others, they'll start the masa cake on the griddle, then transfer it to bubbling oil. The cooked masa is split, then filled with minced (ground) pork, punchy chorizo or cheese and chillies. It's finished off with a sprinkling of shredded lettuce, chopped onion and the usual dollop of hot sauce. You could call it a Mexican pastie, or an edible work of art.

Finding It

Choose from a huge array of *gorditas* at Gorditas Doña Julia, which has a few outlets in Zacatecas, for about 8 pesos (US$0.80) each.

Tasting

Eating a *gordita* is an art form unto itself, a delectable task that requires some dexterity. The problem is one of allure; you want to get your teeth deep into that burnished parcel as soon as you possibly can, but without either exploding the whole thing down your front or burning your tongue to a crisp. Thick, dense and chewy *gorditas* are best; avoid those wafer-thin wretches that miss the point.

An endless choice of fillings are laid out alongside the griddle and boiling oil, in earthenware bowls. Here the fun really starts. Do you go for the *chile con queso* (poblano chillies, lolling in a rich cheese-and-tomato sauce), *pollo deshebrado* (shredded chicken) or the seasonal *flor de calabraza* (squash-blossom)? This is all about a wonderful melange of tastes and textures. Some *gorditas* have a crunchy outer layer, the perfect contrast to the melting meat, while others are softer than a cumulus cloud. The onions and lettuce offer cool relief, while hot sauce adds its usual welcome kick.

Origin

Yet another of Mexico's myriad ways with masa, the *gordita* is simply a variation on the cooked tortilla theme. It's highly likely that these fat cakes were eaten way before Columbus and his crew arrived. *Gorditas* tend to be a speciality of northern Mexico, although they're found across the country.

* VARIATIONS * In Tampico you'll find little griddle-baked versions called *bocoles*. As to the rest...there are endless arguments as to what the correct stuffing and texture is. As ever with Mexican food, there is no definitive answer. Find what you like, and stick with it.

Recipe Gordita

This recipe features a classic shredded beef filling. Note that *masa harina* (instant corn flour) is not the same as regular cornflour (or cornstarch). It's used specifically in Mexican cooking.

YOU'LL NEED

600g (1¼lb) boneless beef chuck steak, cut into 4 pieces

3 small white onions, diced

4 garlic cloves, peeled and chopped finely

1 tbs vegetable oil, plus oil for frying

2 cups chopped ripe tomatoes

1–2 jalapeño chillies (seeds removed), chopped finely

¾ tsp salt, plus salt to taste

1¾ cups masa harina mixed with 1 cup plus 2 tbs warm water

⅓ cup plain (all-purpose) flour

1 level tsp baking powder

⅓ cup grated cheese (try Romano or parmesan if you can't find Mexican queso anejo)

⅓ cup chopped fresh coriander leaves (cilantro)

METHOD

1. To start the filling, put 8 cups of water and a dash of salt in a saucepan over a medium heat. Add the meat, a third of the onions and half the garlic and simmer for 90 minutes until the meat is perfectly tender. Remove the meat, allow it to cool, then shred it with two forks until it's thread-like.

2. In a saucepan, heat 1 tbs vegetable oil over a medium heat. Add half the remaining the onions and cook until golden, then add the garlic and cook for another minute. Add the tomatoes and jalapeños, letting them simmer until any liquid has cooked out, then add the shredded meat and salt to taste. Simmer for a couple of minutes then remove from the heat.

3. To make the actual *gorditas*, combine the *masa harina* with the water and mix until a dough forms. Knead in the flour, baking powder and salt and work it until you have a smooth dough that's easy to handle. (Add a little more water if needed.) Cut the dough into 10 portions and roll each into a ball.

4. Put a heavy skillet (frying pan) on a medium heat. (Add a little oil if it's not a nonstick pan.) Flatten each ball of dough into a chunky disc around 6mm (0.25in) thick and cook in batches for about 90 seconds on each side. They should look crispy and slightly browned but not be cooked right through. Once you've cooked them all, set them aside.

5. Warm up your beef filling if necessary, and have your cheese, coriander leaves and remaining diced onion good to go.

6. In a heavy skillet, pour in vegetable oil to a depth of 0.5in and heat it to a sizzle. Fry the *gorditas* one at a time, turning them after about 15 seconds. When they've puffed up and gone crispy (around 45 seconds), take them out and drain them on paper towel.

7. Once they're all fried, use a sharp knife to gently cut an opening around the edge of the *gordita* and fill it with the meat, and garnish it with cheese, coriander leaves and onion.

MAKES 10

* Gözleme *

TURKEY

Dubbed 'Turkish crepes' by some, these stuffed flatbreads are served fresh in Turkey's many outdoor markets – watching them being made is almost as much fun as eating the finished product!

What is It?

Made with yeast-based dough, *gözleme* are rolled flat, stuffed, and cooked on a hot griddle until small brown spots or 'eyes' (*'goz'* is Turkish for eye) appear. The large pancakes are then generally chopped into squares for individual consumption. Common fillings include minced (ground) lamb or beef, spinach, fetta cheese, potatoes and eggplant.

Origin

Savoury-dough pastries date back thousands of years in Turkey, and *gözleme* is no exception. Originally from rural Turkey, especially the Anatolian regions, *gözleme* migrated to the cities to serve as fast food for busy traders and marketgoers. Today it's common to see *gözleme* vendors – often older women – sitting in markets and shop windows cooking their dough on large round griddles called *sacs*. In more recent years, Turkish immigrants have taken *gözleme* abroad, where they've become a popular street-fair snack in places as far-flung as Germany and Australia.

Finding It

Istanbul's Grand Bazaar is a great place to seek out *gözleme;* expect to pay 5 Turkish lira (US$2.80).

Tasting

Gözleme is the ideal street snack to keep you energised for long days of shopping for spices, rugs, lamps and all the other things that make Turkish markets so seductive. Simply look out for vendors bent over a circular griddle, cooking up what looks like an oversized crepe. Sometimes you have a choice of fillings, other times you simply eat whatever today's special might be. The vendors fold the pancakes as quickly and delicately as origami, browning them on the griddle then chopping them into squares. Whatever the filling – spinach and salty white cheese, savoury minced lamb, richly spiced eggplant – the *gözleme* are delectable, their flaky dough yielding to the soft interior. Bite into one, and suddenly American-style fast food seems about as appealing as eating a wet sock. Bye bye Big Mac, hello *gözleme*.

* TIPS * Eat your *gözleme* Turkish-style, with a squeeze of fresh lemon and a side of *aryan* (a thin yoghurt and water drink). Finish it off with a cup of teeth-judderingly sweet Turkish tea. Then show your appreciation to your *gözleme*-maker with a hearty '*tesekkür ederim*' (thank you).

* By Emily Matchar *

Recipe Spinach & Cheeze Gözleme

YOU'LL NEED

5¼ cups plain (all-purpose) flour

2½ tsp salt

2 tsp dried yeast powder

1 tsp sugar

1¼ cups water

1 cup spinach, chopped

1 cup fetta cheese, crumbled

½ cup vegetable oil

5 tbs butter

METHOD

1. Sift flour into a bowl, reserving 1 cup of flour. Add salt. Combine yeast and sugar in another bowl, add ¼ cup of water and stir. Make a hole in the centre of the flour, and pour the liquid into the hole, covering the top with some flour. Allow to rise for 10 minutes. Add the rest of the water, stirring thoroughly. Knead the mixture for about five minutes, then cover and allow to rise until it has doubled in size (about one hour).

2. Toss the spinach and fetta cheese together in a medium bowl; set aside.

3. Put the dough on a lightly floured surface, then divide into 10 equal portions. Shape each portion into a ball, and roll each ball with a rolling pin until it forms a rectangle slightly less than 0.5cm thick. Brush the surface with oil. Fold the opposite edge of each square together, bringing the edges together in the centre.

4. Sprinkle the fetta and spinach mixture on half the dough, then fold the other half over to form an oval shape. Seal the edges well by pressing gently.

5. Heat a griddle or heavy skillet (frying pan) and grease the surface with butter. Put the *gözleme* on the griddle and cook until the surface is lightly speckled with brown spots (the 'eyes'). Serve hot, with lemon wedges.

* Gyros *

GREECE

Pronounced 'yee-ross', this pita wrap stuffed with hot, greasy slices of spit-roast meat and dripping with delicious garlicky sauce makes a perfectly satisfying late-night snack.

What is It?

Thin slabs of marinated pork, beef or chicken are cooked slowly on a vertical rotisserie so that the edges are crispy and the inside is tender and juicy. It's eaten in warm, pocketless pita bread and topped with tomato, onion and tzatziki sauce. You'll find *souvlatzidikos* selling this quintessential fast food on almost every street corner in Greece, where it's eaten standing or walking. It's an especially popular end to a night on the town.

Origin

These delicious kebabs have a long history. The name comes from Greek γύρος (turn), which is a calque of the Turkish word *döner;* it was originally called ντονέρ (do'ner) in Greece as well. İskender Efendi of Bursa in northwestern Turkey claims to have invented the unmistakable vertical grilling technique in the 1860s, improving on the ancient horizontal method. *Gyros* reached Greece in the 1920s with Greek refugees from Asia Minor. Unlike *döner, gyros* is typically made of pork. It is seasoned with a distinct spice mix, and typically served with Greek yoghurt or tzatziki sauce.

Tasting

In the cities in Greece, chances are that you're never far from a busy *souvlatzidiko,* where the pungent aroma of seasoned pork, chicken or beef draws hungry crowds looking for a quick bite. If the smell isn't enough to get you interested, the sight of the stacks of tantalising slow-roasting meat surely will be. The cook shaves a steaming portion from the cone right in front of you and serves it on fresh pita warmed on the grill. Onions, tomatoes and tzatziki sauce are the most common toppings, but it's not surprising to find yoghurt, fried potatoes, lettuce and green pepper on offer as well.

It takes both hands to hold a stuffed *gyros* sandwich, wrapped in crinkly waxed paper and a napkin. *Gyros* can be a messy treat if you're not careful; the soft pita can scarcely contain the meat's hot juices. The tangy tzatziki sauce, made of yoghurt, garlic and cucumber, is the perfect contrast to the rich spiciness of the meat, and the crisp vegetables add a refreshing juiciness to the dish.

Finding It

In Athens, head to Monastiraki Sq, where *souvlatzidikos* cluster across from the metro. You'll pay €1.80 (US$2.50) for takeaway.

* TIPS * Be sure to order *your gyros 'me pita'* (with bread), or you could end up with more than you bargained for; if you don't specify, restaurants may assume you want the more expensive, less portable *merida,* a full-plate serving that is larger than many people's appetites. *Gyros* is meant to be eaten on the go; most tavernas include a hefty cover charge in the price of the meal for those who choose to eat in.

* By Meredith Snyder *

Recipe Gyros

Although this recipe isn't cooked on a rotisserie, the meat will have a similar flavour.

YOU'LL NEED

Gyros

1½ tsp sweet paprika

3 tbs sea salt

¼ tsp pepper

¼ tsp ground oregano

1.1kg (2½ lb) boneless pork loin

white wine vinegar

Tzatziki Sauce

2 medium cucumbers, peeled, seeded and diced

1 tbs salt

1 garlic clove, chopped

1 tbs finely chopped fresh dill

2 tbs lemon juice

3 cups Greek yoghurt

To Serve

6–8 pieces of pocketless pita bread

olive oil

tzatziki sauce or plain Greek yoghurt

2 tomatoes, sliced

1 medium onion, sliced

salt

freshly ground black pepper

METHOD

1. Combine the paprika, salt, pepper and oregano in a small bowl.

2. Slice the pork as thinly as possible, then pound to less than 0.5cm (0.2in) thick.

3. Arrange some of the meat slices to cover the bottom of a flat-bottomed dish, then sprinkle with the spice mixture and enough vinegar so that all the pieces are moistened. Continue layering meat, spices and vinegar until all the meat has been seasoned. Cover and let marinate in the refrigerator for at least two hours. While the meat is marinating, prepare the tzatziki sauce.

4. Cut the marinated meat into strips about 1cm wide and 5cm long. Cook in a nonstick frying pan without any oil, on high heat until the meat is browned and slightly crisp.

5. Brush the pita with a thin layer of olive oil and grill until it is warm but not crisp. Arrange the meat on the pita and top it with tzatziki sauce or yoghurt, a few tomato slices, sliced onion, and salt and black pepper, to taste. Roll your pita, wrap it in waxed paper, and serve.

Tzatziki Sauce

1. In a colander, sprinkle the cucumbers with 1 tbs salt and allow them to drain for at least 30 minutes. Rinse and pat dry with paper towel.

2. Combine cucumbers, garlic, dill and lemon juice, and puree in a blender or food processor.

3. Stir this mixture into the Greek yoghurt, and allow to rest in the refrigerator for at least two hours to allow the flavours to blend.

Hainanese Chicken Rice

MALAYSIA & SINGAPORE

Poached chicken served with rice and a bowl of its own broth, this is food as a warm, comforting embrace.

What is It?

Described by many as the 'national dish' of Singapore, this is a seemingly simple dish of slow-poached chicken and rice (pre-fried in chicken fat then cooked, pilaf style, in the chicken broth). A small bowl of broth is served alongside, with light or dark soy sauce and a sauce made of chilli and pounded ginger. It's devoured at all hours of the day and night.

Finding It

Tian Tian, in Singapore's Maxwell Food Centre, always has long queues for its justifiably famous Hainanese chicken rice, with a great chilli sauce on the side. Large serves cost S$3.50 (US$2.80).

Tasting

Take your time, and ask around. Every stall has a slightly different version. You might get lucky and stumble upon the greatest one of them all. But probably not. Everyone has an opinion on Hainanese chicken rice, and most will differ. You're looking for every element to work on its own, and then to combine and create something greater than the sum of its parts. The chicken should be gently simmered so that the meat is alabaster white, and lusciously tender and silken; too dry, and the whole thing's ruined. The rice is laced with garlic and ginger. The dish is served with thin slices of cucumber (for elegant cool and colour), soy sauce and a chilli-garlic paste that should neither under- nor overwhelm. This is all about balance: succulent chicken and fluffy, slightly oily rice. The broth is served on the side, delicate but sustaining. Once you've tried the real thing, you'll *know* what this dish is all about.

Origin

Originally from the tiny southern archipelagic province of Hainan, this dish followed the Hainanese diaspora to Southeast Asia in the 19th and 20th centuries. As is pretty much always the case, it has evolved according to local tastes, and now, in Singapore's many hawker markets, you'll find all sorts of embellishments, from egg and tofu steeped in broth, to *chai boe* (stewed mustard leaves with tamarind and chilli) and innards.

* VARIATIONS * In Melaka you'll find the rice in balls, rather than a bowl. And the Ipoh bean sprouts chicken rice – chicken served with boiled beanshoots and plain white rice – is a speciality of Ipoh in Malaysia. Chilli heat in sauces will vary, too

Recipe Hainanese Chicken Rice

YOU'LL NEED

Chicken

1 whole chicken (1.8kg, 3½lb)

salt

10cm (4in) fresh ginger, peeled and cut into 6mm (0.25in) slices

3 stalks spring onions, cut into 2cm (1in) sections (both the green and white parts)

250g (½lb) pork bones (optional)

1 tbs sesame oil

Rice

2 cups jasmine rice, washed and soaked in cool water for at least 10 minutes

2 tbs vegetable oil

2cm (1in) section of ginger, peeled and minced

3 medium cloves garlic, minced

½ tsp sesame oil

2 cups broth from poaching the chicken

1 tsp salt

Chilli Sauce

6 hot red chillies, chopped

1 shallot, chopped

2 tbs chopped peeled fresh ginger

2 medium garlic cloves, minced

½ tsp salt

⅓ cup fresh lime juice

To Serve

¼ cup dark soy sauce

few sprigs coriander leaves (cilantro)

1 European cucumber, thinly sliced

1 bunch watercress

METHOD

1. Clean the chicken by rubbing it all over with salt then rinse it well inside and out. Pat the chicken dry and season generously with salt inside and out.

2. Stuff the bird with the ginger slices and spring onion. Place the chicken and optional pork bones in a large stockpot and fill with water to cover by about 2cm (1in). Bring the water to a boil over high heat, then lower the heat to a simmer. Cook for about 30 minutes till a thermometer inserted into the thickest part of the thigh reads 75°C (170°F) and the juices of the flesh under the leg run clear.

3. Remove pot from the heat and transfer the chicken into a bath of ice water. Discard the ginger and spring onion but reserve the poaching broth. The quick cooling keeps the chicken meat and skin firm and tender.

4. Drain the soaked rice. In a large saucepan, heat the vegetable oil over medium-high heat. When hot, add the ginger and the garlic and saute a few minutes. Pour the rice and sesame oil into the pot with the garlic and ginger, stir to coat and cook for about two minutes.

5. Add 2 cups of the reserved poaching broth, and salt to taste. Bring to a boil then turn the heat to low, cover the pot tightly and cook for 15 minutes. Remove from heat and let sit (with lid still on) for five to 10 minutes more.

6. While the rice is cooking, remove the chicken from the ice bath and rub the outside of the chicken with the sesame oil. Carve the chicken for serving.

7. Blend the chilli sauce ingredients in a food processor until smooth.

8. Reheat the remaining broth, salt to taste and serve on the side with the other condiments and garnishes.

SERVES 6

Hollandse Nieuwe Haring

THE NETHERLANDS

As street food goes, raw, lightly brined herring is a bit drab, even unappetising. But one bite reveals its secret: this is silky, impeccably fatty essence of the sea.

What is It?

Hollandse Nieuwe *haring* is an official term for a humble fish. To be 'New Dutch herring', the 15cm-long fish must be plucked from the freezing waters of the North Sea early each summer, when it's at its plumpest, then briefly salt-cured. Purists take it straight, but even the garnishes are nothing fancy: white onion and sweet pickle. The herring is served without its head, but with its tail, a natural handle for getting the snack to your mouth.

Origin

In the 14th century, Willem Beuckelszoon revolutionised herring consumption with the invention of gibbing, an alchemy of salt, fish-entrail enzymes and oak casks. The resulting portable protein helped fuel the Dutch merchant ships along the world's trade routes. Today's process is far lighter in salt, and freezers do much of the preservation, so prime-season fish can be put up and eaten year-round, with little loss in flavour. Still, Hollandse Nieuwe season remains a huge event in the Netherlands, with live news coverage of the first haul and happy herring-eaters bingeing in the streets.

Tasting

Hollandse Nieuwe kiosks dot main squares and sit at the tops of canal bridges, handy for cycling customers. The stalls are often bedecked with remarkably uncool posters: a pink-cheeked blonde in a dirndl and a starched white hat, for instance, tipping her head back as she dangles a greyish thing over her open mouth. Fortunately, the real herring experience requires no folk costumes or eating in one gulp. A good vendor will deftly clean and fillet each fish as it's ordered, and in Amsterdam, the fillets are chopped into bite-size squares and served on a small cardboard plate with a toothpick trimmed with a miniature Dutch flag. Each morsel – grey on the outside, but a luscious pink inside – is lightly salty and almost melt-in-your-mouth soft with fat; the optional onion and pickles help offset the richness. Once you're *haring*-savvy, you'll see the stalls everywhere, even at the airport, where a pit stop can instantly revive your brain after a red-eye – thanks, omega-3 fatty acids.

Finding It

The oak-cask-bedecked Hollandse Nieuwe stand on the west end of Amsterdam's Albert Cuypmarkt sells the fish for €3 (US$4.25).

* VARIATIONS * **For a bit more substance, or if you just want to cut the intensity of the fish, order a *broodje haring* – herring in a fluffy white roll. The roll does double duty: not only does it hold the garnishes in place, it also soaks up a bit of the fish oil – think of it as an edible napkin.**

* By Zora O'Neill *

Recipe Broodje Haring

YOU'LL NEED

1 Hollandse Nieuwe herring

small bread roll

1tbs finely chopped whitle onion

3 slices of cucumber pickle

METHOD

Fresh Hollandse Nieuwe *haring* gets exported to fishmongers in the know in early June. Otherwise, you'll have to head to Holland to get proper raw herring. To make your own sandwich, you'll need one small white-bread roll (what the Dutch call a *pistolet*), about 1 tbs of minced mild white onion, and three or four slices of a sweet cucumber pickle. Lay one whole, cleaned herring in the roll (slice the tail off if you prefer), then top with the onion and pickle. That's it – the Dutch are the masters of the minimalist sandwich.

* Hopper *

SRI LANKA

Rich and poor, tourists and locals: everyone in Sri Lanka loves spicing up their breakfasts and lunches with this bowl-shaped pancake wolfed down with a fiery salsa.

What is It?

Having fermented overnight, hopper batter is cooked to form a pancake with creaminess from the coconut milk and a slightly sour taste from the Sri Lankan palm toddy. It's thin, crisp, hemispherical and traditionally accompanied by *katta sambol,* concocted from chilli, onions and limes.

Origins

The Sri Lankan word for hopper is *appa,* a form of *appam* also found in southern India. Tamil literature has mentioned Hindu deities being ritually offered the food for centuries. The *appa* or *appam* are staple sustenance at Sri Lankan and Indian festivals.

Tasting

You don't have to travel far from central Colombo before the real Sri Lanka hits you with typical sensory overload. Dodge the careening tuk-tuks of traditional thoroughfares such as Galle Rd, and make for the vendor stands and roti shops responsible for a hefty dose of the colour and chaos before you. Here, white-shirted men, invariably in teams of two (one to make the batter, one to serve up the hoppers and salsa), lean over sizzling saucepans to produce pancake hemispheres. The dryness of the thin, crispy sides, the heavier, doughier, coconut-cream-infused base and the refreshing aftertaste of salt, spice and lime from the *katta sambol* smack your palate in that order (some roti shops offer a chicken or potato curry instead). Two hoppers is a standard fix: rip off roughly a quarter from the rim down and dunk in the salsa, then wipe your hands on the usually included sheet of yesterday's newspaper.

Finding It

The Dehiwala/Wellawatta areas of Galle Rd in Colombo are best for buying hoppers, from vendors or roti shops. Expect to pay from ₹10/25 (US$0.10/0.30) for a plain/egg hopper.

* VARIATIONS * Add an egg into the batter as it solidifies and you have egg hoppers: a snack transformed into a meal and offered as an alternative by most Sri Lankan hopper vendors. Coconut-milk hoppers (*miti kiri appe*) have extra coconut milk, and are worth asking after. Another important member of the extended hopper family, and a source of national culinary pride, are string hoppers (*idiyappam*) made with rice-noodle spirals.

* By Luke Waterson *

Recipe Hoppers

YOU'LL NEED

Hoppers

2 tsp dried yeast powder

⅛ cup warm water

1 tbs white sugar

370ml (1½ cup) coconut milk (and ¾ cup warm water)

4 cups rice flour

2 tbs sugar

salt to taste

dash of palm wine (optional)

olive oil

1 cup warm water

sugar to taste

Katta Sambol Salsa

2 tbs chilli flakes or chopped fresh red chilli

¼ tsp chilli powder

½ small red onion, finely chopped

1 tbs Maldive fish flakes (available in most Asian markets; omit if vegetarian)

½ lime (juice and grated rind)

METHOD

1. Sprinkle the yeast over the warm water, mix well and add the white sugar. Set aside for 10 minutes. The yeast needs to be frothing for this recipe, so if it is not, start again with a fresh batch of yeast.

2. Divide the coconut milk into two receptacles with a one-quarter to three-quarter ratio. Mix the ¾ cup warm water with the three-quarter portion of the coconut milk. Add this mixture to the yeast mix.

3. Combine the rice flour, sugar and salt (to taste) in a bowl and stir in the yeast/coconut milk mixture a little at a time. Add the dash of palm wine, if you are using it. A thick, smooth, pancake-like batter is what should form as you mix; when it's smooth, cover and leave to stand overnight.

4. The following morning, prepare the *katta sambol* by grinding together the chilli flakes or chopped fresh chilli, the chilli powder, the red onion and the fish flakes with a pestle and mortar, then mixing in the lime. Season with salt and chilli flakes to taste.

5. Put some oil in a small to medium wok and smear across so that all the sides and bottom are covered in a thin, oily sheen. Heat up on a medium heat until the oil is hot. The size/shape of the wok will be the size/shape of your hopper, so the kind of wok you use is important. Made in a large wok, the batter may not hold to make the hopper.

6. While the wok is heating, get the batter mix and thin with as much of the cup of water as necessary to achieve a batter that retains its thickness but pours easily.

7. When wok is sufficiently heated, reduce to a low heat. Then add approximately one-fifth to one-sixth of the batter and immediately swill it around so that the batter is completely covering the bottom and the sides at least two-thirds of the way up. Cover pan and cook on low heat for five minutes, after which time the edges should be crisp and the bottom still slightly gooey.

8. Add the remaining coconut milk with a pinch of salt and sugar to the last two or three hoppers (making *miti kiri appe,* coconut-milk hoppers)

9. Remove hoppers carefully from pan with a flexible spatula that you can get down the sides of and underneath each hopper to preserve the shape.

10. Serve warm with a liberal helping of *katta sambol*.

SERVES 6

* Hot Dog *

USA

Indelibly associated with baseball, carnivals and backyard parties, the humble hot dog is the unofficial food of American summer – for many, it's the very taste of childhood happiness.

What is It?

A traditional hot dog (aka 'wiener', 'red hot' or 'frank') is a sausage of finely minced (ground) pork or beef, which is boiled or grilled and served on a tubular bun of soft white bread topped with a variety of condiments. Often sold by mobile vendors at city parks, sporting events, fairs, zoos and circuses, it's widely seen as a fun, special-occasion food.

Origin

Though sausages have been around since at least the 9th century BC, it took late-19th-century German-American immigrants to slap the meat on a bun and call it a hot dog. The name (no, there's no dog in there!) may have been born from the sausage's resemblance to long, skinny dachshund dogs. Then again, maybe not – hot dogs' exact origins are shrouded in mystery. First sold at fairs and baseball games, hot dogs rose to iconic status with the 1916 founding of Nathan's Famous hot-dog stand at the Coney Island amusement park in Brooklyn, New York.

Tasting

Imagine it's a balmy summer evening at the baseball stadium. Your team's up 3-0, the crowd's in a blissed-out mood, all your friends are there. At the 7th inning stretch, you slip out of your seat and make your way through the crush to the hot-dog stand. The vendor hands you your hot dog, plucked from the grill and wrapped in a silver foil jacket. Without waiting to return to your seat, you roll the foil back and bite in. The meat is hot and salty and perfumed with garlic, its juices dripping into the soft absorbent bun. Condiments – ketchup, mustard, sauerkraut, pickle relish – cut the fattiness with an astringent twist. One, two, three, four bites, and the dog is gone. You line up and do it all over again.

It's hard to eat just one hot dog – perhaps that's why Brooklyn's legendary Nathan's Famous Hot Dog Eating Contest (record: 68 hot dogs in 10 minutes) has been going strong for nearly 100 years!

Finding It

You'll find Nathan's Famous stand at Yankee Stadium, in New York's Bronx district. Expect to pay US$3.

* VARIATIONS * Regional variations on the hot dog abound, as do violent regional rivalries over whose wiener is the winner. New York–style means beef hot dogs topped simply with mustard and sauerkraut or onions, while Chicago-style dogs are so vegie-loaded that they're described as being 'dragged through the garden'. Carolina dogs have coleslaw, Midwestern versions mean chilli and onions, while Arizona's Sonoran dog is smothered in bacon, beans, salsa and Mexican cheese.

* By Emily Matchar *

Recipe Chicago-Style Hot Dogs

YOU'LL NEED

kosher beef hot dogs

hot-dog buns (poppy seed buns are best)

yellow mustard

1 white onion, diced

jar of pickled medium-hot peppers (in Chicago, these are usually called 'sport peppers' – in other parts of the world you can substitute chopped pepperoncini or jarred pickled tabasco peppers)

tomato wedges

dill pickle spears

sweet pickle relish

celery salt

METHOD

1. In a pot or Dutch oven fitted with a steamer rack or bamboo steamer basket, boil about 10cm (a few inches) of water (water should remain below the level of the steamer rack).

2. Reduce the heat to low, place the hot dogs atop the steamer rack, cover the pot and simmer for about six minutes.

3. Two minutes before the hot dogs are done, carefully open the pot and place the buns on top of the hot dogs to steam.

4. After the two minutes are up, carefully remove the buns and hot dogs with a pair of tongs.

5. To assemble, place the hot dogs in the buns, top with mustard, onion, peppers, tomato wedges, pickle spears and pickle relish to taste, then sprinkle with celery salt.

* Jerked Pork *

JAMAICA & CARIBBEAN ISLANDS

Pork, marinated in Scotch bonnet chillies, allspice, sugar, cinnamon and a plethora of other ingredients, is slow-cooked over a smoky woodfire to create this dish, best eaten with the fingers.

What is It?

One of the great Caribbean dishes, jerked (cured) pork was originally smoked over pimento wood and berries. This added extra flavour, along with the dry rub made up of blisteringly hot chillies, the clove-laden tang of allspice and any other spice or herb close to hand. The end result was an earthy yet elegant mix: spicy, sweet and succulent.

Origin

Pork was the original jerk meat, a leftover from the Spanish conquest. Another, less happy reminder of Spanish rule were the Maroons, African slaves left to fend for themselves on the islands, and brutally hunted by the British. The Maroons needed meat that could be easily transported, and kept for a good time, so they came up with a jerk seasoning made from readily available ingredients. It had the added bonus of flavouring the meat; smoked over a fire of pimento wood, the seasoning pierced deep into the meat. This fugitive's meal soon became a finger-licking-good part of Caribbean culture.

Finding It

Scotchies Jerk Centre has outlets in Montego Bay, Ocho Rios and Kingston. Here you can dine in open thatched-roof shelters and enjoy authentic side dishes such as roast breadfruit and yam. Prices range from 170 to 425 Jamaican dollars (US$2 to US5).

Tasting

You'll have no problem spotting the jerk stalls, surrounded as they are in billowing clouds of exquisitely scented smoke. The cooking vehicle of choice is usually a split oil barrel, the coals expertly tended. Pimento wood is less common now, and the smoking of the meat pretty much extinct. Still, the jerk seasoning varies from stall to stall. The meat should be tender and bursting with juice; the heat comes first, a fruity chilli blast, then a sweetness to temper the fire. Each bite should have a whisper of allspice, and a hint of nutmeg or cinnamon. And the crust... Oh, that crust: blackened and sticky, containing the quintessence of the jerk. One portion is never enough.

* VARIATIONS * All over Jamaica you'll find jerked chicken, sausage and fish as well as jerked pork.

* By Tom Parker Bowles *

Recipe Jerked Pork

Make sure to wash your hands very thoroughly after rubbing the marinade into the pork – the chillies pack some serious heat!

YOU'LL NEED

3 medium onions, chopped finely

1 garlic bulb, chopped finely

6 sliced scotch bonnet chillies (can substitute jalapeños)

2 tbs fresh thyme

2 tbs ground allspice

2 tbs sugar

2 tbs salt

2 tsp ground black pepper

1–2 tsp ground cinnamon

1–2 tsp nutmeg

1–2 tsp ginger

½ cup olive oil

½ cup soy sauce

1 lime, juiced

1 cup orange juice

1 cup white vinegar

1.5kg (about 3lb) boneless pork loin

METHOD

1. Roughly chop onions, garlic and chillies. Put them in a blender with all the other ingredients (except the pork) and blend it until you have a smooth sauce.

2. Rinse the pork under cold water and pat dry with paper towels. Put it in a deep dish and, using a fork or paring knife, make small holes in the pork so the marinade can really soak in. Pour about a cup of marinade over the meat and massage it in. Cover and leave to marinate – preferably overnight, but five hours will do if you're pressed for time.

3. Take the meat out the fridge and let it come back to room temperature for about half an hour, before putting it on the grill (you could also bake this in the oven if it's easier) and basting it regularly with the left-over marinade. It should take a little under three hours to cook, so baste it and turn it every 20–30 minutes. The end result should be sticky and dark (because of the sugar). Allow the meat to rest before slicing.

* Juane *

AMAZON BASIN, PERU

Prepare for that long Amazon boat journey as rainforest farmers and fishermen have for centuries, with this concoction of chicken, rice and spices wrapped in a jungle leaf.

What is It?

This age-old stalwart of Peruvian jungle cuisine blends egg-flavoured rice with chicken and olives, but it's the *bijao* leaf that this lot gets trussed up in that defines the dish. The *bijao* blends with the chicken-and-rice filling as the *juanes* get boiled to create a uniquely Amazonian flavour, and the rainforest's most easily transportable meal.

Origin

The conquistadors and the Incas would have been fans of the *juane*. Its simple preparation method meant it was ideal for long-haul boat journeys. It's not clear when the *juane* first became identifiable with John the Baptist (San Juan Bautista) but thus is the name derived: the leaf-wrapped goodie bags are synonymous with the San Juan festival, celebrated across the Peruvian jungle on 24 June.

Tasting

There's something about rice compacted in 'cake' format that enhances the eating experience. Imagine, then, what wonders whisking the rice with egg, black olives, garlicky chicken and a medley of spices from turmeric to bay leaves, and squeezing it together in a leaf that secretes its juices into the rice, can do. Having to unwrap your *juane* like a good old-fashioned present before you can consume it adds to the magic. Then there are those few seconds (or, if you're saving it for later like the local boatmen, hours) while you wait to peel back the leaves and chow down, when the aroma of tenderly cooked chicken and freshly mown grass – the *bijao* taking charge – hits the air and intolerably magnifies that pit in your stomach. Yes, technically all this makes the *juane* more river food than street food, but when you taste it, you'll let us off...

Finding It

You'll find *juane* at any of the Iquitos markets, particularly Belén. Expect to pay 2 to 3 Peruvian *nuevo sol* (US$0.75 to US$1).

* DON'T MENTION THE TAMALE! * Just because the *juane* comes wrapped in a leaf does not make it a *tamale*, as so many blogs and articles apparently think. At best they are long-lost cousins, twice removed. *Tamales* generally have a banana-leaf wrapping, use a corn-dough filling and lack that special *juane* ingredient, *guizador* (a root resembling turmeric).

Recipe Juane

YOU'LL NEED

Garlic Paste

450g (about 1lb) garlic

½ cup olive oil

pinch of salt

pepper to taste

grating of *guizador* root (or fresh turmeric)

Leaf & Filling

1 *bijao* leaf (if unavailable, substitute with banana leaf) per *juane*

½ cup rice per *juane* (white rice is best, but brown rice may also be used)

1 medium chicken breast, diced into chunky segments, per *juane*

2 garlic cloves

1 tsp oregano

1 tsp cumin

pinch of turmeric

2–3 bay leaves

pinch of salt

pepper to taste

handful of black pitted olives

½ egg per *juane*

METHOD

1. In advance, make a garlic paste by topping and tailing the garlic, and placing in a baking dish covered in the olive oil. Sprinkle with salt and pepper, and grate in the *guizador* root. Cover the dish and bake for 45 minutes, then remove cover and bake for a further 15 minutes until the garlic cloves brown.

2. Remove the cloves and in a separate bowl gently squeeze them out of their skins. Pour in the oil from the baking dish and blend with a food processor. Then cool the paste and refrigerate it.

3. Ideally heat the *bijao* leaf over an open flame to improve elasticity, then wipe clean.

4. Cook the rice until slightly underdone.

5. Meanwhile, amply baste the chicken segments in the garlic paste (you do not have to use all the paste). Cook the chicken in olive oil on the hob, turning repeatedly.

6. When the rice is done, ensure it is broken up so that there are no clumps, and mix with the juices from the cooked chicken.

7. Saute the garlic cloves and add to the rice mixture. Add the oregano, cumin, tumeric and bay leaves and season with salt and pepper to taste.

8. Stir in the handful of olives to the rice and spice mixture.

9. Beat in a ½ egg per each ½ cup of rice used, and mix well.

10. Put a scoop of the rice mixture along with the chicken segments (one chicken breast per *juane*) in each *bijao* leaf and tie each firmly with string to leave a 'neck'.

11. Boil the *juanes* in a large pot of water for one hour. Serve hot immediately.

* Kati Roll *

KOLKATA, INDIA

Is it a kebab? Is it a wrap? A souped-up sandwich? A powered-up paratha (fried flatbread)? Enter the *kati* roll – Kolkata's favourite portable snack!

What is It?

A *kati* roll is a tinglingly tasty lamb kebab, rolled up inside a paratha with sauteed onions, chilli and spicy sauce. In the best *kati* rolls, the paratha is brushed with egg on one side and seared on a hotplate to seal in the flavours before everything is tucked into the roll. The end result looks a lot like a Mexican wrap, but the fillings and flavours are indisputably Indian.

Origin

Some claim that the *kati* roll was invented as a portable tiffin (light lunch) for Bengali office workers on the go. Others insist that the dish was cooked up for colonial sahibs who were too fastidious to get their hands dirty while eating. Either way, the first *kati* rolls trundled out of the kitchens of Nizam's Restaurant in Kolkata in the 1930s; once word got out, there was no stopping them. Today, hole-in-the-wall takeaways on busy highways are feted like Michelin-star restaurants for the quality of their *kati* rolls.

Finding It

After a long hiatus, Nizam's Restaurant has returned to Kolkata. The reinvented Nizam's has ditched the colonial decor, but the *kati* rolls still sizzle. Expect to pay ₹25 to ₹90 (US$0.55 to US$2).

Tasting

As with wraps anywhere, the preparation of this 'kebab in a blanket' is a piece of street theatre. During the evening rush hour, when office workers gather for their nightly fix, you'll see vendors rolling this portable feast at breakneck speed. Sizzle, seal, wrap and deliver, sizzle, seal, wrap and deliver, then on to the next customer in seconds flat. The flavours are rich, fragrant and immediate. The softness of the paratha gives way suddenly to the tender meat within, and each bite delivers a crunch of chilli and onion and a swoosh of sauce and spices. *Kati* rolls should be eaten fresh off the *tava* (griddle) when the paratha is still hot through and the sauces and meat juices are still mingling. Vegetarians can get in on the act with *kati* rolls filled with spiced egg, potato and paneer.

* TIPS * **Kolkata's best *kati* rolls are often served in the most unlikely of settings, but any office worker can point you in the right direction and the crowds of eager diners queuing outside will guide you like a beacon. If that sounds too taxing, the latest hot spots are listed in the annual *Telegraph Food Guide*, published by Kolkata's leading newspaper.**

* By Joe Bindloss *

Recipe Kati Roll

YOU'LL NEED

Kati Kebabs

1 tsp ground cumin

1 tsp ground chilli

½ tsp lemon juice

1½ tsp ground coriander seeds

1 clove garlic, crushed

½ tsp pepper

½ tsp ground ginger

1 tbs canola oil

salt to taste

400g (14oz) minced (ground) lamb

Parathas

2 cups atta (wholewheat flour)

½ tsp salt

1 cup water

½ cup ghee

Kati Rolls

1 onion, chopped

2 green chillies, chopped

parathas

1 egg, beaten

kati kebabs

garlic-and-chilli sauce

TIP To spice up your parathas, fold mashed potato, chopped coriander leaves (cilantro), cumin seed and chilli into the dough before you roll it out..

METHOD

Kati Kebabs

1. Grind the spices and other ingredients into a paste, then mix together with the minced lamb, and marinate for about four hours.

2. Form the mixture into long sausage shapes and press onto metal skewers.

3. Grill the kebabs over hot charcoal, or in a hot oven, turning regularly and brushing with extra oil to seal in the flavour.

Parathas

1. Make a simple dough with the flour, salt and water.

2. Take egg-sized balls of dough and rub them with ghee, then set them aside for 30 to 45 minutes.

3. Roll the balls of dough into flat sheets, then heat on a *tava* or hotplate for about 45 seconds on each side until brown spots appear. Brush with a little extra ghee on each side during the cooking process to crisp up the paratha. Set aside.

Kati Rolls

1. Saute the onion and chilli in a wok, *karahi* (a type of pot) or frying pan until the onion begins to turn transparent.

2. Brush one side of each paratha with the beaten egg, cook until the egg sets, then remove from the heat.

3. In the middle of each paratha, add the fried onions and chilli, a *kati* kebab, and a generous squeeze of garlic-and-chilli sauce, then roll tightly and serve.

* Kelewele *

GHANA

A sublime combination of flavours, _kelewele_ is like the spicy, plantain version of french fries, only better.

What is It?

Ripe plantain is sliced into long strips, tossed with salt, ginger and fresh chilli, then deep-fried in vegetable oil, maybe over a charcoal stove. It's served up in a square of newspaper as an evening or after-dinner treat. The plantain tends to curl up in the pot, making little spirals of greasy delight.

Tasting

Kelewele is served after the sun has gone down and the heat of the day has faded. The street-food scene is happening: people are taking walks in the neighbourhood (it's cooler outside than in the house), and roadside stalls are lit with small lamps. The _kelewele_ stall is popular with everyone, but especially couples (it's a traditional first-date food) and pregnant women (_kelewele_ is supposed to be good for pregnancy). When the _kelewele_'s ready, the heat – and some of the oil – seeps through the newspaper that holds it, and no one can wait until it cools to dig in. The crunchy plantain is spicy and sweet, the flavours of ginger and plantain playing off each other, and the heat of the chilli builds with each bite until it burns. The aftertaste is sweetness and pure fire – but you go back for more anyway.

Origin

Nowadays _kelewele_ (keleh-weleh) is fried up all over Ghana, but it's originally a food of the Ga people, from Accra and the country's southeastern coast. The snack was created to use plantains that were going bad: the chilli masked the overripe taste, the ginger warded off nausea, while the frying firmed them up. But not to worry: today's _kelewele_ is made with plantains just ripe enough to be sweet, soft and delicious.

Finding It

Oxford St, in Accra's Osu neighbourhood, is the reigning _kelewele_ capital. A handful of _kelewele_, about 15 pieces, costs 1 cedi (US$0.60).

* **TIPS** * _Kelewele_ goes amazingly well with peanuts, and they're often fried in the same oil; get a small side serving at the same stall. Since the _kelewele_ is crazy spicy, you'll need a drink handy: a cold Alvaro, a nonalcoholic malt-based drink, is the local favourite.

* By Amy Karafin, with Barbara Sarpong *

Recipe Kelewele

YOU'LL NEED

1 cup vegetable oil

2 ripe plantains, sliced into thin strips

2 tbs minced ginger

1 minced chilli (or to taste)

½ tsp salt

METHOD

1. Heat vegetable oil in a small saucepan.

2. Toss the sliced plantains in a bowl with the ginger, chilli and salt; marinate for a few minutes.

3. Fry plantain strips in the oil until golden brown.

* Khao Soi *

NORTHERN THAILAND

Chiang Mai's signature dish is a creamy, spicy Thai comfort curry with noodles two ways.

What is It?

A curry-based noodle dish with chicken, beef, or sometimes pork, *khao soi* is spicy, but not mind-blowingly so, with soft noodles below and deep-fried ones sprinkled on top. Pickled cabbage and lime help to cut through an excess of richness. The dish is mainly eaten in the afternoon and at night.

Tasting

If you're lucky the noodles might still be made manually, with the wheat ground, boiled, stretched and sliced by hand. What you want in the dish is balance: spice, but not so much it overpowers; coconut milk, added in just the right amount so it doesn't overwhelm and make everything dull and overly sweet. The meat should be cooked in the broth, the noodles soft and chewy. The deep-fried noodles on top should shatter between the teeth. Oh, and that pickled cabbage is essential: it adds a welcome sour note, along with the lime. Sit down at the rickety table, and slurp and sip to your heart's content. *Khao soi* satisfies every eating urge.

Origin

Khao soi is thought to have roots in Myanmar (Burma), where Chinese Muslims from Yunnan province brought an early version down to Thailand and Laos. Originally said to be halal (so, pork free), it now can contain pork, as well as the more usual beef and chicken. Curry paste was added later, along with coconut milk.

Finding It

Chiang Mai is the traditional home of *khao soi*. Try the pork version at the long-established and popular Khao Soi Lamduan for 20 baht (US$0.70).

* NOT TO BE CONFUSED WITH... * Same name, different dish. The *khao soi* found in Laos is a soup made with rice noodles, pork, chilli and tomatoes, and bears little resemblence to the Thai version.

* By Tom Parker Bowles *

Recipe Khao Soi

YOU'LL NEED

2–3 cups plus 2 tbs vegetable oil

2½ tbs red curry paste

1 tsp curry powder

½ tsp ground turmeric

1 tsp ground cardamom (optional)

3 cups unsweetened coconut milk

1½–2kg (3–4lb) chicken, cut into 6 pieces

1¾ cups chicken stock

1 tsp sugar

2 tbs fish sauce, or more to taste

700g (1½lb) fresh egg noodles or 350g (¾lb) dried

2–6 dried red chillies

⅓ cup shallots, thinly sliced

¾ cup Chinese pickled mustard greens, chopped

1 lime, cut into wedges

handful coriander leaves (cilantro), chopped

⅓ cup spring onions, chopped

METHOD

1. Heat 2 tbs of the oil in a large, heavy saucepan over medium heat then add the red curry paste, curry powder, turmeric and optional cardamom. Cook, stirring constantly for about two minutes.

2. Add 1 cup of the coconut milk and bring to a boil, stirring well for about 2 minutes. Add 1 more cup of the coconut milk, return to a boil, and again boil for about 2 minutes.

3. Add the chicken pieces, 1 cup chicken stock and remaining coconut milk then bring to a boil again. Simmer and thin the broth as needed with chicken stock or water.

4. Add the sugar and fish sauce. Cover and simmer until the chicken is tender, about 45 minutes.

5. If you're using dried noodles, cook all the noodles in a large pot of boiling water, stirring well till they are tender but firm, about seven minutes or more. If you're using fresh noodles, set aside 1 cup then boil the rest till tender and firm, about three minutes. Drain and rinse well in cold water then add a dash of oil and mix well to prevent the noodles from sticking together. If you used dried noodles, set aside 1 cup of the noodles and dry them in a clean dishtowel.

6. Heat the remaining oil in a large saucepan over medium-high heat. Place the 1 cup of towel-dried noodles or the 1 cup of uncooked fresh noodles into the saucepan a few strands at a time. Fry them, turning once, until crisp and golden. Remove from heat and set aside. Add the dried chillies to the pan and fry for a few seconds until they puff up; set aside.

7. Divide the remaining boiled noodles into 4 bowls. Ladle the chicken curry over the noodles and top with shallots, mustard greens, fried noodles and lime wedges. Add fried chillies to taste. Sprinkle with coriander leaves and spring onion and serve.

SERVES 4

* Knish *

NEW YORK, USA

The sort of thing that keeps you going through cold New York days, the knish is a hefty, round, baked pastry, seriously heavy on the carbs.

What is It?

Usually filled with mashed potato or buckwheat groats (kasha), along with sauerkraut, onions, meat or cheese, wrapped in pastry, then baked, the knish offers very serious sustenance and is commonly eaten for lunch.

Origin

The knish came to New York with the Ashkenazi Jews of Eastern Europe. It's a form of piroshki, but in the early days, when it was sold from stalls as a hot lunch for workmen, the meat disappeared. But as money returned, so did the filling of chopped liver and various kinds of meat.

Tasting

There's nothing subtle about a knish. Comprising mashed potato, sauerkraut, meat, onions, cheese and pastry, this is proper ballast, a carbohydrate hit of the very finest kind. It might be known as the 'humble knish', or 'lowly pie', but there's nothing cheap about its appeal. Bite through the hot, crisp pastry, and you hit thick, fluffy mashed potato, and, at its most basic, just onions – there are endless variations with a sharp hit of sauerkraut and meat, liver or beef. Dip the knish in mustard and eat it while it's hot. One is enough to keep the cold out, but it shouldn't be bland; rather, it should be comfort food that warms the cockles of your heart.

Finding It

Knish Nosh, in Forest Hills (and a couple of other locations in the city), serves a huge variety of knishes for about US$3.50 each.

* VARIATIONS * You can get knishes small, square, deep-fried or grilled, and filled with anything from blue cheese and spinach to sweet potato and broccoli. Purists insist that baked, round and potato-filled is the only way to go.

* By Tom Parker Bowles *

Recipe Knish

This is a very simple traditional potato knish recipe. They're sometimes made in a 'jelly roll' shape then sliced, but we're sticking with a parcel arrangement.

YOU'LL NEED

2 cups flour

1 tsp baking powder

½ tsp salt

2 eggs

2 tbs water

2 tbs oil

2 cups finely diced onions

salt and pepper to taste

2 cups mashed potatoes

1 extra egg, beaten with 1 tsp water, for an egg wash

METHOD

1. Combine flour, baking powder and salt in a large bowl. Make a well in the centre of the flour (imagine you're looking down into a volcano) and pour the eggs, 2 tbsp of water and 1 tbsp of oil into it. Mix everything together gently until a dough is formed.

2. Knead the dough then place in a bowl brushed with oil. Cover it and let it stand for an hour.

3. Preheat oven to 180°C (350°F).

4. In a frying pan, cook the onions in the remaining oil until softened, and season with salt and pepper. Remove from the heat and stir them through your mashed potato.

5. Tip your dough out onto a floured surface and roll out to your desired thickness. Shapes of knishes can vary, but a classic option is to use a pizza cutter to slice the dough into rectangles about the size of an envelope.

6. Place a spoonful of filling on the dough, paint the edges of the dough with egg wash, then fold the corners up and over the filling to form a parcel. Brush over with more egg wash and bake on a tray for 40 minutes.

MAKES 8

* Kuaytiaw *

THAILAND

Kuaytiaw, or Thai noodle soup, is – dare we say it – the hamburger of Thai street food: it's simple, satisfying, cheap and ubiquitous.

What is It?

Kuaytiaw can take a variety of shapes and forms, but the most common version is a simple combination of thin rice noodles, pork broth and pork or fish balls garnished with chopped coriander, beanshoots and a dash of white pepper. Variations on the dish are numerous, and range from versions using a curry-like coconut-milk-based broth to so-called 'boat noodles', served with braised meat and a rich, spice-laden broth.

Origin

As evidenced by the name, *kuaytiaw* is yet another Chinese contribution to Thailand's street food repertoire. Originally introduced via labourers from China, who popularised the dish during the early 20th century, today *kuaytiaw* is hands down the most common street food in Thailand. Versions of the dish involving dried spices and a curry-like broth were probably introduced via Thailand's contact with Muslim traders, while more recent spin-offs and variations have resulted in a vast repertoire of entirely Thai varieties of *kuaytiaw*.

Finding It

Bangkok's Victory Monument is home to several shops that specialise in *kuaytiaw ruea* (boat noodles) for as little as 15 baht (US$0.50).

Tasting

In its most basic form, *kuaytiaw* is Thai comfort food, and doesn't pack the spicy punch of most of its counterparts. Yet despite its apparent simplicity, ordering *kuaytiaw* the Thai way requires a bit of linguistic knowledge, as diners are typically expected to specify what type of noodles they want, as well as their preference for meats or other toppings. Like other Thai noodle-based dishes, *kuaytiaw* comes out of the kitchen relatively bland and customers are expected to season the dish with optional condiments including fish sauce, sugar, dried chilli flakes and vinegar. *Kuaytiaw* vendors span what is perhaps the most diverse spectrum of Thai street eats, and range from gritty, open-air, streetside stalls to flash air-conditioned restaurants. Likewise, the dish functions equally well as breakfast, a late-night snack and anything in between.

* **VARIATIONS** * **Yen ta fo** are noodles served in a red, slightly sweet broth, while **bamee** are egg-and-flour noodles often served with roast pork or crab. If you like your noodles served 'dry', that is, without broth, order your bowl **haeng**, while **kao lao** means that the dish is served with no noodles.

Recipe Kuaytiaw

Good Asian supermarkets will sell ready-mix pork stock powder and pork balls but you can really use any combination of stock and meat. Chicken stock makes a good all-purpose broth, which will go well with most meats.

YOU'LL NEED

300mL (10fl oz) pork or chicken stock

50g (1.7oz) fresh rice noodles or 40g (1.4oz) dried rice stick noodles

5 small pork balls or 2 tbs cooked chicken, shredded

1 tsp white pepper, ground

a handful of beanshoots, trimmed

a handful of coriander leaves (cilantro), chopped

fried garlic or onion flakes

spring onions, chopped

red chillies, chopped

a wedge of lime to garnish

METHOD

1. Boil the stock in a small saucepan.

2. Add the noodles, pork balls and white pepper and simmer for a few minutes until the noodles are cooked.

3. Pour the soup into a bowl and top with the beanshoots and coriander leaves.

4. Garnish with the fried garlic flakes, spring onions and as much chilli as you can handle and squeeze over some lime juice. Serve immediately.

SERVES 1

* Kushari *

EGYPT

Opinions often diverge in Egypt, but one thing almost every Egyptian concedes is that *kushari* – a uniquely Egyptian medley of starches – reigns supreme.

What is It?

Kushari is a delectable, any-time-of-day, year-round whole that is far more addictive than the sum of its humdrum base parts: pasta, rice and lentils. The magic finish comes from a spicy tomato-sauce topping and garnish of fried onions, all enhanced by garlic-vinegar or chilli.

Origin

This cheap, filling and healthy national dish is so popular that some restaurants in Eygpt, particularly Cairo, specialise in this alone. But although *kushari* was the first Egyptian fast food, little seems known about its genesis. Educated conjecture suggests that it may have been created out of poverty – filling fare for people who couldn't afford meat – or that, as vegan victuals, it was influenced by the vegetarian diet of fasting Coptic Christians. Whatever the case, meat – such as small pieces of fried liver, chicken or lamb – is now sometimes back in the bowl.

Finding It

For the best *kushari,* visit Abou Tarek Restaurant in downtown Cairo. Depending on the size, *kushari* portions cost E£2 to E£5 (US$0.35 to US$0.85).

Tasting

Kushari is assembled in just a few seconds – but the experience is downright percussive. In *kushari*-specific restaurants, to which Egyptians of all ilk frequently flock, the cooked ingredients are speedily doled out from what comes to be seen as a drum set of food-filled basins. As it happens, the *kushari* composer raps and taps his spoon against the bowls and basins in a virtuosic display of rhythm. It's loud but mesmerising, a Stomp-style performance that begs an encore. Or is it just that the *kushari*'s so good one bowl is never enough?

* TIPS * **Whether purchased in a specialised restaurant or from a street vendor, *kushari* is often alone on the menu; you need only say what size you want – small, medium or large. There's also usually a choice of sauce: garlic-vinegar or a chilli sauce as spicy as it looks. Many locals also squeeze in some lemon.**

* By Ethan Gelber *

Recipe Kushari

YOU'LL NEED

Tomato Sauce

3 tbs olive oil

½ cup onion, finely chopped

4 garlic cloves, chopped

400g (14oz) tomato puree

¾ tsp ground cinnamon

½ tsp ground cumin

½ tsp salt

¼ tsp ground black pepper

¼ tsp chilli flakes

Kushari

1 cup rice (long-grain)

1 cup lentils (brown or black)

2 tbs white vinegar

½ tsp ground cumin

½ tsp garlic powder

8 tbs olive oil

1½ cups onion, sliced

1 cup pasta (small macaroni or vermicelli broken into small pieces)

METHOD

Tomato Sauce

1. Heat the oil and onions on a medium flame until the latter are golden brown.

2. Stir in the garlic and cook for two minutes.

3. Add the tomato puree, cinnamon, cumin, salt, pepper and chilli flakes. Increase the heat a bit and let simmer, uncovered, until the sauce thickens (approximately 15–20 minutes).

Kushari

1. Simultaneously, but in different pots, cook the rice and the lentils. The lentils should simmer, covered, until tender (20–30 minutes); then, use a strainer to remove the lentils (leaving the lentil water in the pot), placing them directly into a mix of the vinegar, cumin and garlic powder.

2. Heat the oil on a medium flame; add the onions and cook, de-glazing as necessary, until they are lightly browned. Remove from the oil and drain on paper towel.

3. Stir the uncooked pasta into the same oil used for cooking the onions; saute pasta until lightly browned, then place in the used lentil water, bring back to a boil and cook until tender.

4. Assemble the *kushari* in eight bowls: lay down a base of rice, add a blanket of pasta with a few browned onions, and then a cover of lentils. Spoon the tomato sauce on top and trim with a few more onions.

SERVES 8

* Lángos *

HUNGARY

Deep-fried, frisbee-shaped bread puffs rubbed with a clove of fresh garlic and topped with shredded gruyère or emmental cheese and sour cream, *lángos* (lahn-gosh) are a classic, filling and quintessentially Hungarian afternoon snack.

What is It?

Made with potatoes, flour, milk, sugar and salt, *lángos* come in a range of variations, but the classic permutation is the *sajtos-tejfölös-sonkás lángos*, topped with cheese, sour cream and ham. They are found all over the country year-round and are best enjoyed at street-corner or market-stall kiosks on a hot day, and downed with a cold beer.

Finding It

Lángos tastes best at Budapest's Fény Utca market, the 1st-floor stand of which sells 15 different varieties from 180 forint (US$1).

Tasting

The smell that emanates from this warm, soft, doughy snack is simply heavenly, and after you've smeared it with juice from a cut garlic clove, you'll never be able to wolf down another run-of-the-mill pizza-dough fritter again – the *lángos* easily trumps it in taste. Something of a *lángos* revival has spread throughout Hungary in recent years, with growing numbers of street vendors serving customers who are nostalgic for a filling food that feels and tastes very Hungarian. Today you'll often find *lángos* stalls cropping up wherever people are milling about: train stations, beaches along Lake Balaton or the Danube, and weekly fairs and markets during summer in Central Europe. At any of these, you'll find that *lángos* happens to be excellent with creamy garlic soup – just don't plan on kissing anyone afterwards.

Origin

During Hungary's long, cold winters, locals needed some serious substance to keep their bodies warm and fuelled; potato dough fried in lard was the best choice around. This scrumptious snack was originally a by-product of bread making in small rural Hungarian villages. Traditionally, the *lángos* was made from leftover bread dough and baked at the front of a brick oven near the fire – its name derives from the Hungarian word for 'flame' – and would be served for breakfast on bread-baking days.

* VARIATIONS * **Common ingredients and toppings include mushroom, quark cheese, beef, eggplant, *kefir* (fermented milk) and cabbage, but *lángos* can also be enjoyed as a dessert – just top with icing (powdered) sugar or jam.**

* By Roger Norum & Strouhan Martins *

Recipe Lángos

YOU'LL NEED

1 large potato, boiled, peeled and mashed

2½ tsp dried yeast powder

1 tsp sugar

1¾ cups plain (all-purpose) flour

1 tbs vegetable oil

¾ tsp salt

½ cup milk

2 cloves garlic, sliced in half

salt

dill, chopped, to taste

METHOD

1. Place all ingredients (except the garlic, second measure of salt and the dill) in a mixing bowl. Mix the ingredients until moist.

2. Using an electric mixer with a dough hook, knead the mixture for approximately six minutes or until smooth. Place in a greased bowl, cover and let rise until size has roughly doubled.

3. Separate dough into four separate portions, then shape into rounds on a lightly floured board. Cover and let sit for 20 minutes.

4. In a large skillet (frying pan), heat oil to 350°C (662°F). Flatten, then stretch dough to roughly 20cm (8in) diameter. Fry individual dough pieces for about two minutes on each side or until golden brown. Absorb grease by placing on paper towel.

5. Rub *lángos* with garlic clove, sprinkle with salt and chopped dill, then serve.

* Maine Lobster Roll *

MAINE, USA

A summer staple of the New England yacht-set, the lobster roll combines the haute (silky, sea-flavoured lobster meat) and the humble (mayonnaise, white-bread hot-dog buns) to drool-worthy effect.

What is It?

The perfect lobster roll means a maximum amount of lobster-meat chunks (up to 450g or more) mixed with mayo or butter and stuffed into an absurdly small hot-dog bun. It's typically served during summer at a seasonal 'lobster shack' – a roadside stand with walk-up window service and a handful of outdoor picnic benches for seating.

Origin

Once so plentiful it was considered a poor-man's food, lobster got a makeover in the 1800s when New England society women realised they could enjoy the crustacean in salad form, rather than have to do the 'distasteful' work of cracking the shell themselves. In the early 1900s, someone came up with the bright idea of piling the lobster salad on a bun for easy eating, and voila, the lobster roll was born. By the mid-20th century, the lobster roll was a must-eat for the hordes of travellers driving up Maine's coastal highway each summer.

Finding It

Try the lobster roll at Red's Eats, Wiscasset, Maine; you'll pay around US$16.

Tasting

A lobster roll is best enjoyed after a long summer morning of strolling one of Maine's pebbly beaches and swimming in the chilly grey sea. You throw a cover-up over your swimsuit, slip on a pair of thongs (flip-flops), and pad over to the nearest lobster shack. Some shacks are beachfront, while others are found on the outskirts of historic fishing villages or perched atop pedestrian bridges. Wherever the location, a good shack will always have a line (often a loooong line) at lunchtime – don't be deterred! Order at the window, then stake out a picnic table as you wait for your name or number to be called. At last, claim your plastic tray, where an overflowing lobster roll sits wedged inside a tiny paper basket like a giant in a VW Beetle. Depending on the shack, your first bite may be warm and buttery, or cool and mayo-slicked. Either way, it will be perfection: the silkiness of the meat, the softness of the bun, the crunch of celery...summer bliss.

* TIPS * Round your meal out with some other Maine classics – a Moxie soda (Maine's official soft drink), a whoopie pie (imagine a giant, fluffy Oreo cookie) and a scoop of Grape-Nuts ice cream (a breakfast-cereal-based flavour that's as good as it is odd). Wherever there's a lobster shack, there's bound to be an ice-cream stand nearby.

* By Emily Matchar *

Recipe Maine Lobster Roll

YOU'LL NEED

4 x 450–500g (1lb) live lobsters

¼ cup mayonnaise

½ cup celery, diced

2 tbs unsalted butter, room temperature

4 hot-dog buns

4 leaves of Boston lettuce (or other crunchy, mild variety), washed

paprika or cayenne pepper (optional)

METHOD

1. Put the lobsters in the freezer for a few minutes (to 'numb' them before cooking).

2. Bring a large pot of water to a boil and cook the lobsters until they turn bright red (about 10 minutes). Plunge the lobsters into an ice bath to stop the cooking process.

3. Crack the lobsters and remove the tail and claw meat – check out the Gulf of Maine Research Institute's tutorial on eating lobster for tips on meat-removal techniques (www.gma.org/lobsters/eatingetc.html). Pat the meat dry with paper towels, trim it into 1.5cm (0.6in) chunks, then refrigerate until cool.

4. In a large bowl, mix the meat with the mayonnaise and celery.

5. Butter the hot-dog buns and toast them under the broiler (grill) or in a pan until golden brown, then line them with a lettuce leaf and fill them with a quarter of the lobster-meat/mayo mixture. Finish by sprinkling with paprika or cayenne pepper, if desired.

SERVES 4

* Mangue Verte *
SENEGAL

Mangue verte (green mango) has more in common with potato chips than yellow mangoes. On a hot Dakar day, it makes a refreshing combination of salty and crunchy, with a side of juicy tartness.

What is It?

Mangues vertes are the prelude to Senegal's glorious mango season, when sweet, juicy *mangues jaunes* (yellow mangoes) are absolutely everywhere. The unripe version – cut into slices and tossed with chilli, salt or Jumbo (a kind of MSG bouillon cube), and sometimes lime – is edgier and more complex than its sweeter, grown-up self.

Origin

Mangue verte may have evolved from *buggai,* a spicy chutney of green mango boiled and seasoned with – wait for it – chilli and Jumbo. It's served with *thieboudjenne,* the national lunch, and the communal bowl in which it's served is cordially fought over. It may also have travelled up from Guinea-Bissau or Senegal's Casamance region, famous for having the best mangoes. There, green-mango juice is made by sun-drying the unripe fruit for three days, then boiling it in water, and adding sugar.

Finding It

The lanes around Dakar's Marché Sandaga, especially Av Peytavin, are prime *mangue verte* areas. A sachet will cost you 50 CFA francs (US$0.10).

Tasting

Mango season coincides with Senegal's hottest time of year, so green-mango season is a time of bittersweet anticipation. It's sunny, the air is dry, and everyone has begun to walk a little more slowly. Even the women who sell *mangues vertes,* their hair tied up in a riotously colourful scarf, prepare the snack with a graceful slowness. When the time comes, they take the mango of your choosing, slice it into a little bag, and shake it up with the toppings. The mango is hard as an apple, and the first taste is salty and crunchy, followed by the bite of the chilli, like some kind of sublime junk food. But then the mango comes through, its sweetness just a glimmer and its sourness a fruity kick – a burst of energy on a slow, hot day.

* TIPS * **Mangue verte is known to be *dangereux* – it can cause an upset stomach – if the mango is too unripe, so avoid it from October to December. (Lots of kids aren't allowed *mangue verte* during this time, but some can't help themselves and eat it in secret.) They're safe from January to April and taste the best just before yellow-mango season in May and June.**

* By Amy Karafin, with Maïmouna Ciss *

Recipe **Mangue Verte**

YOU'LL NEED

1 green mango

½ small lime (optional)

salt or the powder from a Jumbo or other stock cube

chilli powder

METHOD

Peel the mango, then slice. Squirt a bit of lime juice onto the mango if you like it tangy, and toss. Sprinkle salt and chilli to taste.

* Man'oushe *

LEBANON

Man'oushe is commonly (and unfairly) misprized as simply the Lebanese version of pizza. Instead, it is more like the crispy-crusted snack-emblem of the nation – affordable, delightful, all-purpose and classless.

What is It?

This essential Lebanese flatbread can be cooked in an oven or on a *saj* (like an inverted wok) and almost always sports a flavourful topping, usually *za'tar* (an aromatic mix of wild thyme, sumac, sesame seeds, salt and oil), but also *jibneh* (cheese), *qawarma* (lamb), a cracked-wheat-and-yoghurt mix called *kishk,* and much more. *Man'oushe* is a perfect any-time-of-day treat: cheap, quickly prepared and easily eaten while on the move.

Origin

In Lebanon, back in the day, women brought their dough to community ovens and baked large collective loaves. Then modern times brought commercially produced bread, and bakers shifted to single-serve, spice-mix-smeared breakfast helpings of *man'oushe bil-za'tar.* Today, *man'oushe* is a catch-all term describing the snack of round bread adorned by any number of ingredients able to meet hungry hankerings (sweet, savoury, herbivore, carnivore and omnivore).

Tasting

Given the ubiquity of *man'oushe* in Lebanon and the huge diversity of trimmings, there is no quintessential eating experience associated with it other than the powerful sensory connection with Lebanon. The warm, baked-bread freshness of *man'oushe* and the unique seasoned zing of *za'tar* are, to most Lebanese, the strongest olfactory and gustatory triggers of their home when they travel abroad. This holds true whether they're from the bustle of Beirut's bohemian Hamra or the pastoral ease of the mountainous hinterland, and whether they prefer the thinner, slightly crispier and often larger *saj*-cooked disc of dough or its oven-baked coequal.

Finding It

Starting at 1500 Lebanese pounds (US$1) each, *man'oushe* is available in bakeries – some as tiny as cupboards and selling only *man'oushe* – countrywide.

* TIPS * Easily rolled and wrapped in paper, *man'oushe* is a favourite on-the-go pick-me-up, best with a soft drink, tea or juice. While *man'oushe* is principally a snack, if stuffed with an extra helping of chopped cucumbers, tomatoes, pickles and olives, it can be made into a meal with surprising heft.

* By Ethan Gelber *

Recipe Man'oushe

YOU'LL NEED

- 1 tsp active dry yeast
- 1¼ cups warm water
- 2½ cups white flour
- 1 tsp salt
- 1 tsp vegetable oil
- optional toppings (such as cheese, yoghurt, herbs, sliced cooked lamb)

METHOD

1. Dissolve the yeast in the warm water and set aside.

2. Sift 2 cups of flour and the salt together in a bowl and then slowly stir first the oil and then the yeast water into the flour.

3. Knead the dough for about 10 minutes until it is soft and stretchy. Roll it into a ball and set aside in a cloth-covered, flour-coated bowl for up to two hours, or until the ball has doubled in size.

4. Divide the dough ball into four equal parts and then punch each one down. Let rise for 30 more minutes.

5. Preheat the oven to 200°C (400°F).

6. Roll each of the four parts into a ball and coat with flour (shake off the excess). Then roll them out into 20–25cm (8–10in) discs about 4mm (0.1in) thick. They can be thinner and larger if you have a *saj*.

7. Add toppings (prepared separately).

8. Bake in the oven for 10–15 minutes or until the bottom of the bread is crisp and golden brown. Alternatively, cook on a hot *saj* for three to five minutes.

MAKES 4 PIECES

* Masala Dosa *

INDIA

Excuse me sir, is that your lunch, or a rolled-up copy of the *Times of India*? Like a supercharged crepe, the dosa is the signature dish of the Indian south.

What is It?

At its simplest, a dosa is a rice-flour pancake, crisped on a metal hotplate with a swirl of palm oil or ghee. The classic masala dosa is a paper-thin cone stuffed with a zesty curry of potatoes, onions and dried red chillies, but dosas (or dosai) come rolled, unrolled, stuffed, unstuffed, thick, thin, fermented, unfermented, even stacked in towers like American pancakes, all served with a side order of coconut chutney and *sambar,* a fragrant dipping sauce flavoured with dhal, tamarind and mustard seeds.

Origin

First mentioned in classical Indian poems in the 6th century AD, dosas have been linked to the town of Udupi on the coast of Karnataka, famed for the rich vegetarian cuisine cooked up in its Hindu monasteries. As for the habit of stuffing the dosa with spiced vegetables, legend has it this was a trick to hide the onions, which are said to inflame the passions and lead the faithful away from the path to enlightenment.

Tasting

The golden rule for eating dosas is never wear a white shirt. Dosas are eaten by hand, ripped into pieces and dipped into the fiery crucible of *sambar* and chutney, and drips are almost guaranteed. Start at the crispy extremities, dipping as you go, and savour the heat of the *sambar,* the cool-then-hot zing of the coconut chutney and the texture of the dosa – crunchy at the edges, soft and yielding where the *sabji* (vegetable curry) has soaked into the shell. The setting is often as steamy as the spices – street stalls, roadhouses, station platforms, surrounded by vast crowds of people on the move. This is a meal to consume on the hoof: order, rip, dip and go, leaving only crumbs on the counter. But take a moment to observe the preparation: skilled vendors swirl the batter across the hotplate in concentric circles with the bottom of a steel bowl, like a potter preparing his wheel.

Finding It

Every city south of Mumbai claims to offer the 'best dosas in India' – start your search at train-station canteens and branches of Indian Coffee House. Expect to pay ₹15 to ₹30 (US$0.35 to US$0.70).

★ VARIATIONS ★ Dosas come in a bewildering range of shapes and sizes. As well as the ubiquitous masala dosa, look out for *rava* dosas, prepared with unfermented batter, *methi* dosas flavoured with fenugreek, and set dosas, cooked on one side and stacked in a tower. Topping the pile is the paper dosa, which often exceeds 60cm (2ft) in diameter. In 2009 the Sankalp restaurant in Ahmedabad cooked up a record-breaking dosa measuring 9.7m (32ft) from side to side!

* By Joe Bindloss *

Recipe Masala Dosa

YOU'LL NEED

vegetable oil for cooking

salt to taste

coconut chutney for serving

Onion & Potato *Sabji*

4 medium-sized potatoes

¼ tsp mustard seeds

1 tbs *chana dal* (split chickpeas)

1 onion, thinly sliced

2 green chillies and 1 dried red chilli

4 curry leaves

¼ tsp turmeric

½ cup water

2 tbs coriander leaves (cilantro)

1 tbs ghee

Sambar

2 tbs tamarind pulp

1 cup red lentils

½ tsp ground turmeric

2 dried red chillies

½ tsp mustard seeds

½ tsp fenugreek seeds

4 curry leaves

1 onion, chopped

1 tomato, chopped

2 carrots, chopped

2 tbs *sambar* powder

2 tbs coriander leaves, chopped

Dosa

2 cups rice

1 cup black lentils

1 tsp fenugreek seeds

¼ tsp dried yeast, added to ½ cup water with 1 tsp of sugar

METHOD

Onion & Potato *Sabji*

1. Chop potatoes into quarters and boil with a pinch of salt, then drain, mash coarsely and set aside.

2. Heat oil in a wok or frying pan and add mustard seeds. When the seeds start to pop, add the chickpeas and cook for about a minute.

3. Add onion, deseeded chillies, curry leaves and turmeric and saute for 7 to 10 minutes, until the onions are transparent.

4. Add the water, salt, potatoes, chopped coriander and ghee. Cook until the mixture thickens, stirring continuously, then set aside.

Sambar

1. Soak the tamarind in water for half an hour, then remove the seeds and press the pulp through a sieve to make half a cup of tamarind juice.

2. Boil the lentils with water, turmeric and a little vegetable oil, then drain, wash and mash the lentils and set aside.

3. Heat the vegetable oil in a wok or frying pan, and fry the chillies, mustard seeds, fenugreek seeds and curry leaves until the seeds start to pop.

4. Add the onions and saute until they start to brown, then mix in the tamarind juice and cook for another five minutes.

5. Add the mashed lentils, tomato, carrots and *sambar* powder and cook until the vegetables are soft.

6. Garnish with the chopped coriander leaves.

Dosa

1. Soak the rice, lentils and fenugreek seeds in water overnight in separate bowls, then drain and blend together with the yeast, salt and water to make a thick batter. Cover with a loose-fitting lid, and leave the batter for a day at room temperature to ferment.

2. To make your dosas, heat a little oil on a *tava* (griddle) or frying pan until it starts to smoke, then add a ladle of batter and rotate the pan to create a flat pancake. Cook until golden brown on both sides. Add a spoon of the *sabji* mix to the centre of the dosa and roll into a cone. Serve immediately with *sambar* and coconut chutney for dipping.

MAKES 4–5 DOSAS

* Meat Pie *
AUSTRALIA

As Aussie as koalas, Kylie and the Harbour Bridge, the humble meat pie epitomises the no-nonsense nation's unfussy attitude: cook beef, put in pastry, serve hot.

What is It?

The meat pie is an edible icon. Aussies get through 260 million of them each year – that's 12 per person. These hand-sized bundles of shortcrust pastry are traditionally filled with minced beef, onion and gravy; meat content should be no less than 25% (though 'meat' can encompass ears, snouts, tendons…). Once baked and golden, pies are topped with a splat of tomato sauce.

Origin

Pies may not be uniquely Australian, but nowhere (except, perhaps, neighbouring New Zealand) has embraced the concept of meat-and-pastry snackage with quite such gusto. It's the nearest there is to a national dish, and in 1990 the Great Aussie Meat Pie contest was inaugurated to reward the country's finest exponents.

It was early British settlers who brought the pie to Australia; the first recorded mention appeared in the Melbourne *Argus* newspaper in 1850. Their popularity boomed, and streetside pie carts (originally horse-drawn) proliferated, serving lunch on the go. Save for the horses, little has changed.

Tasting

There are gourmet specimens on sale out there, handmade with posh ingredients such as garlic prawns. And there are many places to buy them: corner shops, pubs, late-night vans. But to appreciate the full Aussie-ness of the humble meat pie, there's only one place to go: the footy. You'll need to jostle with a fair few thousand Australian Rules Football fans to purchase your pie, served hot and slightly soggy in its little paper bag. First things first: unsheathe the golden delicacy and douse with tomato sauce. Second: wolf down while cheering/jeering men in tight, short shorts.

The taste sensations are simple ones: lightly seasoned gravy, robust enough to act as internal glue; meat of not the highest calibre, but satisfying nonetheless; pastry wilted, but just about holding things together. No frills. No nonsense. Very Australian.

Finding It

Try a Four'N Twenty meat pie at Melbourne's MCG stadium while watching an Aussie Rules game. Expect to pay A$4.40 (US$4.70).

* VARIATIONS * You want peas with that? They do in South Australia, where the pie floater is the snack of choice, and an official state heritage icon. An alarming-looking slurry, this dish – popular as a late-night, post-pub munchie – consists of a regular meat pie served upside down (why?) in a sea of thick pea soup.

* By Sarah Baxter *

Recipe Meat Pie

YOU'LL NEED

1 tbs olive oil

1 onion, chopped

400g (14oz) minced (ground) beef

1 tbs cornflour

175mL (6fl oz) beef stock

1 tbs Worcestershire sauce

2 tbs tomato paste

1 tsp Vegemite

4 sheets shortcrust pastry
(or make your own)

1 egg, beaten

tomato sauce

METHOD

1. Preheat oven to 220°C (425°F).

2. Fry onion in oil until soft.

3. Add beef; cook until browned.

4. Combine cornflour and 1 tbs of beef stock; stir. Set aside.

5. Add remaining stock, Worcestershire sauce, tomato paste and Vegemite to meat mixture; stir.

6. Add cornflour mix; stir.

7. Bring to boil, then simmer until thick. Remove from heat and cool.

8. Cut pastry into eight circles, four slightly larger. Press larger circles into pie tins; fill with meat mixture.

9. Place smaller circles over meat; press edges to seal. Brush tops with egg.

10. Bake for 20 minutes or until golden.

11. Serve with tomato sauce.

MAKES 4

* Mohinga *

MYANMAR (BURMA)

Cherished as Myanmar's national dish, *mohinga* is a comforting noodle soup that exemplifies the earthy flavours of the country's cuisine via a combination of lemongrass, shallots, turmeric and freshwater fish.

What is It?

Mohinga combines a fish-based broth, thickened with rice or bean powder and typically containing a combination of shallots and the crunchy inner edible core of the banana tree, with thin round rice noodles. The dish is served topped with a pinch of chopped coriander and accompanied by dried chilli powder and lime, as well as optional toppings such as lentil- or vegetable-based fritters or a hard-boiled duck egg.

Origin

Mohinga is made from an almost exclusively indigenous repertoire of ingredients, suggesting that the dish has its origins in Myanmar. Some suspect that the noodles, which are made from rice via a complicated and time-consuming process that is thought to date back several centuries, are also indigenous to the region. This stands in contrast with most other Southeast Asian noodle dishes, which can usually be traced directly back to China.

Finding It

If you're in Yangon (Rangoon), head to Myaung Mya Daw Cho, where a bowl will set you back K500 (US$0.75).

Tasting

Generally associated with central Myanmar and that region's predominantly Burmese ethnic group, *mohinga* is nonetheless sold in just about every town in Myanmar, typically from mobile vending carts and baskets or basic open-fronted restaurants. *Mohinga* vendors are most prevalent in the morning.

Ordering the dish is a simple affair, as the only optional ingredient is *akyaw* (crispy fritters of lentils or battered and deep-fried vegetables). The thick broth has flakes of freshwater fish (typically snakehead fish), a yellow/orange hue due to the addition of turmeric, and a light herbal flavour, thanks to the use of lemongrass. A bowl is generally seasoned in advance, but dried chilli and limes are usually available to add a bit of spice and tartness.

* **TIPS** * For an authentic Myanmar eating experience, do as the locals do and have a bowl of *mohinga* for breakfast. The dish is standard at Myanmar-style teashops and is great when taken with a cup of sweet tea. *Mohinga* is also sold from mobile vendors after dark and makes a cheap and filling late-night snack.

* By Austin Bush *

Recipe Mohinga

Banana stems look like fibrous white leeks and taste very similar to the fruit. If you're unable to find them in Asian grocery stores, try substituting water chestnuts. To prepare the rice, toss in a heated pan until the grains are browned and slightly burnt (but not stuck to the pan) and crush using a mortar and pestle or a spice grinder. The amount of gram flour can also be doubled in place of the toasted rice.

YOU'LL NEED

1 tbs vegetable or canola oil

1 onion, finely diced

1 tsp ginger, crushed

1 tsp turmeric

2 tbs shrimp paste

2 red chillies, chopped

60g (2oz) banana stem, sliced thinly

2 stalks of lemongrass, sliced thinly

3 cups fish stock

50g (1.8oz) gram flour

50g (1.8oz) rice, toasted and ground

500g (1lb) dried thin rice noodles

200g (7oz) firm white fish, such as haddock, pollack or sea bass, sliced

lime wedges, fried onions, extra chopped chillies and fresh coriander leaves (cilantro) to serve

METHOD

1. Heat the oil in a saucepan and fry the onion, ginger, turmeric, shrimp paste, chillies, banana stem and lemongrass until the onion has softened.

2. Add the stock and whisk in the gram flour and toasted rice. Simmer for approximately 15 minutes until the soup has thickened.

3. Add the rice noodles and continue simmering until the noodles are cooked.

4. Add the fish and cook for a further five minutes.

5. Serve immediately with a wedge of lime and garnished with fried onions, chopped chillies and coriander leaves.

SERVES 4

* Murtabak *
MALAYSIA & SINGAPORE

A stuffed pancake bursting with anything from lamb to egg to onions to peanuts, *murtabak* are a culinary symbol of the Muslim presence across Southeast Asia.

What is It?

Murtabak is essentially a filled pancake, often resembling a crepe that has been rolled and chopped into squares. (It also comes in a sweet form in Indonesia, known as *martabak manis*, which has a thicker dough with a texture that recalls a smooth waffle.) Eaten as a snack food, it's found in markets, food courts and street stalls across Singapore and Malaysia.

Origin

Believed to have been invented in India in the Middle Ages, *murtabak* was brought to Southeast Asia by Tamil Muslim traders, who have been trading in the region since as early as the 10th century. Since arriving on the Malay peninsula, *murtabak* styles have multiplied to reflect local tastes and ingredients – Chinese-style egg and green onion is a favourite filling in Singapore, while a side of spiced curry is common in Malaysia.

Tasting

Across Singapore and Malaysia, snacking is practically a national sport. And all sports must have their stadiums, right? In these countries, this means chaotic, colourful night markets and hawker centres (outdoor food courts), where food vendors outdo each other to prove that their dishes are the best. Imagine stumbling, bleary eyed, into a Singaporean hawker centre at 8am after a night on the town. '*Murtabak*?' asks a man behind one of the centre's many counters, tilting his head at you. Sure, you nod, and the next thing you know, you're feasting on a warm golden pancake, stuffed with heavily spiced minced (ground) lamb and onion, the pastry flaky in your mouth. Wash it down with a few cups of hot, sugar-laced tea, and you'll be fortified for another night of fun.

Finding It

Try the Zam Zam restaurant in Singapore, where you can find *murtabak* for 4 Singaporean dollars (US$3.30).

* **VARIATIONS** * *Murtabak* **is but one of many pancake-type street foods popular in the region. Also look out for** *roti* **(flatbread served with a side of curry, condensed milk, lentils or almost anything else you can imagine),** *dosa* **(south Indian crispy stuffed crepes) and** *popiah* **(fresh spring rolls in a wheat-flour pancake).**

* By Emily Matchar *

Recipe Murtabak

YOU'LL NEED

Dough

3 cups white flour

1 tsp salt

1 tsp ghee

1 cup lukewarm water

½ cup vegetable oil

Filling

2 tbs ghee, plus extra for greasing

1 onion, finely sliced

2 garlic cloves, crushed

½ tsp ginger, freshly grated

1 tsp turmeric powder

1 tsp garam masala

500g (1lb) minced (ground) lamb

2 eggs, beaten

salt and pepper

2 tbs coriander leaves (cilantro), finely chopped

1 bird's eye chilli, finely chopped

METHOD

1. Put the flour and salt in a large bowl and add the ghee, mixing with your hands.

2. Add the water and mix until a soft dough is formed, then knead for an additional 10 minutes.

3. Divide the dough into six equal-sized balls and put them in a bowl with the oil. Allow to sit for an hour.

4. Meanwhile, prepare the filling. Heat the ghee over medium heat and fry the onion until it's soft, about five minutes.

5. Add the garlic and ginger and fry until the onion is golden brown. Add the turmeric and garam masala and stir.

6. Add the meat and cook, stirring constantly, until well browned.

7. Beat the eggs in a small bowl with the salt and pepper and set aside.

8. On a smooth oiled surface, take one of the dough balls and flatten it with a rolling pin. Press and stretch the dough with your fingers until it's so thin that it's nearly translucent.

9. Heat a griddle or heavy pan on high and grease it with more ghee. Quickly transfer the dough to the griddle, using the rolling pin to drape the dough to aid the transfer.

10. Pour a small portion of beaten egg onto the dough and spread it around with a spoon to cover the centre.

11. Add one-sixth of the meat filling, then fold the dough over lengthwise.

12. When one side browns, flip the pancake, adding more ghee to the griddle if necessary.

13. Cook until golden brown and crisp on both sides.

MAKES 6

* Otak-Otak *

SINGAPORE, MALAYSIA & INDONESIA

A hand-held pâté that comes in its own 100% natural (and fully biodegradable) package? For convenience, deliciousness and environmental friendliness, this spicy Southeast Asian treat takes first prize.

What is It?

Found cooking over beds of hot coals in Singapore, Malaysia and Indonesia, *otak-otak* is a spicy paste made from fresh fish, onions, eggs and a vast array of herbs and spices then grilled inside broad green leaves (usually from banana or pandan trees). The heating process turns the paste into a gelatinous pâté, which can be mixed with other dishes or eaten straight from the leaf.

Origin

In the Bahasa Indonesia and Malay languages, the word *'otak'* means brains. But don't let this keep you from trying *otak-otak*; the name comes from the colour and consistency of the dish, not its ingredients. Originating in Malaysia and Indonesia, *otak-otak* migrated to Singapore, where it quickly became a hawker-centre staple. Food-obsessed Singaporeans are said to cross the causeway into Muar in southern Malaysia for a taste of that town's *otak-otak* (said to be the region's best).

Tasting

At first glance, the sight of long green leaves charring side by side may lead the uninitiated into thinking that *otak-otak* is some sort of grilled tropical vegetable. But the charred green leaf is the packaging only – unwrap an aromatic *otak-otak* and inside you'll find a gelatinous cake that's somewhere between paste and pâté in consistency, spicy and aromatic (with just a hint of the ocean).

Otak-otak is best eaten at a streetside stall or inside a hawker centre, perhaps with a bottle of Tiger beer or an iced Milo (depending on your taste in beverages). Though generally eaten as a side dish with other items (skewered chicken or grilled prawns make for a great combination), four or five *otak-otaks* should be enough to hold you over until your next meal (which, if you're Singaporean, might occur within minutes).

Finding It

Supposedly the best place for *otak-otak* is the strip of hawker stalls nicknamed 'Glutton Street' in Muar, Malaysia (Jln Haji Abu just off Jln Ali). One Singapore dollar (US$0.77) will get you two or three sticks.

* VARIATIONS * While *otak-otak* is generally made with fish (mackerel and snapper are the most popular choices), variations using crab and prawns can sometimes be found. A steamed variety of *otak-otak* is often served in Peranakan restaurants in Singapore and Malaysia. Called *'otak-otak* Nonya', the Peranakan variety generally tends to be a bit moister.

* By Joshua Samuel Brown *

Recipe Otak-Otak

This recipe comes to us from Ruqxana Vasanwala at Cookery Magic in Singapore (www.cookerymagic.com).

YOU'LL NEED

400g (14oz) deboned mackerel, minced

1 small onion, finely chopped

1 egg, lightly beaten

½ small turmeric leaf, thinly sliced

2 kaffir lime leaves, thinly sliced

2 tbs laksa leaves (Vietnamese mint), thinly sliced

1 tbs oil (optional)

½–¾ cup coconut cream

1 tbs sugar

salt to taste

banana leaves, cut into 20cm x 10cm (8in x 4in) size; microwave for one minute to soften

Spice Paste

1cm (0.5in) turmeric root (or ¼ tsp powdered turmeric)

2–4 red chillies

4 pieces galangal, sliced (ginger can be substituted)

1 lemongrass stalk

3 candlenuts

2 garlic cloves

6 shallots

1 tsp belacan (shrimp paste), dry-roasted

METHOD

1. Grind the spice paste ingredients to a fine paste.

2. Combine the spice paste with all the other ingredients (except banana leaves) in a mixing bowl. Adjust taste with salt and sugar.

3. Spoon 2 tbs of the mixture onto each banana leaf. Fold the leaf and secure it with a toothpick on both ends.

4. Grill or barbecue for about 10 minutes and serve.

* Oyster Cake *

HONG KONG, CHINA

These hand-span-sized, savoury-smelling, deep-fried omelettes are tweaked Asia-style with a gluttonous dozen or so fat oysters and a smattering of aromatic herbs, condiments and chilli.

What is It?

Several tricks of the trade perk up the traditional egg-and-flour omelette concoction, and variations abound. Starch is added to make the batter thicker, handfuls of Asian herbs add zest, and pork lard can give the outer casing an addictive crunch. Oysters are obviously key, and though the cakes are sometimes served in restaurants, downing one of these down-to-earth delicacies in a night market is not only a meal in itself, it's the easiest way to imbibe a dozen oysters in the shortest possible time.

Origin

Keep your eyes and ears open. Oyster cakes are also known as oyster pancakes or oyster omelettes. In China you might hear them referred to as *ah oh chian* (Fujian), *o'jian* (Hong Kong) or *orh lua* (Taiwan). The variations on the name, the distinctive ingredients and the different cooking styles (panfried or deep-fried) allude to the dish's peripatetic evolution. It originated in the southern Chinese seaside provinces of Fujian and Guangdong, where seafood is king. From here, migratory influences have seen it surface in Taiwan and Hong Kong, and further afield in Malaysia, Singapore and the Philippines.

Tasting

Night markets are the ideal hunting ground for seeking out oyster cakes. Look for the stack of Chinese-style melamine plates wrapped in greaseproof paper. Behind them, there'll be a little old lady with a spatula in hand who will pour batter, spring onion and a ladle brimming with sloppy oysters into a bowl, before dunking it into the deep-fryer. Once cooked, the still-sizzling golden cake is doused in chilli sauce, sprinkled with market-fresh coriander and upended into a brown paper bag complete with wooden chopsticks.

A yin-and-yang-esque equilibrium between crunch and flavour is paramount for the perfect oyster cake. Too much oil and the grease forms a layer on your tongue, too much starch and the texture is chewy and gelatinous. The best have a thin outer layer of crunch, like a hash brown, and an inner eggy flavour. Coriander takes the edge off the fat. And chilli sauce? Well, that's the icing on the oyster cake.

Finding It

Temple Street Night Market, Jordan and Yau Ma Tei, New Territories; and Four Seasons Pot Rice, Yau Ma Tei are the places. You'll pay HK$20 (US$2.56) for a small oyster cake, HK$40 (US$5.13) for a large one.

* **VARIATIONS** * Those kings of street food, the Taiwanese, sometimes refer to the oyster cake as their national dish. Their panfried version, filled with Chinese vegetables, is more common than Hong Kong's variety. The Singaporeans have a collective pride about oyster cakes eaten in childhood and the associated egg, oyster and pork-lard aromas. Their cake has a thicker, smoother outer layer of crispiness that cracks like an egg when you bite into it.

* By Penny Watson *

Recipe Oyster Cake

YOU'LL NEED

12–15 fresh oysters or 20 from a jar of refrigerated shucked oysters

4 eggs, beaten

pinch of salt

pinch of white pepper

1 cup rice flour

40g (1.4oz) tapioca starch

150mL (5fl oz) water

25mL (¾ fl oz) peanut oil

2 garlic cloves, finely sliced

10mL (⅓ fl oz) soy sauce

20mL (⅔ fl oz) rice wine

4 spring onions, roughly chopped

2 tbs coriander leaves (cilantro), roughly chopped

chilli sambal (optional)

METHOD

1. Rinse oysters briefly in fresh water, then sit them in a colander to drain.

2. Hand-beat the eggs, salt and pepper in a bowl.

3. In a separate bowl, mix rice flour, tapioca starch and water together and stir until it becomes a thin batter.

4. Heat large pan until hot. Add a glug of peanut oil. When the oil is hot, pour in batter, swirl it around the base of the pan and cook for about 15 seconds.

5. Pour in egg mixture and leave until bottom layer is cooked and top layer is almost set.

6. With a wooden spoon, push the mixture to all sides of the pan, creating a small hole. Pour in remaining oil and garlic, and saute.

7. Repeat with oysters, soy sauce and rice wine until oysters are warmed through and mixture is set. Remove from pan.

8. For night-market authenticity, cover with spring onion and coriander leaves, and serve with a big dob of chilli sambal or similar.

Pane, Panelle e Crocchè *

PALERMO, SICILY, ITALY

The top draw at Palermo's outdoor food stalls is this unusual, North African–influenced sandwich stuffed with chickpea fritters and potato croquettes.

What is It?

As the name implies, *pane, panelle e crocchè* has three distinct components. The *pane* (bread) is Palermo's traditional sesame-seed roll. Next come the *panelle*: rectangular fritters made from chickpea flour, lightly seasoned with mint or parsley, salt and pepper and fried in hot oil till golden. Last come the *crocchè*: mashed-potato croquettes sometimes blended with egg, parsley, mint or breadcrumbs before frying.

Origin

Panelle trace their origins back to the Arabs who ruled Palermo in the 10th century. While chickpeas were already known throughout the Mediterranean, it was the Arabs who developed the technique of grinding them into flour, and who introduced sesame seeds to Sicilian kitchens. Over time, potato croquettes were added to the mix, creating an affordable, carbohydrate-intensive treat popular with everyone from labourers to students, for breakfast, lunch or an afternoon snack. Some *friggitorie* (fry-shops) stamped patterns onto the *panelle;* most popular were *panelle* with fish designs, legendarily prized by the poorest Palermitans as a low-cost alternative to fried fish.

Tasting

Step into Palermo's streets on a sunny morning and you'll be greeted by a cacophony of vendors singing out the virtues of their produce. Follow their voices into Palermo's dense tangle of back-alley markets, navigating past mounds of fresh artichokes, strawberries, tomatoes and eggplants, through stalls piled with olives, sausages and cheeses. Eventually you'll reach the humble street carts where *panelle* are sold, their presence announced by the crackle of oil and the stacks of golden fritters just emerging from the fryer.

Best when crisp and hot, these fried delights are soul-satisfyingly soft and tooth-pleasingly crunchy, their flavours punctuated with wonderful hints of sesame from the all-enclosing roll. To complete the experience, shake on a little salt, squeeze on some lemon juice, and bite in!

Finding It

Try the Ballarò market, just southwest of Palermo's Quattro Canti crossroads, or Friggitoria Chiluzzo on Piazza Kalsa. You'll pay around €1.50 (US$2.15).

* VARIATIONS * **Some vendors offer tasty extras such as fried eggplant. You can ask for *fedde* – simple slices of eggplant layered in with your *panelle* and *crocchè*; or, for a uniquely Palermitan experience, look for the so-called *quaglie* (quails) – whole eggplants cut lengthwise into 1cm strips joined at the stem, which fan out like a bird's feathers when deep-fried.**

* By Gregor Clark *

Recipe Pane, Panelle e Crocchè

The chickpea fritters and potato croquettes are surprisingly easy to make but best tackled in big batches.

YOU'LL NEED

2 sesame-seed bread rolls, sliced lengthways

vegetable or canola oil for deep-frying

Panelle (Chickpea Fritters)

250g (9oz; about 1 cup) gram flour

1½ cups water

salt and pepper to season

Crocchè (Potato Croquettes)

500g (1lb) potatoes, peeled

1 tsp cornflour

a handful of fresh parsley, chopped

salt and pepper to season

METHOD

1. To make the chickpea fritters, combine the gram flour and water in a saucepan over medium heat. Season well with salt and pepper.

2. Bring to the boil while continuously stirring to remove any lumps until the mixture becomes thick like a paste.

3. Remove from the heat. Using a wooden spoon, take dollops of the mixture and spread it thinly – about 0.5cm (0.2in) thick – on the entire surface of a round plate.

4. When the mixture has cooled on the plate, slice into eight even triangular sections (like a pizza) using a butter knife.

5. Fry the fritters in a deep-fryer or heavy-bottomed saucepan.

6. To make the potato croquettes, boil the potatoes until soft.

7. Mash with the cornflour and parsley and season well with salt and pepper.

8. Take a golf ball-sized amount of the mixture and shape into croquettes.

9. Fry the croquettes in a deep-fryer or heavy-bottomed saucepan.

10. To assemble the sandwich, put a few slices of the chickpea fritters and two or three potato croquettes in the bread roll and serve immediately.

MAKES AT LEAST 2 SANDWICHES WITH PLENTY OF LEFTOVERS!

* Pastizzi *

MALTA

Pastizzi are savoury, diamond-shaped pastry puffs, often (inaccurately) called 'cheesecakes' in English. Diminutive, divine and most delectable when steaming hot, they're irresistibly, quintessentially Malta.

What is It?

The two most common *pastizzi* fillings are creamy ricotta cheese (*pastizzi ta' l-irkotta*) and spicy pea mash (*pastizzi tal-pizelli*). They're a calorie-rich frill devoured anytime, although usually at breakfast, as an afternoon snack and on Sunday mornings – early, when nocturnal revellers are staggering home hungry, or late, as churchgoers are returning from Mass.

Origin

Food historians have found mentions of *pastizzi* by merchants prior to the 16th century, when Malta's fabled Knights Hospitaller fortified the capital of Valletta. More than that may never be known, however, as the local cuisine is a heady mix of many cultural influences and the once-resident Phoenician, Greek, Carthaginian, Roman, Byzantine, Ottoman, Arab, Italian and British populations.

Finding It

A single *pastizz* costs €0.30 to €0.40 (US$0.40 to US$0.54) in *pastizzeriji* throughout Malta. Particularly notable for its quality pastries, the town of Rabat has its Crystal Palace (which opens at 4am), a true traditional *pastizzi* mecca.

Tasting

The Maltese discuss and eat *pastizzi* the same way young newlyweds cavort in public on their wedding night: with tender devotion thinly disguising animal ravenousness. No matter what time of day it is, whether you're on the street, in a nondescript *pastizzeriji* at 5am or at home with friends, eating *pastizzi* is serious business. Hot treat in hand, everyone pauses to absorb the initial sensory wave of buttery, cheesy, spicy delight. The first bite detonates the crust, spraying pastry crumbs over everything, followed swiftly by the hot, intoxicating surge of filling. For both first-timers and aficionados, it's visceral. The proof is that there's always room for just one more.

* **WORD PLAY** * Brave linguists beware: probably due to the pastry's shape, *pastizz* (the singular of *pastizzi*) is a slang term for female genitalia. That said, the Maltese expression 'selling like *pastizzi*' is the equivalent of 'selling like hotcakes'.

* By Ethan Gelber *

Recipe Pastizzi

YOU'LL NEED

300g (11oz) ricotta cheese

2 eggs

handful of parsley (finely chopped)

salt and pepper

750g (26oz) puff pastry

egg wash

METHOD

1. Combine the ricotta, eggs, parsley and seasoning. Mix thoroughly.

2. Roll out the puff pastry so that it is quite thin. Measure and cut out circles that are approximately 9cm (3.5in) in diameter.

3. Brush the egg wash along the edges of each circle. Drop a dollop of the filling onto the centre of each and then fold it in half, sealing along the joined edge.

4. Coat with egg wash and then bake in a medium-hot oven for 30 minutes or until the pastry is golden brown.

* Peso Pizza *

CUBA

A faithful streetside hunger-buster since the economic sanctions of the post-Soviet era, peso pizza is testimony to Cuba's turbulent past and a refreshing change from the touristy restaurants that dominate today's eating scene.

What is It?

It's pizza, although with toppings that are usually limited to cheese, tomatoes, pickles and mustard. More importantly, it's history: an invention of the woefully lean period that hit Cuba after the Soviets left. Equally importantly, it's dirt-cheap sustenance in a poverty-crippled country where food is often an overpriced luxury.

Origins

Origins are everything with peso pizza, and that's because they will possibly rock your world more than the taste. Since the US embargo took effect in the 1960s, Cuba had been relying heavily on the Soviets for trade (they bought Cuban sugar at inflated prices) but, following the Fall of the Wall, Russia pulled the plug on this arrangement. The rug was pulled from under the Cuban economy, too, and financially woeful times ensued... Necessity being the mother of invention, delights like grapefruit-rind steak and pizza for a peso cropped up, using basics and leftovers to fill bellies.

Tasting

Why the long queue outside such a humble-looking booth? Queuing is a Cuban specialty right up there with cigars, so the wait for peso pizza might be the longest prequel to buying street food you'll ever have. But when the other options are an ice-cream man, a bland restaurant or a poorly stocked local shop, peso pizza is a sure-fire winner. The crust is thin and crunchy. The toppings are an unlikely assortment of tomatoes and a pungent, Swiss-style cheese (giving an acquired, slightly bitter taste) with additions of pickles, mustard and, on very good days, pork offcuts or salami. And it's Cuba's most enjoyable snack. This is mainly because you eat peso pizza like calzone, folded over with the ingredients whammed together and hitting you all at once. Savour it. This is the taste that fed Cuba when precious little else was. This is the taste that defied capitalism.

Finding It

Vendors sell peso pizza along San Rafael Blvd (between Prado and Infanta) in central Havana for anywhere from 5 to 10 Cuban pesos (US$0.20 to US$0.40).

* **VARIATIONS** * **The favoured (and endearingly quirky) method of eating peso pizza is by folding it in half – it's no wonder Cuba's classic snack has garnered the nickname 'Cuban Sandwich' (Sandwich de Cubana). US embargo–fuelled food scarcities mean that it's sometimes hard to find, but it's totally worth it. Gather up the Cuban pesos you'll need to pay and step outside tourist-package Cuba for the real, taste bud–altering deal.**

* By Luke Waterson *

Recipe Peso Pizza

To get the right 'made-in-Havana' pungency and texture, we suggest a blend of Swiss cheese and American muenster. If you don't have muenster, try substituting aged brick cheese, Danish Esrom or gouda.

YOU'LL NEED

1 x 30cm (12in) thin-crust pizza base (either store-bought or homemade)

mustard

tomato paste, unseasoned

Swiss cheese and American muenster cheese to taste (one to three ratio)

dill pickles, sliced

leftover roast or slow-cooked pork, shredded

adobo seasoning

METHOD

1. Preheat the oven to 230°C (450°F).

2. Spread some mustard over the pizza base, then add a liberal amount of unseasoned tomato paste.

3. Grate the desired amount of cheese and mix together. Sprinkle half the grated cheese mixture over the base. Authentic peso pizza should have more cheese than tomato, so the tanginess of the cheese comes through.

4. Add the dill pickles and some pre-cooked shredded pork , then top with the remaining cheese.

5. Sprinkle with *adobo* seasoning and bake for six to eight minutes or until the crust is golden brown. Fold in half to serve.

* Phat Kaphrao *

THAILAND

While *phat kaphrao* might not have the same sort of instant name recognition as, say, *phat thai*, this spicy, herbal, meaty stir-fry is actually the go-to one-dish meal for many Thais.

What is It?

The Thai word *kaphrao* means 'holy basil' (*Ocimum tenuiflorum*), the essential ingredient in this stir-fried dish. In *phat kaphrao*, the plant is fried with some protein – typically minced (ground) pork or chicken, but it can also be seafood – along with coarsely chopped garlic, chillies and, sometimes, chopped long bean. The dish is seasoned with fish sauce and a pinch of sugar, served over rice and usually crowned with a fried egg.

Origin

Phat kaphrao is a relatively recent introduction to Thai cuisine and didn't become commonplace until about 50 years ago, although holy basil has probably been used in Thai cuisine for a long time. In ancient India, the herb was used in ayurveda and it has long been considered a sacred plant among Hindus. Like many Thai street-food dishes – and particularly because *phat kaphrao* is fried in a wok – the dish most likely has at least partial Chinese origins.

Finding It

Any *raan ahaan taam sang* (made-to-order) restaurant or stall in Thailand will serve *phat kaphrao* – just look for the case of ingredients. On the street it costs 30 to 50 baht (US$1 to US$1.65).

Tasting

Unlike other street dishes in Thailand, there generally aren't any vendors who specialise only in *phat kaphrao*. Rather, the dish is typically sought out at *raan ahaan taam sang* (made-to-order) carts, stalls and restaurants. These establishments do a huge variety of dishes and are recognised by a tray or case of raw ingredients. A diner will generally have a look at what ingredients are available and place his or her order directly with the cook. The steaming dish emerges from the wok a few minutes later. Although *phat kaphrao* is predominately salty and spicy, it is always served with a small bowl of finely sliced chillies in fish sauce and sometimes a squeeze of lime – the Thai equivalent of the salt shaker.

* VARIATIONS * It's thought that beef was used in the original *phat kaphrao*, but today many Thais are reluctant to eat beef, so minced pork, chicken, seafood and even fish balls or fermented pork sausage are used instead. The dish is almost always spicy as a matter of course, but if you can't take the heat, tell the vendor to make it *mai phet* (not spicy).

* By Austin Bush *

Recipe Phat Kaphrao

This dish is traditionally very spicy so use the number of chillies below as a guide and feel free to add as many more as you can handle. Beef or chicken may be substituted for the pork.

YOU'LL NEED

¼ cup plus 2 tbs fish sauce

6 bird's eye chillies, chopped

1 tbs lime juice

1 tbs coriander leaves (cilantro), chopped

5 tbs peanut (groundnut) or vegetable oil

4 garlic cloves, peeled and coarsely chopped

400g (14oz) minced (ground) pork, preferably a coarse consistency

1 tsp white sugar

½ cup water

3 large handfuls of holy basil leaves

steamed rice and 4 fried eggs to serve

METHOD

1. Make the fish sauce seasoning by mixing the ¼ cup fish sauce with four of the chillies, the lime juice and coriander leaves. Set aside.

2. Heat the oil in a wok over medium heat.

3. Fry the garlic and the rest of the chillies but do not let the garlic go brown.

4. Add the pork mince and stir-fry until nearly cooked. Season with the remaining fish sauce and the sugar.

5. Add the water and simmer for a few minutes until some of the water has evaporated.

6. Remove the wok from the heat and stir in the basil.

7. Serve on a bed of steamed rice, topped with the fish sauce seasoning and a fried egg.

SERVES 4

* Phat Thai *

THAILAND

Phat thai is the most famous Thai dish in the world, and understandably so: how do you go wrong with gooey strands of noodles, crunchy peanuts, tart lime and singed egg?

What is It?

To make *phat thai*, thin rice noodles are fried with bits of tofu, dried shrimp, salted radish, shallots and egg, and seasoned with fish sauce, tamarind extract (and/or vinegar) and sugar. The fried noodles are then topped with ground peanuts, Chinese chives and beanshoots and are served with a slice of lime and a side of crunchy vegetables.

Origin

Phat thai, which allegedly dates back to the 1930s, is a relatively recent introduction to the Thai kitchen and, despite the nationalistic name, is in many ways more of a Chinese than a Thai dish. Both noodles and the technique of frying are Chinese in origin, although the dish was invented in Thailand and its seasonings are characteristically Thai. Today, the dish is quite possibly Thailand's most popular culinary export and remains a popular one-dish meal in Bangkok and central Thailand.

Finding It

Bangkok's Thip Samai has been serving *phat thai* for nearly 50 years; a dish costs about 30 baht (US$1).

Tasting

Although nowadays *phat thai* is sold in restaurants, it's still very much an important part of the street-food repertoire. Stalls and carts selling *phat thai* also tend to serve *hoy thot*, a crispy mussel omelette. Both are generally fried on the same flat, round surface, but some vendors choose to fry *phat thai* in a wok, skilfully allowing the flames to singe and burn the noodles. *Phat thai* is among the milder Thai street dishes and diners are expected to boost the flavour of their noodles with a personalised mixture of fish sauce, sugar, dried chilli and ground peanuts – the standard condiments for the dish. And in the very Thai effort to incorporate seemingly every possible flavour, *phat thai* is served with sides that possess a slightly bitter taste, including banana flower and garlic chives. In contrast to the version you might find at your local restaurant, true *phat thai* is a largely vegetarian dish containing only dried shrimp and fish sauce, although modern versions of the dish sometimes include fresh shrimp or prawns.

* VARIATIONS * **Variations on the dish include *phat thai hor khai*, where the noodles are artfully wrapped in a paper-thin omelette, and a particularly decadent version using *man kung* (fat from the heads of prawns, also known as tomalley). One Bangkok restaurant makes the dish using strands of crispy green papaya instead of the usual rice noodles from Chanthaburi Province.**

* By Austin Bush *

Recipe Phat Thai

Have all the ingredients prepared and ready to go next to your wok as the dish takes very little time to cook. The duck eggs may be substituted with chicken eggs, and the red shallots with French shallots or brown onions but the rest of the ingredients are key to the dish's salty, sweet and sour taste, and should be easily available from a well-stocked Asian supermarket.

YOU'LL NEED

4 tbs tamarind concentrate

6 tbs palm sugar

2 tbs fish sauce

5 tbs peanut (groundnut) or vegetable oil

8 red shallots, coarsely chopped

3 duck eggs

300g (11oz) fresh rice noodles; or 250g (9oz) dried rice noodles blanched in boiling water

60g (2oz) firm tofu, cut into cubes

2 tbs dried prawns, rinsed and dried

1 tsp salted radish, rinsed and dried and finely chopped

2 tbs roasted peanuts, coarsely chopped

2 handfuls of beanshoots, trimmed

1 handful of Chinese chives, sliced into 2cm (1in) lengths

extra beanshoots and roasted peanuts, fresh chillies and lime wedges to serve

METHOD

1. Mix the tamarind concentrate with the palm sugar and fish sauce until the sugar dissolves. Set aside.

2. Heat the oil in a wok over medium heat.

3. Fry the shallots until they begin to colour.

4. Crack in the eggs and stir them until they resemble scrambled eggs.

5. Turn up the heat and add the noodles. Add the tamarind mixture and let simmer for a few minutes until the noodles have absorbed some of the sauce.

6. Stir in the tofu, dried prawns, radish and peanuts and continue stirring until most of the sauce is absorbed.

7. Add the beanshoots and chives and stir for a few minutes.

8. Transfer to a bowl, top with more beanshoots and roasted peanuts and serve immediately with fresh chillies and lime wedges on the side.

SERVES 4

* Pho *

VIETNAM

The breakfast of champions, this fragrant and delicately spiced Vietnamese noodle soup is the perfect wake-up call on a steamy Hanoi morning.

What is It?

You could call it noodle soup, but to put it so plainly would be a grave injustice. *Pho* is so much more: it's divine beef stock (with lingering notes of onion, ginger, star anise and coriander), freshly made rice noodles, mild chillies and crunchy beanshoots, topped with slices of beef, brisket, chicken, tendon or meatballs and a squeeze of lime.

Finding It

The Quan An Ngon restaurant in Hanoi is a little bit more expensive than the average street stall – a bowl might cost 45,000 dong (US$2.15) here instead of 20,000 dong (US$0.95) elsewhere – but the garden is gorgeous and the *pho* exemplary.

Tasting

Dawn is breaking across Vietnam and the background hum of scooter engines has yet to reach its mid-morning crescendo. The *pho* sellers have set up stalls, some little more than a battered collection of metal pans, while others include plastic tables and gleaming trolleys. Whatever you choose, it's the broth that matters. This is the heart and soul of *pho* and should be rich and deeply flavoured, hinting of star anise, cardamom and coriander. The noodles should be freshly made, soft with a hint of firmness, while the chillies are mild, rather than fierce. Beanshoots add a satisfyingly crunchy texture. A dash of fish sauce, a squeeze of lime, and breakfast is ready. Grab a wobbly chair, sit back and slurp.

Origins

Pho has its origins in the cuisines of France and China and was popularised around the end of the 19th century. The Vietnamese took the rice noodles from their northern neighbour and a taste for red meat from the colonialists, and in the process managed to create something entirely new. Some say *pho* (pronounced 'feu') is derived from the French dish *pot au feu*, while others argue that it is Chinese in origin, stemming from a Cantonese word for noodles, *fan*. The debate, as ever, rages on unabated. Both have equal claim to the title.

* REGIONAL VARIATIONS * *Pho* tends to be more simple and traditional in the north, like all food in Vietnam. There is less meat and fewer herbs – sometimes even none at all. You'll usually find just chillies and lime. Down south, things are more ornate. Fresh Thai basil, sawtooth herb and coriander are some of the herbs used to garnish the soup, while the broth might contain more chillies and even peanuts.

* By Tom Parker Bowles *

Recipe Pho

YOU'LL NEED

Broth

10cm (4in) piece of ginger,
halved lengthwise

2 yellow onions, halved

cooking oil

2.25kg (5lb) beef marrow bones,
preferably leg and knuckle
(can substitute with oxtail bones)

4.75L (5 quarts) of water

1 cinnamon stick

1 tsp coriander seeds

1 tbs fennel seeds

5 star anise

2 cardamom pods

6 whole garlic cloves

¼ cup fish sauce

2 tbs sugar

1 tbs salt

Noodles & Adornments

225g (½lb) beef steak

450g (1lb) dried flat rice noodles,
prepared for soup as per packet
directions

10 sprigs mint

10 sprigs coriander leaves (cilantro)

10 sprigs Thai basil

12 sawtooth coriander leaves

½ yellow onion, thinly sliced

2 limes, each cut into 6 thin wedges

2–3 chilli peppers, sliced

450g (1lb) beanshoots

hoisin sauce

hot chilli sauce

METHOD

Broth

1. Place ginger and halved yellow onions on a baking sheet, brush with cooking oil and put on the highest rack under a heated grill (broiler). Grill on high until ginger and onions begin to char. Turn over to char the other side for a total of 10–15 minutes.

2. Boil enough water in a large pot to cover the beef bones and continue to boil on high for five minutes. Drain, rinse the bones and rinse out the pot. Refill the pot with the bones and the 4.75L of cool water. Bring to the boil then lower to a simmer. Remove any scum that rises to the top with a ladle or skimmer.

3. Place the cinnamon stick, coriander seeds, fennel seeds, star anise, cardamom pods and garlic cloves in a mesh bag (alternatively, *pho* spice packets are available at speciality Asian food markets already in a bag) and add to the broth pot along with the charred onion and ginger and the fish sauce, sugar and salt and simmer for 1½ hours.

4. Discard the spice pack and the onion and continue to simmer for another 1½ hours.

5. Strain the broth and return it to the pot. Adjust salt, fish sauce and sugar to taste.

Noodles & Adornments

1. Slice the beef as thin as possible across the grain.

2. Follow the directions on the package to cook your noodles (cooking varies between types and brands).

3. Bring the broth back to a boil.

4. Arrange all the other adornments next to your serving bowls.

5. To serve, fill each bowl with noodles and raw meat slices. Ladle the boiling broth into the bowls – this will cook the beef slices.

6. Garnish with the remaining herbs, thinly sliced onion, lime wedges, chillies, beanshoots and sauces and serve immediately.

SERVES 8

* Pierogi *

POLAND

Tasty, cheap and satisfying, these crescent-shaped doughy delights are a Polish icon, with the variety of fillings limited only by the imagination.

What is It?

The highly versatile Polish version of the Chinese dumpling or Italian ravioli comes stuffed with either savoury or sweet fillings. It can be boiled, fried or baked and eaten as an appetiser, main course or dessert. Pierogi are not just a street snack but can be found everywhere in Poland, from church *festyns* (charity fundraisers) and milk bars to high-end restaurants. Classic fillings include *ruskie* (potato and cheese), *z miesem* (meat), *z kapusta* (cabbage) and *z owocami* (fruit) for sweet tooths.

Origin

Variations of stuffed dumplings can be found all over Europe and Asia, but the exact origin of pierogi remains unknown. A Dominican monk named Jacek, better known as the patron saint of pierogi, is generally credited for their popularisation by distributing them to the poor. This, in addition to their ease of preparation, has cemented their reputation as peasant food. An indelible part of the Polish culinary landscape, this simple and sustaining food is likely to be associated with life behind the Iron Curtain by older generations. In recent years bolder and more creative filling combinations have led to their resurgence and increased popularity among a wider audience. Yet for many Poles, a plateful of pierogi is still comfort food at its best, with the carefully imprinted fingers on the edges of handmade dumplings a soothing reminder of home.

Tasting

Don't be fooled by the appearance of pierogi as a seemingly bland and stodgy pocket of dough. The best pierogi are soft and pillowy, and their infinite variety means you can match your mood with the filling of your choice. No Polish family gathering is complete without the humble classic potato and cheese, but equally popular and a must-try is cabbage and sauerkraut. Savour its rounded tartness and be pleasantly surprised by the lack of the usual sharpness or smelliness associated with cabbage. While wandering Poland's historical market squares, the moreish meat or *kielbasa* (a garlicky Polish sausage) pierogi will provide all the sustenance you need for the day ahead. The savoury mince and pasta-like dough topped with sour cream and fried onion is a hearty meal in itself, the Polish equivalent of instant noodles in a bowl. At the height of berry season in summer, treat yourself to sweet, refreshing blueberry or strawberry pierogi, served with lashings of cream.

Finding It

Stuff yourself silly with pierogi of all kinds at Krakow's Annual Festival in August, where the most exotic filling is awarded a statue of St Jacek. Winning combinations have included apples and rose petals, broad bean and bacon, and cherries and poppy seeds. A plate of three pierogi at the festival can be had for 10 to 15 złoty (US$3 to US$5).

* PAIRINGS * **Wash down a plate of pierogi with a local brew of refreshingly crisp Zywiec beer.**

* By Johanna Uy *

Recipe Pierogi

This recipe is for *pierogi ruskie* (pierogi with potato, cheese and onion stuffing). If you are unable to find twarog cheese, you can use quark cheese or fresh farmer's cheese as an alternative. This recipe makes approximately 60 pierogi, which at four or five pieces per serving is not really an enormous amount. Any leftovers can be frozen after simmering, then thawed and lightly fried in a little oil when ready to eat.

YOU'LL NEED

Dough

4 cups plain (all-purpose) flour

1 tsp salt

1 egg

2 tbs olive oil

1 cup warm water

Filling

2 large potatoes for mashing

125g (4.4oz) twarog cheese

1 medium onion, finely diced and lightly fried in olive oil

To Serve

olive oil for frying

sour cream for garnish

METHOD

1. Peel the potatoes and add them to a pot of boiling water. They should cook until soft.

2. While the potatoes are boiling, prepare the dough. Sift the flour and salt on a flat surface and then, with your hands, mix in the egg, oil and half the water.

3. Knead the mixture for approximately 10 minutes, adding the rest of the water a little at a time (as you may not need all of the water), until you end up with a soft, elastic dough. Wrap the dough in plastic or cover with a damp cloth so it does not dry out while preparing the filling.

4. When the potatoes are soft, and while still hot, push them through a sieve or a potato ricer (aerating the potato this way, rather than mashing them, will result in a fluffier filling). Combine the potato with the cheese and half of the fried onion. Season well and set aside.

5. Unwrap the dough and roll it out flat on your workspace to about 3mm (0.1in) thickness. Use a glass tumbler or cup to cut out circular shapes in the dough.

6. Put a teaspoon of filling in the centre of each circle. Fold the circle in half into a semicircle and seal the ends by pinching them together with your fingers.

7. To cook, place the pierogi in a pot of simmering (not boiling) water. Once they rise to the surface a few minutes later, remove them from the pot.

8. To serve, lightly brown the boiled pierogi for a few minutes in olive oil, then garnish with sour cream and remainder of fried onions.

* Pizza al Taglio *

ROME, ITALY

Baked in giant metal trays, sliced in thick rectangular slabs and paid for by weight, Roman pizza is for fun on the run.

What is It?

Pizza al taglio is a rectangular piece of pizza in the Roman style. Traditionally, it should have an unrisen crust, which makes it rather different from the version found in Naples, with its chewy, billowing and blistered edges. *Pizza bianca* is the classic cheeseless version, while *rossa* has only tomato sauce.

Finding It

The best *pizza bianca* (and *rossa*) can be found at Forno Campo de' Fiori in Rome, for about €1.50 to €2.50 per square (US$2 to US$3.50).

Tasting

Good pizza, whether *al taglio* or Neapolitan, is all about the crust. Any fool can slather on some tomato sauce and scatter a few toppings over it all. But only the masters can create a crust that renders all conversation useless. Avoid any place with a spongy, crust. You want to find somewhere with yelpingly expectant crowds and queues of uncooked pizza, waiting for the oven to disgorge its treasure. The smell is overwhelming, the wait excruciating. Point at what you want and indicate how much. The cooks will then cut, weigh and hand it over, wrapped in a paper napkin, to be eaten like a sandwich. The crust is brittle, the toppings spread with a generous hand. Don't worry about manners – scoff it down before it cools. That's what the Romans do. Albeit, in a rather neater way.

Origins

All pizza evolved from unleavened flatbreads, and the Persians and Greeks both claim credit. But it's the Italians who mastered the art. Although the ingredients are simple, pizza perfection is elusive. To succeed, you need a white-hot wood-burning oven and the best ingredients you can afford. The Roman version has a much thinner crust, and, historically, it was a flat bread. You'll find all sorts now, but crisp and thin is still king.

* **VARIATIONS** * *Bianca* and *rossa* are just the beginning: potato and rosemary, sausage and spinach, artichoke and *cime di rapa* (broccoli rabe). *Pizza al taglio* can include anything you can think of, really. But remember, the crust is king. The toppings are mere frivolous embellishments.

* By Tom Parker Bowles *

Recipe Pizza al Taglio

YOU'LL NEED

30g (1oz) yeast

2 cups warm water

7 cups plain (all-purpose) flour

1½ tsp salt

2 tbs olive oil, and extra to
oil baking trays

toppings of your choice – tomato
sauce, mozzarella, fresh basil,
anchovies, olives...

METHOD

1. Dissolve the yeast in one cup of the water, then combine all dough ingredients and mix gently until a dough forms. Knead the dough, either by hand or using an electric mixer with a dough hook, until you have an elastic texture and satin finish.

2. Transfer the dough to an oiled bowl, cover it and leave it in a warm spot until it doubles in size.

3. Lightly grease your baking trays and preheat your oven to 220°C (425°F). On a floured surface, divide the dough into four portions, and roll out each one to fit your trays, trimming as needed.

4. Drizzle a little olive oil over the rolled-out bases, then start creating your signature pizza, using whatever toppings take your fancy. Just a couple of simple ingredients will do. Bake for roughly 15 minutes or until the crusts are pleasingly golden. Cut into neat rectangles to serve.

MAKES ENOUGH FOR 4 RECTANGULAR DOMESTIC PIZZA TRAYS

* Poisson Cru *

FRENCH POLYNESIA

If flower-scented air and turquoise lagoons could be blended into a dish, *poisson cru* would be it: raw fish and vegetable salad dressed with lime juice and coconut milk.

What is It?

Bite-sized chunks of fresh, raw fish (usually tuna) are briefly marinated in lime juice, mixed with vegetables such as cucumber, tomato and grated carrot, and then doused in coconut milk. Sometimes a touch of garlic is added. The dish is served with white rice and is eaten for breakfast, lunch or dinner.

Finding It

Few places can beat the dining experience at the Place Vaite *roulottes* in Papeete, the capital of French Polynesia. Expect to pay around 1000CFP (US$12).

Tasting

Sweet from the coconut, tart from the lemon, savoury from the fish, *poisson cru* is as refreshing as a tickle of trade wind and goes down best to the strum of a ukulele. It's usually prepared by Polynesian hands in humid kitchens and ladled into rectangular plastic takeaway dishes alongside a heaping portion of steamed rice. It's eaten for dinner at a *roulotte* (mobile food van), among families sharing the dish alongside *steak frites* (steak and chips) and chow mein, the night sticky with smoke from open-air grills. The rice soaks up the coconut flavour of the sauce and softens the crunch of the vegetables; the raw tuna takes on the texture of a firm mousse torte, tender and silky. The lingering scent of flowers in the evening air adds the final touch to gustatory paradise.

Origin

Seafood has probably always been eaten raw in Polynesia, particularly by fisherman who often spent several days at sea and had no choice in the matter. The Japanese introduced the idea of sashimi (eaten in French Polynesia as a heap of thinly sliced raw tuna on a bed of rice) in the last century while European and Chinese cultures introduced their own vegetables and spices to the islands during early contact.

* VARIATIONS * *Poisson cru à la chinoise* (Chinese-style *poisson cru*), also found all over French Polynesia, is made with chunks of raw fish marinated in oil and vinegar and then mixed with Chinese pickled vegetables; no coconut milk is added. Ginger and sometimes garlic are used in moderation and the flavour is more sour than the classic *poisson cru au lait coco*.

Recipe Poisson Cru

YOU'LL NEED

500g (about 1lb) fresh yellowfin tuna cut into 2.5cm (1in) cubes (salmon, swordfish, bonito and other deep-water fish can also be used)

¾ cup fresh lime or lemon juice (or a mix of both – they shouldn't be too sour)

2 tomatoes, chopped

½ small onion, finely chopped

1 cucumber, finely chopped

1 carrot, grated

1 green capsicum (bell pepper), thinly sliced (optional)

1 cup coconut milk (canned is OK but fresh is best)

salt and pepper

spring onion or parsley, chopped (optional)

METHOD

1. Take the tuna chunks and soak in a bowl of seawater or lightly salted fresh water (locals swear this makes the fish more tender) while preparing the vegetables.

2. Remove the tuna from the salt water and place in a large salad bowl. Add the lemon or lime juice and leave the fish to marinate for about three minutes.

3. Pour off about half to two-thirds of the juice (depending on how tart you like it), then add the vegetables and toss together with the fish.

4. Pour the coconut milk over the salad and add salt and pepper to taste.

5. Garnish with chopped spring onion or parsley and serve with white rice.

* Poutine *

QUEBEC, CANADA

It may be a 'damn mess', but it's a damn delicious mess. It's the Quebecois creation called *poutine*, potatoes swimming in gravy and sprinkled with cheese.

What is It?

Poutine starts with a mound of french fries (chips) hot from the fryer, which are then buried in a salty brown gravy and topped with fresh cheese curds. The gravy is typically made with chicken stock, but you'll also see veal, beef and occasionally vegetarian versions. The best cheese curds are so fresh that they make a squeaky sound when you bite into them.

Origin

Poutine is Quebec slang for 'a mess'. According to legend, in 1957 a customer walked into a restaurant in Warwick, northeast of Montreal, and asked the owner, Fernand Lachance, to toss some cheese curds in with his potatoes. Lachance complied but reportedly said, '*Ça va faire une maudite poutine!*' ('That's going to make a damn mess!') Jean-Paul Roy, a restaurateur in nearby Drummondville, claimed that he invented the complete *poutine* a few years later when he mixed gravy as well as cheese curds into the fries.

Tasting

Stab your fork into the pile of potatoes and pull out a starchy spear, drenched in gravy and dripping with cheese. It's not elegant, but it's a perfect cure for the munchies after a last call at the pub. It's a staple of ski resorts, casual eateries and chip stands, too – fast-food stalls sell burgers, hot dogs and sometimes fried fish along with *poutine*. Wherever you're indulging, let your *poutine* sit for a minute or two, so the cheese begins to melt and soak into the gravy. Don't wait too long or the potatoes will get soggy. You want the ideal balance of crisp potato, soft cheese and gooey gravy.

Finding It

For *poutine* anytime, head for La Banquise in Montreal, open 24 hours. A plate typically costs around CAD$6 to CAD$14 (US$6 to US$14).

* VARIATIONS * Although *poutine* originated in Quebec, you can now find it across Canada – this down-home dish has even gone upscale. In high-end dining rooms, its trendy toppings might include braised short ribs, duck confit and even foie gras. In Quebec, *poutine* is pronounced 'poo-*tin*'.

* By Carolyn B Heller *

Recipe Poutine

A classic *poutine* is usually made from St Hubert packet sauce and fresh cheese curds which are readily available in Quebecois supermarkets. Shredded mozzarella and ready-mix chicken gravy are acceptable substitutes.

YOU'LL NEED

Homemade chicken gravy

2 cups chicken stock

1 tbs butter

2 tbs flour

Fries

5 potatoes, peeled and sliced into fries

vegetable oil for frying

400g (14oz) fresh cheese curds

2 cups chicken gravy, either from a packet or homemade

METHOD

1. Prepare the gravy. If using a ready-mixed sauce, simply warm according to the packet instructions.

2. If making your own gravy, melt the butter in a saucepan and stir in the flour until it becomes a yellow paste.

3. Slowly whisk in the stock, ensuring it is free of lumps.

4. Let simmer for approximately 10 minutes until the volume reduces by about a third. Remove the sauce from the heat and set aside.

5. While the gravy is simmering, rinse the potatoes in cold water and dry thoroughly.

6. Deep fry or shallow fry the potatoes until golden brown.

7. Place the fries in a shallow bowl and top with the cheese curds and smother with the gravy. Serve immediately.

SERVES 4

* Pretzel *

USA

Fat, warm and twisted, these salt-sprinkled chewy breads stand shoulder to shoulder with that other New York classic that takes a squirt of mustard – the 'dirty water' hot dog.

What is It?

Soft pretzels are a knot of boiled then baked dough, the surface shiny thanks to the oven's heat. The key is a crisp surface, dotted with fat crystals of salt, and a hefty, malleable heart that requires some serious chew. A generous smear of yellow mustard is mandatory.

Finding It

Sigmund Pretzelshop in the East Village is second to none, a true bite of old-fashioned pretzel joy. Pretzels with seeds, herbs, cheese or cinnamon cost US$3 each.

Tasting

Alas, the vast majority of vending-cart soft pretzels are sorry, sullen shadows of the real things. They're often either dry and horribly stale or woefully undercooked and dripping with grease. But at their best, though, soft pretzels have a texture that makes the jaw whoop with delight; they're big and chewy, but never drab and overwhelming. Eaten fresh from the oven, the crust should be blistered with a healthy shine. Crack and crunch, then proper doughty heft. And the shape twisted by hand. This is one street food that has long left the pavement. The best are to be found in small local bakeries.

Origin

Although New York and Philadelphia may claim them as their own, pretzels are European to the core. Originally a Lenten bread of the Italian early Middle Ages (the characteristic shape is said to depict a monk in prayer), it was known as either *bracellae* (little arms) or *pretiola* (little reward). This turned into the German *Bretzel*, or pretzel. And it was the Germans who turned the pretzel into an art form. They soon spread across central Europe; the pretzel has been a baker's emblem since the 12th century. It probably sailed across the Atlantic with the German emigrants who settled in Pennsylvania in the 19th century. Sturgis Pretzel House, near Lancaster, Pennsylvania, was founded in 1861 and is still going strong.

* VARIATIONS * Philadelphia is where it all started and there are plenty of fine bakeries there too. Miller's Twist, Federal Soft Pretzel and DiPalma Soft Pretzel all have their acolytes.

Recipe Pretzels

The use of bread flour (which contains more gluten than all-purpose flour) gives these soft pretzels that trademark chewiness. This dough can be made either by hand or with a mixer.

YOU'LL NEED

2¼ tsp dried yeast powder

⅛ tsp fine sea salt

2 tsp sugar (for the dough)

1 cup warm water

1 cup bread flour

2 cups plain (all-purpose) flour

2 tbs butter, softened

2–3 tbs vegetable oil

¼ cup bicarb soda (baking soda)

1½ tbs sugar (for the cooking water)

1 tbs coarse sea salt

1 tsp water

1 egg, beaten

METHOD

1. In a small bowl, briskly stir yeast, fine sea salt, sugar and warm water together until the sugar has dissolved. Let the mix stand until it starts getting frothy (usually in under 10 minutes).

2. In a large, separate bowl, place the flours and softened butter and start rubbing the butter into the flour with your fingers until it takes on the look of coarse breadcrumbs.

3. Gently pour the foamy yeast mixture over the flour and stir with a wooden spoon. When combined, gather up the dough and start kneading it on a lightly floured surface for a few minutes – until it's smooth and not still sticking to your fingers.

4. Brush the insides of a large bowl with a light coating of vegetable oil. Put your dough in the bowl, flip the dough over so it gets coated in oil, then cover the bowl with plastic wrap and place it in a warm spot to rise and double in size. This should take about an hour. In the meantime, lightly brush a couple of baking trays with vegetable oil.

5. When the dough has magically doubled, take it out of the bowl and cut it into 12 pieces. To make the pretzel shape, roll a piece of dough into a long rope (around 45cm or 18in long). Lie it on your bench in a U-shape, then bring the ends together and twist them twice to make a loop. Flip the ends down to the base of the loop and gently press them onto the dough. When you've made all your pretzels, place them on an oiled baking tray and let them rise for 20 minutes.

6. Preheat your oven to 250°C (475°F). Meanwhile, boil a large pot of water and add the bicarb soda and sugar. Gently lower pretzels into the water (you can cook them in batches) and cook for a couple of minutes on either side, until they get puffed up and have a slight sheen. Remove from the water and allow to drain on wire racks before transferring them onto the oiled baking trays.

7. Combine the teaspoon of water with the beaten egg, then brush pretzels with the mixture and sprinkle with coarse sea salt. Bake until golden – around 15 minutes. Eat fresh and slathered in mustard.

MAKES 12

* Pupusa *
EL SALVADOR

Often described as the national dish of El Salvador, these fat, stuffed tortillas available on every street corner fulfil your every dietary need: bread, meat, cheese and vegetables.

What is It?

Similar to the Mexican *gordita*, the *pupusa* takes a fat handmade tortilla of masa (dough made from maize flour) and stuffs it with appetite-sating *queso* (cheese), *chicharron* (in El Salvador, this means ground pork) or *frijoles* (beans) – or a blend of all three. It's then cooked on the griddle and served hot. Piled high close by is *curtido* (a mildly spicy and sharp coleslaw) and tomato salsa.

Tasting

El Salvador is not exactly feted for its native food, but a decent *pupusa* is a world-class bite. There's barely a street, from main thoroughfare to winding dirt track, where you won't find a *pupuseria*. And it's adored by peasant and politician alike. Make sure yours is cooked fresh before your eyes – not so much for reasons of hygiene, but pure, visceral pleasure. They taste so much better fresh off the hot plate. Cheap, rich and filling, the quality is generally high, while the *curtido* (usually available in mild or spicy) cuts a vinegary swathe through all the stodge. Go for a mix of cheese, beans and pork for the ultimate hit, all washed down with a bottle of local Suprema beer. It's as satisfying a lunch, eaten perched on a rickety plastic chair, as you'll find anywhere in the world.

Origins

Another ancient Central American dish, these were already being cooked up almost 2000 years ago. Archaeologists have found cooking equipment used to make *pupusas* in Joya de Ceren, often described as El Salvador's Pompeii. Until the middle of the 20th century, they were said to be a speciality of the central regions alone. But as the population became mobile in the 1960s, they spread not just across the country, but to neighbouring states as well.

Finding It

A famous spot overlooking San Salvador, Los Planes de Renderos has local beer, local bands and some of the best *pupuserias* in town. *Pupusas* cost US$1.

* **VARIATIONS** * One variation is the **pupusa de arroz**, made with rice flour, which is a speciality of Olocuilta, east of San Salvador. You can also find them at numerous stalls in the capital.

Recipe Pupusas

YOU'LL NEED

Pupusas

2 cups masa harina (maize flour)

1 cup warm water

assorted fillings: for a cheese filling, grate a combination of your favourite cheeses (try mozzarella or Swiss) and add a hit of minced green chilli; for a quick pork version, you can blend cooked bacon with a zingy tomato sauce; or you can even used leftover potatoes pepped up with jalapeños – invent your own!

Curtido

½ green cabbage, shredded

1 carrot, grated

4 cups boiling water

½ cup water

½ cup apple cider vinegar

½ tsp salt

1 jalapeño or serrano chilli, minced

3 spring onions, minced

METHOD

Pupusas

1. Mix the *masa harina* with the water to form a malleable dough that is firm but not dry. Add water in small increments if needed. Cover and leave to rest for five to 10 minutes.

2. Divide the dough into even portions and roll each piece into a ball. Make a deep indentation into the dough with your thumb – big enough to accommodate a small spoonful of filling. Pinch the dough closed over the filling then gently flatten the ball into a disc in the palm of your hand.

3. Place a disc between two pieces of wax paper and carefully roll it out with a rolling pin until it's about 6mm (0.25in) thick.

4. Place an oiled skillet (frying pan) over a medium to high heat and cook pupusas for one to two minutes on each side, until they are browned and a little crispy. Serve with the *curtido* and salsa.

Curtido

1. Place the cabbage and carrots in a large bowl. Pour over the boiling water to cover the vegetables and set aside for about five minutes. Then drain in a colander, pressing out the liquid.

2. Return the cabbage mixture to the bowl and toss with the remaining ingredients. Cover and chill for a couple of hours (or preferably overnight) to lightly ferment.

MAKES 4–5 PUPUSAS

* Red Red *

GHANA

The only thing better than Ghanaian dishes may be their names. Hot, sweet and spicy, red red pairs beans with fried plantains and *zomi* (red palm oil).

What is It?

The key to red red is one of the reds: *zomi* is a special palm oil with a rich nutty taste. Onions and chilli (also red) are fried in the *zomi* and added to black-eyed peas, then topped with more *zomi* and *gari* (fermented, dried cassava powder). Sweet, ripe plantains (*koko*; another red) – thickly sliced, salted and deep-fried in vegetable oil – accompany the beans.

Origin

Everyone loves red red, but it's a favourite of the Ewe ethnic group and may have migrated from Ewe country in eastern Ghana (the Volta Region) and Togo. There, as in Accra, beans are an inexpensive protein, which makes red red Ghana's national cheap lunch. Over time, *gari* was added for texture and, since it expands with water, as a cheap stomach-filler; *shito* (shee-to; peppery fish sauce with spices) was added for heat.

Finding It

Red red is good everywhere, but in the Community 12 region of Tema, it's extraordinary. Prices vary with serving sizes: a light-lunch portion costs one cedi (US$0.60).

Tasting

Red red's natural habitat is 'chop bars' (little shacks serving lunch) and roadside stands. If you wait near others who are already eating, you'll hear, 'You are invited!' – the traditional polite offering to share food. The scene is crowded, with office workers and working-class people alike breaking for lunch, while a woman with a basket of pineapples on her head passes by, ready to cut up one of her fruit for dessert. The red red is hot and the oil on the plantains still sizzling when it is served on a dried plantain leaf (or, less interestingly, a plate). The beans are soft and salty and the plantains are soft and sweet with crispy edges – the tastes are meant to be together. The *gari* gives it an extra crunch, the *zomi* gives it depth and the *shito* gives it a kick.

* **VARIATIONS** * **The Ga people sometimes switch out *koko* for *akrakruo*: a super-ripe plantain mashed and mixed with ginger and chilli for spice and cassava flour for form. The gooey mash is spooned into the fryer to make golden, crunchy, spicy plantain blobs.**

* By Amy Karafin, with Gladys Noi *

Recipe Red Red

Try African grocery stores for these ingredients.

YOU'LL NEED

1½ cups dried black-eyed peas

salt

3 ripe but slightly firm plantains

½ cup *zomi* plus a little extra for taste (vegetable oil can be used in a pinch)

salt

2 small onions, finely sliced

minced fresh chilli

2 garlic cloves, sliced (optional)

2 ripe tomatoes, diced

3 cups vegetable oil

shito to taste (omit if vegetarian)

1 tbs *gari*

METHOD

1. Rinse the peas and then let them soak for an hour minimum.

2. Drain the peas and rinse them again.

3. Cook peas in a saucepan with 3 cups water. Bring to boil for a minute or two then reduce heat and let simmer until soft (about 45 minutes). When they are finished cooking, drain, toss in a couple of pinches of salt, and set aside.

4. Chop the plantains in four, cutting at a diagonal so the slices make a wedge-like 'spoon'. Dribble water over them and sprinkle salt to 'cure' them (it increases their sweetness). Let them sit for a few minutes.

5. In another saucepan, heat ½ cup *zomi*. Add onions and chilli (garlic optional) to the oil once hot; stir until crispy. Add the tomatoes and stew until soft.

6. Heat up some vegetable oil in a third pan and add the plantains, a few at a time, stirring to ensure even frying (a couple of minutes will usually do it). Remove when golden brown.

7. Add the *zomi*, onion and chilli mixture to the finished peas. Dribble some more *zomi* and some *shito* on top and then sprinkle *gari* over it. Serve with fried plantains. Red red is eaten with the right hand: use the plantain to pick up the peas.

* Roasted Chestnuts *

EUROPE

No other aroma evokes the spirit of winter and festive holidays more vividly than roasted chestnuts. One whiff of their distinctly sweet and earthy smell will have you humming *that* Christmas tune in no time.

What is It?

Street carts peddling paper cones or bags full of the shiny, brown thick-skinned nuts with their mustard-hued kernels are a ubiquitous presence on the streets in winter and at Christmas markets all over Europe.

Origin

Chestnuts have been part of the human diet since the time of the ancient Greeks, who wrote about their flatulence-inducing properties. Ground as flour, they provided a starchy fix for rural families in mountainous areas where cereals were not easily grown. The rock-hard casings of fresh chestnuts are difficult to peel unless roasted, as was historically done in front of the fire during long winters. Roasted chestnuts were sold on the streets of Rome as early as the 16th century, but chestnuts as a staple food have gradually gone out of fashion. These days roasted chestnuts are more popularly consumed as a winter treat.

Tasting

Few can resist the smoky, heavenly waft of roasting chestnuts from a street cart on a chilly day. Snacking on a bag of hot chestnuts freshly roasted over an open fire, or on open coals as they do in Padua, is the quintessential European holiday-season experience. The unpleasantness of raw chestnuts is miraculously transformed, with their sweet taste and fuller flavour emerging only after a good roasting. In Rome, street vendors go the extra mile and arrange individual chestnuts about to burst in their split shells in neat gold-and-brown rows. As nuts go, chestnuts are literally tough ones to crack. Peeling them while still warm is all part of the ritual and your efforts will be rewarded with their delicate and nutty taste and the rich texture of a baked sweet potato. A winter promenade is made all the more delightful with a bag of these simply roasted, unadorned nuts.

Finding It

Soak up the festive holiday atmosphere of the historic Cologne Christmas Markets with a hot bag of freshly roasted chestnuts and some mulled wine, at about €5 (US$7) per bag.

* USEFUL FACT * Chestnuts are surprisingly nutritious: they are very low in fat and the only nut that contains Vitamin C.

* By Johanna Uy

Recipe Roasted Chestnuts

Scoring the chestnuts is critical to prevent them from exploding in the oven. Of course, chestnuts can also be roasted over an open fire, or you could invest in a chestnut pan, which has holes on the bottom for roasting over the open flame of a gas stove top. A street vendors' secret is to boil the chestnuts first for about 15 to 20 minutes before grilling and giving them that 'roasted' look.

YOU'LL NEED

500g (1lb) chestnuts

METHOD

1. Preheat the oven to 200°C (400°F).

2. With a small, sharp knife, carefully score a cross or a slit on each chestnut. Place the chestnuts in a shallow roasting tray with slit sides facing up.

3. Roast until the skins break open and the nuts are soft, approximately 30 minutes.

4. Serve in paper cones with mugs of mulled wine.

* Sabih *

ISRAEL

Felafel's little brother combines fried eggplant and hard-boiled egg with tahini, *amba* (Iraqi-style mango chutney) and freshly chopped vegies to create a cheap, filling and healthy meal in a pita pocket.

What is It?

Hard-boiled egg turned brown by long hours of simmering and deep-fried slices of young eggplant are placed in a pita lined with tahini, *amba* and (often) hot sauce. Boiled potato, chopped parsley and tomato and cucumber salad round out the pita's stuffing, which is salted, sprinkled with finely ground pepper and, finally, garnished with dollop of tahini.

Origin

Traditionally eaten by Iraqi Jews on Saturday morning, *sabih* – known as *bid babinjan* (egg in eggplant) back in Baghdad – was brought to Israel by Iraqi immigrants in the early 1950s. For years appreciated mainly in Ramat Gan and Givatayim, Tel Aviv suburbs with large populations of Iraqi Jews, the dish has recently created a buzz among Israel's young and trendy set, especially in ultrahip Tel Aviv.

Tasting

Ask an Israeli of Iraqi origin where to find the best *sabih* and chances are you'll hear about long-ago Sabbath mornings in Baghdad. Traditionalists swear by the old-time recipes, on offer in hole-in-the-wall shops with chest-high glass cases and a few bar stools, while modish *feinshmekerim* ('connoisseurs' in Israeli slang and Yiddish) often champion sleek eateries with bright wall menus that feature audacious fusion dishes. But what everyone is looking for is the perfect mixture of complementary flavours and contrasting textures. As you bite through the pita – so fresh it's still warm! – the diverse ingredients take centre stage for cameo roles and then merge into the background harmonies: warm, molten eggplant meets crunchy, spring-green parsley; juicy-fresh tomato chunks nuzzle up to soft morsels of egg; tangy *amba* mixes with crisp slivers of onion; and the heat of green chilli is mellowed by creamy tahini.

Finding It

Hippo in Tel Aviv serves up both tradition and innovation for about 17 shekels (US$5).

* VARIATIONS * **Every *sabihiyya* (*sabih* shop) has its own recipe. Some places leave out the traditional boiled potatoes, while others – to the outrage of purists – incorporate elements adopted from other types of Israeli street food, such as hummus, slices of pickle, *s'chug* (Yemenite hot chilli paste), pickled chilli peppers, Argentine *chimichurri* sauce, arugula (rocket) leaves and even quinoa salad.**

* By Daniel Robinson *

Recipe Sabih

YOU'LL NEED

4 eggs

onion peels

1–2 young *baladi* (Levantine heirloom) eggplants

1–4 potatoes, depending on size

salt and pepper

tahini paste

1 garlic clove

1 tsp lemon juice

2–4 fresh tomatoes

4 Mediterranean (Persian) cucumbers

1 onion

mildly hot green chilli peppers

handful of parsley

vegetable oil

4 fresh pita

amba

METHOD

1. Add the eggs and lots of onion peels to a large pot of cold water, bring to a boil and then let simmer for several hours until the whites of the eggs have turned light brown. (Another way to achieve this effect is to simmer the eggs in black tea).

2. Slice the eggplant into strips 2cm to 3cm (0.8in to 1.2in) wide and 0.75cm (0.3in) thick, place on a strainer one layer thick, add salt and let it sit for an hour (this removes the bitterness).

3. Peel the potatoes, cut them into chunks 1cm (0.4in) thick and boil with a pinch of salt. Remove them from the pot, sprinkle with salt and finely ground pepper and set aside.

4. Place 3 or 4 tsp of tahini paste in a small bowl and add enough water to create a thick liquid. Crush the garlic clove into paste and add to the tahini along with the lemon juice, and some salt and pepper. Stir thoroughly.

5. Chop the tomatoes and cucumbers (equal quantities of each) into pencil-eraser-sized cubes. Finely dice the onion and chop the chilli peppers into almost microscopic bits; add both to the salad.

6. Chop the parsley and set aside.

7. Deep-fry the eggplant slices in vegetable oil for seven or eight minutes.

8. Take a pita bread and make a horizontal slit near one edge. Spread some tahini inside and add a smear of *amba* (not too much or it will overpower everything else).

9. Place slices of eggplant and potato along one wall of the pita.

10. Place chopped parsley and tomato-and-cucumber salad on top of the eggplant and potato. Sprinkle with salt and finely ground pepper.

11. Crush a peeled brown egg with a spatula (yes, just mush it) and place it on the wall of the pita opposite the eggplant and potato.

12. Add salt, pepper, chopped parsley and a dollop of tahini to the top of the pita. Press the pocket together so it will fit in your mouth.

SERVES 4

* Salteña *

BOLIVIA

Sure, chomp your coca leaves to combat lofty Andean altitudes, but for conquering the cold, this elusive, juicier cousin of the empanada is the de facto edible solution.

What is It?

A portable pastry stuffed with beef, pork or chicken stew, Bolivia's best-loved culinary treat uses gelatine as the secret to its success. The setting agent is mixed with the meaty filling (called *jigote*), so it hardens in the refrigerator overnight. This then slowly melts once it's baked in its pastry case next morning – keeping the *salteña* crisp on the outside and gooey on the inside.

Finding It

The best *salteña*-seeking spots in La Paz are Plaza San Francisco (centre) and Avenida Aniceto Arce (Sopocachi). Expect to pay around two bolivianos ($0.30) for one.

Tasting

The women in their bowler hats on the back-street intersections of La Paz with their loaded trolleys steaming into the chilly morning don't need to call: the customers will come flocking. There is no set rule – no fixed time or place – for when and where these *salteña* sellers will show. '*Que es?*' ('What's that?') you ask in anticipation with the smells of meat, oregano and garlic already wafting over. The answer is far from certain: the filling could be made up of *pollo* (chicken), *carne de res* (beef) or *cerdo* (pork). Seldom has street food looked so uniform (look for the golden-brown mounds of half-deflated pastry rugby balls) yet varied so much in taste. What provides the wow factor is how the meat blends not just with the miraculously still-crunchy pastry, but also with the 'secret ingredients' that could be hard-boiled egg, olives or even raisins.

Origin

Argentine dictator Juan Manuel de Rosas exiled one Juana Manuela Gorriti and her family from the city of Salta to Tarija, Bolivia, in 1831. The Gorritis needed to make money in their new home and so invented an elaborate empanada to sell on the street. So the story goes, anyway. Gorriti grew up to marry future president Manuel Isidoro Belzu Humerez, although whether she wooed him with tasty pastries remains unknown.

* THE GOLDEN RULE * Seize the moment: *salteñas* appear around 7am and are usually gone by midday. Devour them from the top corner down so the pastry acts as a bowl for the filling – until the inevitable happens and the juices spill out all over your hands and chin.

* **By Luke Waterson** *

Recipe Salteñas

YOU'LL NEED

Filling

½ cup margarine

1½ cups chopped white onion

2 garlic cloves, crushed

¼ cup ground cayenne mixed with a little water

1 tsp oregano

¼ cup of parsley, finely chopped

¾ cup boiling water

1 tsp ground cumin

2 tbs white sugar

1 tsp vinegar

½ beef stock cube

2 tsp salt

½ cup potato, chopped

2 carrots, chopped

¼ cup green peas

680g (1½ lb) lean chicken/beef/pork (boned and diced)

1 cup beef broth made with 1 beef stock cube

1 tsp ground black pepper

1 tbs gelatine (usually 1 packet) dissolved in 1½ cups boiling water

½ black olive per salteña

3 raisins per salteña

1–2 slices boiled egg per salteña

Dough

6 cups plain (all-purpose) flour

¾ cup margarine, plus extra for glazing

3 eggs, beaten

2 tbs white sugar

1 cup lukewarm water

1½ tsp salt

METHOD

1. Start by making the filling. In a large cooking pot, melt the margarine and then add the onion, garlic, cayenne, oregano and parsley. Saute over low heat for 10 minutes.

2. Add the boiling water, cumin, white sugar, vinegar, beef stock cube and half the salt. Simmer over low heat for 35 to 45 minutes until a reddish oil comes to the surface of the mixture.

3. Meanwhile, boil the potatoes, carrots and peas until cooked, then drain and put off to the side.

4. Raise the temperature of the simmering mixture slightly and add the meat in small amounts. Cook for 15 minutes, stirring frequently.

5. Add beef broth and the cooked vegetables. Season with pepper and mix well.

6. Add the dissolved gelatine to the stew and mix thoroughly. Then allow to cool.

7. Transfer mixture to a large bowl, cover and refrigerate overnight.

8. Before making the dough the next day, first preheat the oven to very hot: 240°C (475°F).

9. Sift the flour into a bowl. Melt the margarine until sizzling then add to the flour and mix quickly. Let cool for five minutes.

10. Add the eggs, sugar, lukewarm water and salt. Knead to form a dry dough. Cover the dough and let stand for 10 minutes.

11. Separate the dough into approximately 20 to 25 balls, then roll flat with a rolling pin to form circles approximately 0.5cm (0.2in) thick and 13cm (5in) in diameter.

12. On each circle, distribute the black olives, raisins and hard-boiled egg slices along with a spoonful of the chilled meat filling. Leave space for the dough to close around the filling.

13. Wet the edge of each circle with water, then fold to seal the filling within. Pinch the edges shut to ensure the dough is sealed.

14. Position the *salteñas* on a floured baking tray with the sealed edges facing upward. Glaze if desired by brushing with melted margarine. Bake for seven to 10 minutes. Serve warm.

MAKES 20–25 *SALTEÑAS*

* Samosa *

INDIA

Pint-sized triangular pockets of spicy goodness, the humble samosa – with its crisp pastry shell encasing a soft mashed-potato filling – is one of India's most iconic street snacks. Deservedly so!

What is It?

Savoury shells prepared from *maida* flour, samosas are most commonly stuffed with a vegetarian mixture comprised of spiced potatoes, onions, peas, coriander and green chillies. The plump pastry pockets are deep-fried in vegetable oil until golden brown then served hot with fresh tamarind, coriander or mint chutney. Downright delicious and incredibly nourishing, samosas certainly fit the bill when it comes to tantalising the taste buds and filling the belly.

Origin

Samosas are believed to have first originated in pre-10th-century central Asia where they were known as *samsas*. Thanks to flourishing trading routes between central and south Asia, they were introduced to India somewhere between the 13th and 14th centuries. They were traditionally cooked around campfires during night halts on overland trade journeys, not only because they were nutritious and easy to prepare, but also due to the convenience of carrying them cold en route. Old manuscripts describe subsequent 'royal' versions of the little pastry parcels being filled with everything from walnuts and pistachios to prime cuts of minced (ground) meat.

Tasting

No matter how confounding the tangling lanes may be, it's surprisingly easy to find a samosa-*wallah* (samosa vendor) in the most bustling of bazaars – just follow your nose. Once you've navigated the spicy aroma trail to the samosa-*wallah*, your tummy will continue to rumble as you watch the puffy savoury triangles bob like little sailboats on a sea of spluttering oil. When each side of the pastry parcel is fried to golden perfection, the vendor scoops it out and serves it with a splodge of tangy chutney. Sinking your teeth into the warm, flaky pastry to its soft, piquant potato centre is nothing short of an in-mouth flavour festival, with the multifarious sights and sounds of the bubbly Indian bazaar adding extra zing to the samosa experience.

Finding It

Samosa vendors are found in virtually every bazaar and every other street corner in India. One samosa costs around ₹8 (US$0.18).

* VARIATIONS * Southern twists to the typically northern samosa include slight variations in how the pastry is folded as well as differences in the ingredients used for the filling. In parts of south India, samosas may completely omit potatoes and instead contain fried cabbage, onions, carrots, peas and curry leaves. Unlike the north, samosas in the south are quite often served straight up, without any chutney at all. The health conscious bake their samosas instead of deep-frying them.

* By Sarina Singh *

Recipe Samosas

Making your own pastry for this traditional north Indian vegetarian version is easy and will reward you with texture that you simply won't get from the store-bought variety. While fiddlier, you may find the more compact shape of mini-samosas easier to deep-fry if you are using a heavy-bottomed saucepan instead of a deep-fryer.

YOU'LL NEED

Dough

1 cup plain (all-purpose) flour

2 tsp semolina flour

¼ tsp salt

1 tbs vegetable or canola oil

¼ cup lukewarm water

Filling

2 tbs vegetable or canola oil

½ tsp cumin seeds

⅓ cup green peas

2 green chillies, seeded and chopped

½ tsp coriander seeds, ground

½ tsp garam masala

2 large potatoes, peeled, boiled and diced (not mashed)

1 tsp amchur (mango powder)

vegetable oil for deep frying

mango chutney to serve

METHOD

1. To make the dough, combine all the ingredients in a mixing bowl.

2. Knead with your hands until the dough is soft, smooth and elastic. Set aside to rest for at least 20 minutes.

3. To make the filling, heat the oil in a small saucepan and lightly fry the cumin seeds.

4. Add the green peas and cook for a couple of minutes.

5. Add the chillies, coriander seeds and garam masala and stir for another couple of minutes.

6. Add the potatoes and gently mix through (so as not to crush the potatoes) until coated in the spices.

7. Stir through the *amchur*, put the mixture in a bowl and let it cool.

8. When the dough has rested, knead it lightly and divide into two balls. Keep dividing each ball until you end up with eight balls, or 16 if you are making mini-samosas.

9. Using a rolling pin, flatten out the first ball into a circular shape about 1mm (0.04in) thick and cut each circle in half.

10. Hold one half flat in the palm of your left hand and lightly moisten the edges of the dough with water.

11. Form the semicircle into a cone shape by joining and pressing on the cut edges to seal it into shape.

12. Stuff the cone with the filling and close the cone into a triangular shape by pinching and sealing the top edge. You should now have a triangle-shaped stuffed samosa.

13. Repeat with the rest of the dough.

14. If not using a deep-fryer, heat the oil in a saucepan and test for readiness by dropping in a tiny piece of dough. The oil is ready if it sizzles and comes up to the surface gradually.

15. Fry the samosas until golden a few at a time. Do not overcrowd the pan.

16. Serve immediately with mango chutney.

MAKES 8 LARGE OR 16 MINI-SAMOSAS

* Samsa *

CENTRAL ASIA

This lightly spiced mutton-filled pastry has been a perennial favorite among the hungry caravan men, spice merchants and travellers along the Silk Road throughout the centuries.

What is It?

Samsas are square-shaped pockets of minced (ground) meat, onion and spices that are cooked on the inner wall of a tandoori clay oven.

Origin

The *samsa* (also spelled *somsa*) originated in the ancient city-states of Samarkand, Bukhara and Khiva, located in modern day Uzbekistan. It was a popular street snack among merchants and Silk Road travellers, who stocked up on the meat pies before a long journey. Abul-Fazl Bayhaqi (AD 995–1077), a Persian historian, mentioned the *samsa* in his work *Tarikh-e Mas'oudi* (Masoudian History). *Samsas* eventually made their way to other stops on the Silk Road, including the legendary cities of Kashgar, Yarkand and Hotan (in modern-day Xinjiang, China). The concept was also brought to India in the 13th century, where it evolved into the samosa, the famed deep-fried staple that is today found throughout the subcontinent.

Tasting

Deep in every bazaar of central Asia stands the venerable *samsa* chef, his black smock streaked with white ash, sleeves rolled up to the elbows and a white cap covering his head, jauntily tilted to one side. At the crucial moment – known only through his years of experience – he peers through the oven smoke and scoops up his golden-brown bounty using a large iron ladle attached to a metre-long (3ft-long) wooden handle. The smell of mutton fat rises from the serving pans and mingles with the other heady scents of the spice market. Hungry patrons purchase *samsa* by the plateful and huddle over small tables, a hair's breadth away from the chaos of the bazaar. The first bite of a fresh *samsa* is dangerously hot as steam escapes the small meat pie; care must be taken not to burn your lips. Once your palate becomes acclimated to the intense heat, you'll begin to appreciate the deliciously juicy mutton, the savoury onion, the aromatic spices and the crisp, buttery envelope that combine to create a true taste of Central Asia.

Finding It

The quintessential place to try *samsas* is the famed Sunday Livestock Market in Kashgar (China). One *samsa* costs 1 yuan (US$0.16).

* VARIATIONS * The size, shape and filling of a *samsa* can vary greatly across the region. In Xinjiang, the *samsas* are small and square-shaped. In Uzbekistan and Kyrgyzstan, *samsas* tend to be larger and either round or triangular in shape. The minced meat filling can include potato, greens, cheese or pumpkin. Dough is usually a simple unleavened dough, but a flaky, layered filo pastry also exists.

* **By Michael Kohn** *

Recipe Samsas

Dicing the meat will be easier if it's frozen. Vegetarians can replace the meat filling with chopped vegetables.

YOU'LL NEED

Filling

225g (½lb) diced beef

1 cup chopped onions,

1 tbs chopped garlic

¼ cup cubed mutton fat

1 tsp cumin

1 tsp salt

1 tsp pepper

Dough

2½ cups plain (all-purpose) flour

1 egg

½ cup warm water

2½ tbs margarine, melted

METHOD

1. In a mixing bowl, combine the diced beef, chopped onions, garlic and cubed mutton fat. Add the cumin, salt and pepper. Mix well and refrigerate for 45 minutes.

2. Prepare the dough by combining the flour, egg and water. Kneed the dough until it attains a thick consistency, but don't overwork it. Roll it into a tube shape and then slice it into sections, each a little bigger than a golf ball.

3. Preheat the oven to 200°C (400°F).

4. Sprinkle some flour on your work surface and roll out the ball-shaped pieces of dough into a rectangle with a rolling pin. Lightly brush the dough (on both sides) with melted margarine.

5. Using a spoon, add a dollop of the meat mixture to the centre of the dough. Then fold the edges of the pastry over the meat mixture in either a triangular or rectangular shape. Press the corners and edges together to prevent leakage. Repeat.

6. Place the *samsas* on a greased baking sheet, seam side up. Bake for 25 minutes until the tops are golden brown.

MAKES 15 *SAMSAS* (3 SERVINGS).

* Sarawak Laksa *

SARAWAK, MALAYSIA

Tangy, spicy, oh-so slurpable and lip-smackingly good, Sarawak laksa is a supremely satisfying way to begin the day. It's the dish Sarawakians most often crave when they're away from Borneo.

What is It?

Sarawak laksa brings a hot, tangy broth – made with a paste of chilli, garlic, shallots, peanuts, galangal (a relative of ginger), candlenuts and lemongrass – together with *bee hoon* (vermicelli) noodles and an array of tasty toppings with toothsome textures: beanshoots, omelette strips, chicken slices, shrimp and chopped coriander leaves. Diners squeeze calamansi lime on top and decide how much *sambal belacan* (a fiery local shrimp paste) they can handle.

Origin

Most purveyors of Sarawak laksa are, like *bee hoon* noodles, of Chinese origin, but in the finest Malaysian tradition this pungent dish brings together a variety of culinary influences, including classic Nyonya (Peranakan) ingredients such as *sambal belacan* and coconut milk. Sarawak laksa, the ingredients of which do *not* include curry, shares little more than its name with the laksa dishes popular in Peninsular (West) Malaysia and Singapore, such as *asam laksa* (fish soup made with sour tamarind) and curry laksa (featuring a fusion of curry and coconut milk).

Tasting

You're in Kuching and it's 7.30am, so following a tip from a local contact you stroll to a cafe famous for its Sarawak laksa. It's a modest establishment in an old Chinese shophouse, with a faded sign in Chinese and English, an open-air front, white-tile walls and crowded tables surrounded by red plastic chairs. Ceiling fans, arrayed below rows of neon-tube lights, churn the humid air. Men and women – mostly Chinese, but also Malay and Dayak – read newspapers or chat in a babel of dialects as they dig into oversize bowls with chopsticks and spoons. Inside each one, a tangle of white vermicelli noodles, swimming in oil-flecked broth, is topped with crunchy beanshoots, orange-white shrimp, strips of light yellow omelette, chicken bits with shredded edges and bright green coriander leaves. Occasionally, someone silently adds a dollop of fiery *sambal belacan* or a squeeze of calamansi lime. The air is redolent with the tang of chilli, galangal and lemongrass and the heady aromas of coriander and coconut milk.

Finding It

Chong Choon Cafe (Jalan Abell, Kuching), situated three blocks southeast of the Sarawak Plaza, serves up bowls for 4.50 Malaysian ringgits (US$1.50).

* VARIATIONS * **Each laksa shop prides itself on its particular secret recipe. Take a tour of Kuching's most hallowed ones and you'll find versions with viscosity that ranges from runny to puree, lots of coconut milk (which mellows the *sambal belacan*) or just a little, and varying degrees of heat. Halal variations prepared by Muslim Malays tend to be spicier, with more pepper and less coconut milk.**

* By Daniel Robinson *

Recipe Sarawak Laksa

YOU'LL NEED

Sarawak laksa paste

8 cups water

8 prawns

2–3 cups chicken stock

½ cup coconut milk

2–3 eggs

2 handfuls *bee hoon* noodles

1 handful beanshoots

100g (¼lb) shredded chicken breast

coriander leaves (cilantro), to garnish

1 lime

sambal belacan

METHOD

1. In a pot, bring 8 cups of water to the boil then add Sarawak laksa paste. Stir every few minutes for 30 to 45 minutes.

2. In a separate pot, boil the prawns in chicken stock, remove and slice lengthwise.

3. Add chicken stock to Sarawak laksa pot. Simmer over a low flame.

4. Pour liquid into a third pot through a fine mesh strainer to remove any solid particles. Continue to simmer.

5. Add coconut milk to taste. Stir broth every few minutes.

6. Beat the eggs and cook a very thin omelette, then slice it into strips.

7. Soak the *bee hoon* noodles in hot water until soft and then place in boiling water for three minutes. Transfer the noodles to two medium-sized bowls.

8. Add beanshoots, shredded chicken breast, halved prawns and omelette strips to the bowls.

9. Ladle just enough broth into the bowl to cover the noodles.

10. Garnish with chopped coriander leaves and squeeze the juice of half a lime into each bowl.

11. Add *sambal belacan* to taste.

SERVES 2

* Sfiha *

BAALBEK, BEKAA VALLEY, LEBANON

These bite-sized morsels have a sweet-and-sour pomegranate punch that sums up the taste of Lebanon in one mouthful.

What is It?

Sfiha combines the best bits of both pizza and pie. The meat filling is spiced up with mint, tahini, yoghurt and drizzles of pomegranate molasses with a final result that is purely Levantine. Baked in the oven until the dough is golden and the filling sizzling, these miniature meat pies are perfect for snacking on in the sun.

Finding It

Rue Hajjar in Baalbek is home to the *sfiha* bakeries. A plateful of pastries will set you back 6000 Lebanese pounds (US$4).

Tasting

On a sun-drenched Baalbek day, there's no better way to street feast after clambering over the Roman ruins. Luckily, the *sfiha* bakeries are only a stone's throw from the tumbled columns themselves. Pull up a chair at a dinky pavement table and order up your plate. The tiny parcels arrive freshly baked, their filling bubbling and the corners pinched in to keep it from oozing out. Drench your piled-high plate with lemon and add a dollop of yoghurt before tucking in.

They're quick to eat – two mouthfuls at the most – but with the solidly satisfying savouriness of summer's myriad flavours. The mint-kissed juicy lamb has a nutty tahini twist topped off by the sharp smack of piquant pomegranate. When it's just crumbs left on your plate, it's the toasted crunch of pine nuts that you're left to relish.

Origins

The original *sfiha* source is unknown, leaving the Syrians and Lebanese to argue over who created it first. The name itself derives from the Arabic root-word 'to flatten', maybe a reference to spreading the meat mixture along the dough. In Baalbek, where *sfiha* production is something of an art form, traditionally it's the butchers who create the meat filling, each with their own special recipe. Customers then take the filling to the bakeries to finish off the cooking.

* VARIATIONS * During the 1880s, huge numbers of Bekaa Valley Lebanese immigrated to South America, which has resulted in *sfiha* becoming one of Brazil's most beloved street-food snacks as well. This emigrant version uses beef instead of lamb (due to the scarcity of sheep) and lime juice as a substitute for pomegranate molasses. It also lost its open top, becoming instead a closed triangular pastry.

* By Jessica Lee *

Recipe Sfiha

This recipe makes approximately 24 pies. Note that it's fine to use basic pizza dough for the crust. Pomegranate molasses or thickened sauce can be found at Middle Eastern or Turkish specialist supermarkets.

YOU'LL NEED

Dough

1 cup warm milk

1 tsp dried yeast powder

1½ cups plain (all-purpose) flour

1 tbs olive oil

1½ tbs sugar

½ tsp salt

Filling

⅓ cup pine nuts

500g (1lb) minced lamb

1 large onion, finely diced

1 large tomato, chopped

1 handful fresh mint or coriander leaves (cilantro), finely chopped

2 tsp salt

1 tsp allspice

¼ tsp cinnamon

¼ tsp cayenne pepper

2 tbs yoghurt

1 tbs tahini

1 tbs pomegranate molasses

2 tbs butter

METHOD

1. In a bowl combine the milk and yeast, stirring quickly so that the yeast dissolves. Set aside in a warm place in your kitchen for around five minutes (the mixture will begin to froth when ready).

2. Meanwhile, sift your flour into a separate bowl and stir in the olive oil, sugar and salt. Once your milk mixture has begun to froth, add this to the other ingredients and mix well.

3. Cover the bowl with a cloth and set aside for five minutes.

4. After allowing the dough to sit, knead it thoroughly for around 10 minutes, until it becomes more elastic in consistency.

5. After you're done kneading, cover the dough with a cloth, place it in a warm spot in your kitchen and allow it to rise for one to two hours until it has doubled in size.

6. Once the dough is ready, you can begin preparing the filling. First, lightly toast the pine nuts in a frying pan.

7. In a large bowl, combine the meat, onion, tomatoes, mint, salt and spices.

8. Add the yoghurt, tahini, pomegranate molasses, toasted pine nuts and butter and mix well.

9. Divide your dough into walnut-sized balls by rolling them between your palms.

10. Place the dough balls on a floured surface and use a rolling pin to flatten each ball into a circle, about 8cm (3in) in diameter.

11. Place 1 tbs of the meat filling in the middle of each circle, flattening the mixture into a cube-like shape.

12. Lift the edges of each circle up to encase the filling by pinching the corners together.

13. Brush an oven tray lightly with olive oil and place the pastries on it.

14. Bake at 180°C (350°F) for 30 minutes or until the pastry is golden and the filling sizzling.

15. Serve with wedges of lemon and dollops of natural yoghurt.

* Som Tam *

THAILAND

Spicy, tart, crunchy, salty and sweet – five reasons why *som tam*, a green papaya 'salad', is quite possibly Thailand's best loved street-food dish.

What is It?

Som tam is made by slicing or shredding crispy unripe papaya into long strands that are then bruised in a mortar and pestle with fish sauce, lime juice, sugar, MSG, chilli, garlic and often slices of tomato and long bean. The result is a refreshing and often ballistically spicy salad that functions equally well as part of a meal or as a stand-alone snack.

Origin

Som tam most likely has its origins in neighbouring Laos, where it's known as *tam maak hung* and is a culinary staple. Residents of northeast Thailand, who have many cultural and culinary links with Laos, most likely introduced the dish to the rest of Thailand during their stints as migrant labourers as early as the 1950s. It didn't take long to catch on, and *som tam* can now be found in virtually every corner of the country.

Tasting

Although more and more restaurants in Thailand are serving the dish, *som tam* is still largely associated with the rickety street stalls and carts run by residents of northeast Thailand. As is the case with much Thai-style street food, ordering *som tam* requires a fair bit of advance discussion, with diners typically stating exactly how many chillies or how much sugar they prefer. This is usually done via direct conversation with the woman – and it's always a woman – operating the mortar and pestle. Thais from northeastern Thailand tend to prefer 'Lao' style *som tam*, which contains *plaa raa*, a type of unpasteurized fermented fish sauce, and crunchy chunks of eggplant. Most others go for 'Thai' *som tam*, which is generally somewhat sweeter: it contains peanuts and dried shrimp and is seasoned with bottled fish sauce. Either way, the generous application of both chilli and lime juice provide the defining flavours of *som tam*: spicy and tart.

Finding It

Som tam is sold just about everywhere; vendors can be identified by their tall clay or wood mortar. You'll pay around 30 baht (US$1).

* TIPS * *Som tam* is often eaten on its own, but is best accompanied with a basket of sticky rice. To eat like a northeastern Thai, roll a small ball of the rice in your hand and dip it into the spicy dressing or pinch both the rice and a bit of the *som tam* with your fingers.

* By Austin Bush *

Recipe Som Tam

Try to make this salad a couple of hours before serving so that the papaya can absorb all the flavours.

YOU'LL NEED

4 tbs palm sugar

3 tbs fish sauce

2 tbs tamarind concentrate

4 tbs lime juice

4 garlic cloves

salt

4 bird's eye chillies

3 tbs roasted peanuts

3 tbs dried prawns, rinsed and dried

8 cherry tomatoes, quartered

4 snake beans, chopped

3 cups green papaya, shredded

METHOD

1. Make the dressing by mixing the palm sugar, fish sauce, tamarind concentrate and 3 tbs of the lime juice.

2. Using a large mortar and pestle, crush the garlic with some salt, then add the bird's eye chillies, roasted peanuts, dried prawns and the rest of the lime juice and pound until it resembles a coarse paste.

3. Add the cherry tomatoes and snake beans and lightly bruise (but do not crush) with the paste.

4. Put the green papaya in a large salad bowl, stir in the paste and the dressing and gently toss with a large spoon.

5. Serve as a side dish in a Thai banquet or with steamed rice and raw vegetables such as cabbage and green beans.

SERVES 4

* Spring Roll *

CHINA

The spring roll is a crisp, paper-thin pastry wrapped around a dazzling array of fillings. Bite, crunch, grin.

What is It?

Found throughout China and much of Asia, spring rolls take a thin flour-and-water pastry and use it to encase all manner of ingredients, from carrots and beanshoots to shrimp, pork and duck. They're eaten at all times of the day, as a cheap snack or part of a full meal.

Origins

These date right back to the Eastern Jin dynasty (AD 317–420), when people would cook up thin flour cakes and eat them with vegetables to celebrate the beginning of spring. Then, they were known as 'spring cakes'. Later on, in the Ming and Qing dynasties, there was a custom of 'biting spring' – eating the cakes to welcome in the new season. In time the 'spring cake' evolved into the spring roll.

Finding It

The Donghuamen Night Market, off bustling Wangfujing St in Beijing, is quite touristy, but the busy stalls selling spring rolls are excellent (about 5 yuan each, or US$0.80). And if you're feeling brave, you can combine the experience with sampling the more adventurous snacks on offer at the market, like deep-fried crickets or scorpions.

Tasting

Crisp and fresh – that's the secret to the greatest spring rolls. You want the pastry to be golden and brittle, and the filling to leap around the mouth in great joyous bounds. This contrast lies at the heart of the spring roll's appeal. On the street, make sure they're cooked before you. They sit in neat rows, pale and soft, ready for the bubbling cauldron. A dash of vinegar is the perfect foil to the spring roll, and you'll find this, together with soy sauce, served alongside.

* **VARIATIONS** * You'll find endless versions across Asia, including the egg roll, a spring roll dipped in an egg wash. In Singapore, you'll find them stuffed with dried shrimp; in Korea, they're known as *chungwon*. Uncooked rice-paper rolls, like the Vietnamese *bo bia*, are different again, being soft rather than crisp.

Recipe Spring Rolls

YOU'LL NEED

Filling

2 cups beanshoots

6 dried shiitake mushrooms

2½ tbs oyster sauce

1 tbs chicken broth (water is an adequate substitute)

2 tsp light soy sauce

1 tsp sugar

2 tbs oil for stir-frying

55g (2oz) canned bamboo shoots, finely sliced

½ red capsicum (bell pepper), diced

1 medium carrot, grated

salt and pepper to taste

Rolls

18–20 spring roll wrappers

1 egg, lightly beaten

4–5 cups oil (for deep-frying)

METHOD

Filling

1. Rinse and drain beanshoots. Soak the dried mushrooms in warm water. Let the beanshoots dry and the mushrooms soak for 30 minutes.

2. Squeeze excess water out of the mushrooms, then slice thinly.

3. Mix the oyster sauce, broth, soy sauce and sugar into a small bowl. Set aside.

4. Spread 2 tbs hot oil around a frying pan. Once sizzling, stir-fry the vegetables. Begin with dried mushrooms, then add bamboo shoots, followed by capsicum, beanshoots and grated carrot.

5. Stir in the oyster-sauce mixture and add salt and pepper to taste.

Rolls

1. Lay one wrapper with a corner towards you, then paint the edges with lightly beaten egg.

2. Place 2 tbs of the filling across the bottom half, not quite to the edges. Fold the bottom corner of the wrapper over and tuck it under the filling, fold in the left and right sides, then roll. Brush the top corner lightly with beaten egg, fold over and seal.

3. Place the roll seam-side down on a baking sheet and brush lightly all over with oil. Repeat with the remaining wrappers and filling.

4. Heat the oil for deep-frying to hot, then add several spring rolls at a time and cook until crispy and golden brown (approximately three to four minutes). Remove, then drain on a paper towel. (Healthy alternative: instead of frying, bake the rolls for 12–15 minutes at 180°C (360°F) until golden and crisp.) Serve with plum sauce or sweet-and-sour sauce for dipping.

MAKES ROUGHLY 20 ROLLS

* Stinky Tofu *

TAIWAN

Of the typical dishes on offer in night markets around Taiwan, the one that really separates the casual tourist from the hard-core foodie is a pungent local favourite known as stinky tofu.

What is It?

Taiwanese street chefs take fresh firm bean curd and let it ferment in a brine solution for anywhere from a few days to several months. After it gains a pungency that'll turn heads from a block away, the fermented tofu is deep-fried and served with sour pickled cabbage and fiery hot sauce.

Tasting

Taiwan's vibrant night markets are filled with strange sights, sounds and smells, and perhaps the strangest of all is stinky tofu. You'll likely smell it before you see it – it's sold from a small stand consisting of a deep fryer, dripping rack and little else. Your nose might suggest that someone's left a block of limburger cheese out in the sun or is maybe deep-frying unwashed socks. But fear not, for as any Taiwanese will enthusiastically tell you, '*Stinky tofu smells bad, but it tastes good.*' Give in to culinary adventure and try a plate; you'll discover a snack that's crispy on the outside and soft within, with a flavour not too far removed from ripe camembert. Stay in Taiwan long enough and you may even develop a taste for the stuff.

Finding It

Easier to find at night and generally served outdoors, stinky-tofu stands are a common fixture in night markets and elsewhere throughout Taiwan (and can also be found less commonly in Hong Kong and coastal China). Expect to pay 50 to 60 Taiwan dollars (US$1.65 to US$2).

Origin

It's likely that this pungent dish migrated to the island along with settlers from China's southeast coast during the early days of Han Chinese settlement in the 17th century. It's possible that stinky tofu's inventor was someone in a predicament similar to the first person to eat *nattō* (a sticky, odorous Japanese dish consisting of fermented soybeans); namely, a resourceful hungry person looking for a way to make a spoiled soy product palatable and discovering in the process a way to make it delicious.

* VARIATIONS * If the classic deep-fried variety isn't hard-core enough for you, another (and some say smellier) option is to get the stewed version. Generally served in restaurants, *mala* stinky tofu is the same fermented tofu as its street-food cousin, served in a spicy chilli-based sauce. The texture is softer and the flavour somewhat more intense.

* By Joshua Samuel Brown *

Recipe Stinky Tofu

Stinky tofu is not a dish most folks make at home. For one thing, to make it requires a fermentation process lasting weeks or even months. For another thing, it stinks. This recipe produces a reasonable (though less odiferous) version that gives a genuine approximation of the night-market variety.

YOU'LL NEED

2 blocks of fresh, extra-firm tofu

2 jars *kimchi* (pickled cabbage, available from Korean supermarkets)

vegetable oil, for deep-frying

METHOD

1. Cut the tofu into 5cm (2in) cubes and place in a bowl with the liquid from both jars of *kimchi*. A shallow bowl works well, as the liquid should cover the tofu. You can also layer the *kimchi* itself between the tofu for an extra kick.

2. Cover the bowl with an airtight cover and set aside on a counter or, if the weather is warm, outside (warmth promotes fermentation). After about 48 hours you should notice some fermentation occurring – the liquid should be slightly fizzy, and there may be a mild (though not unpleasant) smell coming from the bowl. The longer you let it sit, the more pungent the tofu.

3. When you're ready to cook the tofu, heat up enough oil so that your cubes will be fully (or almost) covered. Squeeze any additional liquid from your cubes and fry until they're golden brown.

4. Drain and serve with *kimchi* and hot sauce. Whereas street-vendor stinky tofu (with its long fermentation time) has a flavour similar to a ripe camembert, yours might taste more like a mild brie – not a bad place to start for the uninitiated!

* Taco *

MEXICO

If maize is the heart of Mexican food, then the taco, a soft corn tortilla stuffed with all manner of ingredients, is its soul. Eaten at every hour of the day, this is Mexico's first love.

What is It?

The most ubiquitous street food in Mexico, tacos are rolled tortillas (made of ground maize slaked with nixtamel, or calcium hydroxide) stuffed with different fillings. The two basic types are *tacos de guisados,* with prepared fillings such as *cochinita pibil* (slow-cooked pork), and *tacos de carne,* with every kind of meat, from chopped roast pork to spicy mutton or goat stew. In coastal regions, you'll find fish tacos too.

Origin

Pigs, chickens, cows, goats, sheep and coriander were all introduced to the Americas by early Spanish invaders. But the taco is the only true pre-Hispanic dish that remains untouched and unchanged, adored by the Olmec, Maya and Aztec civilisations alike. *Tacos al pastor* is a Mexico City classic and a dish with Middle Eastern roots. Brought to the city by Lebanese emigrants in the 1950s, it's a doner kebab made from pork rather than lamb.

Tasting

If it's a good taco stall, there'll be a queue. Always look for that queue. As the sweet scent of cooking meat mingles with cigarette smoke, diesel fumes and the ever-present smell of warm tortillas, your appetite will be honed to an almost unbearable edge. Smile, but hold your ground as you advance through the hungry crowds. Don't worry if the stall is little more than a bicycle with a propane heater, or a rundown pushcart. It's the food, not aesthetics, you're after. Four tacos make a civilised start, and you can always come back for more. Extra lime, salt and hot sauce will always be close by, so you can personalise and pique the palate. The Mexicans are elegant eaters, managing to envelop all manner of ingredients in neat rolls, and munch without spilling a morsel. Novices might find things a little more difficult, but after a few goes, you'll eat like a pro. The taco might seem simple, but that contrast between soft tortilla and crisp pork is sublime. If food here is religion, then the taco is God.

Finding It

For the finest *tacos al pastor* in Mexico City, it has to be El Huequito, meaning 'hole in the wall'. That's literally what it is, and you eat your fill on the sidewalk. But you'll find them at stalls everywhere, costing between 5 and 10 pesos (US$0.40 to US$0.80).

* VARIATIONS * You name it, they've got it. *Carnitas, cochinita pibil* (a speciality of the Yucatán Peninsula), *al pastor, camerones* (prawns) and *pescado* (fish) are all there. For the more offally inspired, try the *tripa* (tripe) and *sesos* (brain). The *tacos de ojo* (eyes), though, are a more acquired taste.

* By Tom Parker Bowles *

Recipe Tacos

YOU'LL NEED

500g (1lb) minced (ground) beef

garlic salt, to taste

16 corn tortillas

olive oil for frying

3 serrano chillies, chopped (you can substitute jalapeños)

1 medium onion, sliced finely

1 tomato, diced

1 bunch coriander leaves (cilantro), chopped

2 avocados, sliced

2 limes, cut into wedges

salt, to taste

METHOD

1. In a frying pan, cook the ground beef with a couple of dashes of garlic salt until browned. Drain off any fat and set aside.

2. Take your tortillas and lightly brush them with olive oil. Put a large frying pan on a high heat and lightly fry the tortillas so they are still soft but have got a bit of colour on them. Remove from the heat and let them drain on paper towels.

3. Now to assemble the tacos. Place a spoonful of meat on each one, then add the chillies, onion, tomato, coriander leaves and avocado. Squeeze a wedge of lime across it, sprinkle with salt, roll it up and serve. You can also add grated cheese, shredded lettuce, salsa – whatever you like.

MAKES 16 TACOS

* Takoyaki *

OSAKA, JAPAN

Takoyaki are small, hot, crisp golf balls of octopus-spiked batter, bought from vendors in the street and either slathered with sauce, mayonnaise and shaved bonito flakes, or carefully dipped into a sharp *ponzu* sauce.

What is It?

A ball of crisp, puffy wheat batter encases a sweet, tender chunk of octopus. The mixture is poured onto a specially designed hotplate with shallow indentations, like ping-pong balls hewn in half. A few spring onions might be thrown on top, then the whole thing cooks until golden. Once done, it's dusted with *aonori* (green seaweed powder), sprinkled with *katsuobushi* (bonito flakes) or doused in mayonnaise or *takoyaki* sauce, similar to a thick Worcestershire sauce.

Origin

The use of wheat can be traced back to the French influence on Japanese cuisine in the 17th century. There are records of a thin crepe popular in both Tokyo and Osaka, which evolved into dishes such as *okonomiyaki*, a thick egg pancake weighed down with toppings, and *choboyaki*, small batter balls cooked in a special pan. But it is Endo Tomekichi, a *choboyaki* vendor in Osaka, who is seen as the creator of *takoyaki*. He began, in the mid-1930s, to add octopus to his *choboyaki*, along with more flavourings to the batter. Now, it's one of the great traditional foods of Osaka, and found across the country.

Tasting

As is often the case with street food, it's the smell that grabs you first, especially on an icy Osaka night. A hint of onion, a whisper of cephalopod. But most of all, the rich fug of cooking batter. The cooking process is every bit as delectable as the eating. A ladle of milky batter is poured into dozens of tiny moulds, sizzling as it hits the hot metal. Chunks of tentacle are dropped in each one, covered by a handful of spring onion and *tenkasu* (little crunches of tempura batter). Then the real art begins. With pointed steel chopsticks, the cook works with astonishing speed and precision, poking and turning each ball, creating a perfect golden sphere. Once done, they're packed into a polystyrene box and anointed with thin strands of mayonnaise, a thick coating of the rich, sticky *takoyaki* sauce and a layer of smoky shaved bonito. Grab your cocktail stick and dig in. The shell is firm and chewy, bursting open to reveal a scalding hot, creamy and not-quite-set mass of batter. The fat chunk of octopus is the final treat, something to chew on while you attack the next.

Finding It

Juso, Osaka's red-light district, has some excellent stalls: try Karitoro Takoyaki, where for 300 yen (about US$3) you can get six.

* **VARIATIONS** * Some put secret spices in their batter, others pickled ginger and *dashi* (stock). Everyone will have their own recipe, which they proclaim 'the best'. The recipe for the *takoyaki* sauce changes with each stall, and you can also flavour them with *ponzu* and soy sauces.

Recipe Takoyaki

These scrumptious dumplings are meant to be eaten hot straight out of the pan – the lightly crisp morsels lose their crispness in under a minute. If you don't have a *takoyaki* pan, then a Pancake Puff pan or *ableskiver* pan (for Danish pancakes) works well.

YOU'LL NEED

Batter

1 large egg

1⅓ cups water

1⅓ cups cake flour, or 1 cup plain (all-purpose) flour and ⅓ cup cornflour

1½ tsp baking powder

½ tsp salt

1½ tsp sugar

1½ tsp instant *dashi* powder

Filling

250g (½lb) boiled octopus, or substitute 3 large cooked shrimp, cut into small, thumb-sized cubes

2 tbs pickled ginger, finely chopped and squeezed to remove moisture

2 tbs spring onions, finely chopped

2 tbs green cabbage, finely chopped

1–2 tbs canola oil

Garnishes

3 tbs mayonnaise (optional)

3 tbs Worcestershire sauce

1½ tbs *aonori*

½ cup *katsuobushi*

METHOD

1. Whisk egg and water. Mix flour, baking powder, salt, sugar, and *dashi* in a bowl. Form a hole in the centre, then whisk in the egg mixture until smooth, as with pancake batter. Transfer to a measuring cup. Set aside for 15 minutes.

2. Heat a *takoyaki* pan over medium heat. Brush oil into each well.

3. Once pan is just sizzling, pour batter into the pan to just shy of the rim.

4. Add one or two pieces of octopus or shrimp and ample pinches of ginger, spring onion and cabbage to each well.

5. Wait one minute until the edges have begun to set and/or small bubbles have formed at the rim. Use skewers to loosen each dumpling at the top edge and flip it over.

6. Continue turning and rotating the dumplings until they attain a uniform light brown colour and are crisp (usually about five minutes). Move the dumplings to a plate using a skewer or tongs. Oil and repeat the cooking to make more dumplings.

7. Splash the mayonnaise and Worcestershire sauce on top of each dumpling, followed by the *aonori* and the *katsuobushi*. Serve hot.

MAKES ABOUT 16 DUMPLINGS

* Tamale *

MEXICO

Breakfast bliss or twilight snack, these steamed, corn-husk-clad masa delights are comfort food, Mexican-style. Filled with anything from pork to pineapple, this is hand-held ballast of the finest kind.

What is It?

Sweet or savoury, spicy or bland, the tamale has a version for every palate. Chicken or pork filling with salsa (red or green) or mole (a thick, complex sauce) are the most popular, along with poblano chillies and cheese. The whole package is then wrapped in corn husks or banana leaves and steamed until soft and seductive.

Origin

Found all over Central and South America, tamales are an ancient food that pre-dated the arrival of Europeans by millennia. There's evidence of their existence as far back as 8000 BC; they were a staple for Aztecs, Mayans, Olmec, Toltecan and even Inca civilisations. Like the taco, this is a truly ancient food.

Tasting

Look for vast steel containers (*tamaleras*) leaking steam, which loiter on pretty much every street corner. This is a snack for even the most cautious of gastronauts, as all those hours of steaming make for a particularly safe mouthful. This is glorious super stodge and you'll struggle to eat more than two. The wrapper is not edible and is to be discarded once finished. The fillings, whether savoury or sweet, are mere bit parts when compared to the main event, the steamed dough itself. It should sing of maize, with the sort of texture that softly and subtly succumbs to the onslaught of teeth. *Atole*, a thick porridge-like drink sweetened with coarse sugar, cinnamon and vanilla, is usually sold alongside tamales.

Finding It

Tamales Especiales in Coyoacan, Mexico City, lives up to its name. All homemade and a member of Mexican Slow Food, it has takeaway during the week with the option to sit in the garden on Saturday and Sunday nights. Tamales will set you back 10 to 15 pesos each (US$0.75 to US$1.20)

* **VARIATIONS** * **Every region has its own special tamale, ranging in shape from the square and small to the 1.2m (4ft) long. And the masa flour can be coarse or fine ground too. In Oaxaca, you'll find them stuffed with black mole and wrapped in banana leaves, whereas up in the northwest, you'll find them made with pineapple and sweet brown beans. Some are stained pink and filled with raisins and dried fruit (*tamales de dulce*), while others might not have any filling at all (*tamal sordo*).**

* By Tom Parker Bowles *

Recipe Tamales

YOU'LL NEED

Filling

500g (1lb) pork loin

1 large onion, halved

1 garlic clove

4 dried California chilli pods (similar to poblano chillies)

2 cups water

1½ tsp salt

Dough

500g (1lb) dried corn husks

⅔ cup lard (can use vegetable shortening)

300mL (10fl oz) beef stock

2 cups *masa harina* (maize flour)

1 tsp baking powder

½ tsp salt

1 cup sour cream

METHOD

1. Put the pork, onion and garlic in a large cooking pot and cover with water. Bring it to the boil, then reduce to a simmer until the meat is tender and thoroughly cooked. (This should take about two hours.)

2. Deseed the chillies (use rubber gloves to avoid transfer-burn!) and simmer them in a pot with 2 cups of water for 20 minutes. Remove from the heat. When it has cooled, blitz both the chillies and water in a blender until smooth. Strain it, add the salt and set aside.

3. When the pork is done, shred it with two forks and stir in one cup of the chilli sauce.

4. Soak corn husks in warm water.

5. With an electric mixer, beat the lard (or shortening) with a tablespoon of beef stock until it whips up and becomes airy. Stir the *masa harina*, baking powder and salt together in a separate bowl and gradually add to the shortening mix, adding more broth as needed until you have a dough with a bouncy texture.

6. Drain corn husks and pat dry. Spread the dough over the husks (no thicker than 6mm or 0.5in), put a spoonful of the pork in the middle and fold the sides of the husk inwards like you're packaging up a parcel. Place in a steamer and cook for an hour.

7. When they're done, peel away the husks, pour over a little of the chilli sauce and top with a knob of sour cream.

* Walkie-Talkies *

SOUTH AFRICA

Walkie-talkies are gluten-full feet and protein-packed heads. Literally. Perhaps they're not the most appetising-looking stewed chicken parts, but in South African townships, walkie-talkies are low-priced, lip-smacking, pluck-giving delights.

What is It?

Walkie-talkies are cooked chicken feet ('walkies') and heads ('talkies') . A large quantity is boiled together to facilitate the removal of chewier bits. The pieces are then seasoned and cooked according to taste. They are cheap year-round treats that are flavourful and high in protein.

Origin

During the apartheid years in South Africa, farmers of European origin favoured the meatiest parts of the chicken. The leftovers – like the heads and the feet – were given to workers and people in the townships, who adapted them to their culinary needs, usually for children. Although the key ingredients are no longer free today, they are sold cheaply to locals. That may of course change now that Simba-brand potato crisps come in walkie-talkie chicken flavour too!

Finding It

Although best known at inner-city taxi ranks and in the townships of Durban and Soweto, walkie-talkies (also known as *tincondvo*) are market titbits sold countrywide for about 10 rand (US$1.40) a kilogram.

Tasting

Township markets are always abustle, brimming with a wonder of sights, sounds and smells. Adding to the rumpus are walkie-talkies. Some are just boiled, with added salt and spices; others are stewed with onions, green peppers and tomatoes; lately, they are grilled too. Whatever the style, you stick the feet in your mouth toes first and then scrape the skin and meat off with your teeth. The rest can be chewed up for the bone marrow. It takes a bit of determined crunching, but not as much as required for the head, which gets eaten whole, except for the beak.

* **ALTERNATIVES** * The meat treats of South Africa run the gamut from typical *braai* (barbecue) and chewy biltong (cured meat) to *ulusu* (animal-stomach stew) and 'smilies' (roasted sheep heads cooked into a toothsome grin). There's really no avoiding them, so why not start with walkie-talkies, something relatively harmless? Try *umqombothi* (traditional grain-brewed beer) as a chaser.

* By Ethan Gelber *

Recipe **Walkie-Talkies**

This recipe includes both the traditional style and a 'tasty' variation.

YOU'LL NEED

Traditional Style

500g (1lb) chicken heads

500g (1lb) chicken feet

1 tsp oil

salt

1 cube chicken bouillon

spices of your choice

Tasty Style

6 tbs oil

2 medium onions, thickly sliced

salt

2 green peppers, thickly sliced

4 medium tomatoes, thickly sliced

1 cube chicken bouillon

spices of your choice

METHOD

1. Wash the chicken heads and feet thoroughly. Place together in boiling water for about one minute to soften them.

2. Remove from water (keep it boiling for traditional style walkie-talkies) and then cut off the beaks, clean the feathers from the head and peel the tough outer layer of skin off the feet. If desired, pull out the toe nails.

Traditional Style

3. Place the cleaned heads and feet back in the boiling water. Add oil and a pinch of salt. Cook on medium heat for 10 minutes.

4. Add a cube of chicken bouillon and other spices to taste. Maintain medium heat for an additional 20 minutes (or 10 minutes for a less tender result). Drain and serve.

Tasty Style

3. Heat 3 tbs oil in a frying pan over medium heat. Add the onions and a pinch of salt. Continually stir the onions, deglazing as necessary, until they are lightly browned. Add another 3 tbs oil, the chicken heads and feet, green peppers, tomatoes and any desired spices (like a cube of chicken bouillon). Cover and cook over medium heat for 10 to 15 minutes, stirring from time to time. Remove and serve. Eat with cooked maize (South African 'pap').

* Yangrou Chuan *

(E)
(✋)

NORTHWESTERN CHINA, BEIJING & OTHER URBAN AREAS

From the urban canyons of Beijing to the far-flung reaches of Kashgar, grilled skewers of *yangrou chuan* unite migrant workers, party cadres and the nouveau riche alike.

What is It?

A deceptively simple snack with as many variations as one might expect in a nation of over a billion people, *yangrou chuan* is basically bite-sized bits of mutton skewered on a wooden stick, coated in a mixture of cumin, salt and chilli pepper and grilled to perfection over a bed of coals.

Origin

This particular method of serving mutton reflects the tastes and traditions of central Asia, specifically the Uighur people of China's northwestern Xinjiang Province. Most purveyors of *yangrou chuan* either hail from this region or are Hui (Chinese Muslims).

Tasting

Imagine yourself out on an evening stroll in urban China. Perhaps you're in one of Beijing's *hutong* neighbourhoods, or maybe on a side street off a busy avenue in Xi'an. The smell of smoky grilled meat and a faint trace of cumin wafts through the air. Approaching the grill (one small enough to be carried away should the police come calling), you see a fellow alternately fanning the coals and spinning skewers of meat, announcing in Mandarin: '*Yangrou chuan! Yi tiao yi kuai!*' ('Mutton kebabs! One yuan per stick!'). The presence of a small crowd surrounding the grill and buying up skewers as fast as the vendor can make them is a good sign. Join the throngs and order half a dozen – they're the perfect evening snack.

Finding It

Yangrou chuan are fairly easy to find throughout northern China. In Beijing, head to Guijie in the Dongzhimen or Wangfujing districts. They cost about 1 yuan (US$0.15) per stick.

* MEDICINAL PROPERTIES * According to traditional Chinese medicine, mutton is said to warm the spleen, stomach and kidneys, and is thus beneficial for those suffering from colds, coughs, bronchitis or general chilliness. Spend a winter north of the Yangzi River and mutton may become your best friend!

* By Joshua Samuel Brown *

Recipe Yangrou Chuan

YOU'LL NEED

12 skewers

500g (1lb) boneless leg of lamb

⅛ cup (30mL) vegetable oil

2 tbs ground cumin

2 tbs chilli pepper

salt

pepper

METHOD

1. If using bamboo skewers, soak them for an hour in water (to prevent them from burning) and prepare charcoal grill or barbecue.

2. Cut the meat into small pieces about the size of a walnut.

3. Add about five to eight pieces of meat per skewer.

4. Put your oil on one plate, and mix the spices on a second.

5. Roll the skewers in oil first, then the spice mix.

6. Grill the skewers for about two to three minutes on each side. The meat should be cooked but not too dry.

* Zapiekanka *

POLAND

When Poles need a quick snack, they head for the serving window of a *zapiekanka* stand. These long toasted rolls with succulent toppings are guaranteed to stave off hunger pangs.

What is It?

The *zapiekanka*'s base is an open-faced flat bread roll – basically, half a baguette. Onto this are spread sliced mushrooms and cheese, as well as additional toppings such as ham or garlic. The roll is then toasted until the bread is crisp and the cheese has melted. Ketchup and/or mayonnaise is then squirted generously on top.

Origin

Poland's communist era is quickly receding into the past and, for the most part, is hardly missed. However, one positive legacy that it did leave the world is *zapiekanka*. For one reason or another, this humble street food rose to prominence in the 1980s, when it became a popular snack served from stands where the proprietors prepared the ingredients from scratch, turning out delicious, inexpensive stomach fillers. No doubt they were handy energy boosters for the strikers who finally brought down the communist regime at the end of the decade.

Tasting

Decide first on the size of *zapiekanka* you want – some are up to 50cm (20in) long – then select the toppings. Although traditionally these were fairly simple, in recent years the *zapiekanka* has lived up to its billing as the Polish pizza by taking on ever more exotic elements (Hawaiian *zapiekanka* with pineapple, anyone?). Once your order is served up, you'll experience the satisfying crunch of toasted bread, followed by the palate-pleasing combination of cheese, mushrooms, a tangy sauce and whatever other toppings you've chosen. It's a warm and filling sensation. In recent years, *zapiekanka* outlets have faced competition from kebab shops, so it's become harder to find a truly dedicated *zapiekanka* creator. As always, ask a local for the best stand and beware the microwave oven – it's guaranteed to turn out a soggy, tasteless shadow of the real McCoyski.

Finding It

A popular destination for a *zapiekanka* fix (about 5 złoty or US$1.75) are the stands within Plac Nowy, in the Kazimierz district of Krakow.

* TIPS * The *zapiekanka* tends to be served with a more than generous (some would say excessive) amount of ketchup and mayo, so feel free to say '*bez sosu*' if you'd rather have it without the sauce. Don't be surprised if it arrives with ketchup anyway, through sheer force of tradition.

* By Tim Richards *

Recipe Zapiekanka

YOU'LL NEED

200g (7oz) mushrooms

1 baguette

100g (¼lb) thinly sliced ham

120g (4¼oz) edam (or any other hard cheese that melts easily)

ketchup

mayonnaise

METHOD

1. Cut the mushrooms into thin slices and then saute over medium heat until cooked.

2. Cut the baguette lengthwise into two long pieces.

3. Layer the ham, cooked mushrooms and cheese on the flat surfaces of each piece.

4. Toast under a grill until the cheese has melted and the bread is crisp.

5. Smother with ketchup and mayonnaise, then serve.

* Sweet *

Recipe

(E) **Easy** - A very basic recipe, eg, putting together a sandwich or tossing salad ingredients.

(M) **Medium** - Suitable for the average home cook.

(C) **Complex** - Several parts to make, or lots of ingredients to prepare, or a specific technique involved that may take some practice.

Utensils

 Hands

 **Knife * Fork * Spoon**

Chopsticks

Drinks

Note Definitions for words in blue in the recipes can be found in the glosssary on page 214.

* Açai na Tigela *

COASTAL BRAZIL

Based on the frozen pulp of the Amazonian superfood açai, this popular granola-and-syrup-topped kiosk treat is a delectable start to the day.

What is It?

The antioxidant- and protein-rich açai berry starts life on a palm in the Brazilian Amazon, but *açai na tigela* is a fruity concoction that's most popular on the coast. It consists of açai pulp topped with banana, granola and guarana syrup: a perfect early-morning pick-me-up.

Finding It

In Rio, find vendors along the Copacabana and Ipanema Beaches or at juice shops like Ipanema's Polis Sucos. Expect to pay between three to four Brazilian reals (US$1.90 to US$2.60) for a bowl.

Tasting

If you thought street food was unhealthy, greasy or the domain of hungry, hard-working locals, think again. Not with this fruity serving of superfood. You could easily find yourself queuing for your *açai na tigela* alongside the bronzed gods and goddesses of the Brazilian jet set. Reams have been written on the nutritional advantages of this little berry, but honestly, even if it were packed with more calories than a treble-cream doughnut, you'd still want to treat yourself to this. The berry's deep purple wells up in the bowl when blended and its dominant notes of blueberry and dark chocolate are the perfect complement to that dreamy, creamy, crunchy breakfast combo of banana and granola. It's laced with a hefty dose of guarana syrup, and with the average guarana fruit containing significantly more caffeine than a coffee bean, *açai na tigela* is a great way to get over the previous night's shenanigans.

Origins

The health benefits of the açai berry were known to Amazon tribes for centuries. Other Brazilians began enjoying the fruit after doctors started to extol its virtues in the 1950s. By the 1970s kiosks and juice bars in Rio were selling *açai na tigela* (açai in a bowl) made with frozen açai pulp: the time it took to transport açai from the Amazon to the coast meant the fruit would spoil if shipped fresh.

* AÇAI IN THE AMAZON * For the rare opportunity to sample açai fresh, make the trip out to its Amazon birthplace where you'll find it consumed in a very different way. The berries are traditionally served in gourds called *cuias* and eaten with tapioca and (occasionally) honey. They can be salty or sweet.

* By Luke Waterson *

Recipe Açai na Tigela

YOU'LL NEED

100g (¼lb) frozen açai pulp

1 banana

granola

generous squeeze of guarana syrup (or honey)

2 ice cubes

METHOD

1. Blend together half the banana, the frozen açai pulp, the guarana syrup and the ice cubes until fairly smooth. Avoid blending too long or the pulp will start to melt. Pour into a bowl.

2. Slice the remaining banana and add over the top of the fruit blend along with the granola and a further dollop of guarana syrup. Serve immediately.

* Baklava *

GAZIANTEP, TURKEY

Renowned from Greece and Turkey to the countries of the Middle East, baklava is the ultimate expression of the delicate craft of the region's skilled pastry chefs.

What is It?

One of the most delicate desserts on the planet, baklava is carefully crafted from gossamer-thin sheets of *yufka* (filo pastry). Fold in a filling of finely chopped pistachio or walnuts, layer with melted butter and drown the whole shebang in syrup to create a mid-afternoon snack perfect with a robust Turkish coffee.

Origin

Baklava is thought to be based on ancient recipes from central Asia that were perfected during the Ottoman Empire. Early Uzbek and Azerbaijani recipes were more rustic than the refined variations developed in the imperial Ottoman kitchens, where up to 40 separate layers of filo pastry were used. The southeast Anatolian city of Gaziantep is now renowned for the world's finest pistachio baklava, with the soil surrounding the city producing *fistikli* (pistachios) of unique flavour and aroma. Master baklava bakers train for up to 20 years and have been known to add up to 100 layers of impossibly thin pastry into one dish.

Tasting

Discovering the best of baklava is all in the delicate sound it makes when you first bite into it. The gossamer-light top layers of filo pastry should fold gently when it's in your mouth, with the subtle release of pressure and flavour producing an almost inaudible *kshhhh* sound. The freshest of pistachios should combine with carefully layered pastry and syrup to perfectly balance crunch and collapse, offering subtle resistance when bitten, but not threatening the need for dental reconstruction. With more than 180 pastry shops, Gaziantep offers the opportunity to discover the *kshhhhh* of the world's best baklava on virtually every street. Try it still warm from the oven – a local breakfast variation is to dip baklava in milk – or as the perfect dessert after an evening meal in the elegant dining room of the İmam Çağdaş restaurant. Between meals, you're bound to still find room for a couple of baklava-and-coffee stops throughout the day.

Finding It

Try the Güllüoglu pastry shop in Gaziantep, where it sells for around six Turkish lira (US$3.50). There is also a Güllüoglu branch in Istanbul.

* VARIATIONS * Entering a Gaziantep pastry shop is an opportunity to sample tasty local variations. *Saray sarmasi* is a special round baklava, while *söbiyet* – a culinary cousin of sherbet – is rolled baklava crammed with pistachio and cream. Other regional Turkish variations include *kus gözü* ('bird's eye' baklava) from Antalya, and *gelin bohça* ('bridal dress' baklava) from Kahramanmaras. It's a city also renowned for Turkey's finest ice cream, so good luck choosing between sweet treats.

• By Brett Atkinson •

Recipe Baklava

Adapted from Selen Rozanes at Turkish Flavours (www.turkishflavours.com)

YOU'LL NEED

1 cup water

1½ cups sugar

juice of 1 lemon

180g (6oz) butter, melted

450g (1lb) filo pastry sheets

340g (11oz) walnuts and pistachios, finely chopped

ground pistachio nuts

METHOD

1. Preheat the oven to 160°C (325°F).

2. To make the syrup, pour the water and sugar into a heavy pan. Bring to a boil while stirring continuously.

3. Once the sugar is dissolved, reduce the heat and add the lemon juice. Simmer for around 15 minutes. Once the syrup has thickened, leave the mixture to cool in the pan.

4. Brush the melted butter across the bottom and sides of a 30cm (12in) baking dish.

5. Place a sheet of filo pastry in the bottom of the pan and brush carefully with melted butter. Trim the edges of the filo pastry if you need to make it fit. Continue until you have used half the sheets of filo pastry, making sure that you brush each one with butter.

6. Press the sheets carefully into the corners of the dish, and trim the edges if they extend outside the top of the dish.

7. Spread the chopped walnuts and pistachios on top of the last buttered sheet. Continue layering the remaining half of the filo pastry sheets, brushing each one with melted butter.

8. Brush the top of the final sheet and then cut straight lines right through all the layers, from the top to the bottom, to form small diamond shapes. It's essential to use a sharp knife to do this.

9. Bake in the oven for around one hour until the top is golden. Increase the temperature for the final few minutes to ensure a golden finish.

10. After baking, remove the baklava from the oven and slowly pour the cooled syrup over the hot pastry. Return to the oven for two to three minutes so that the syrup is soaked up.

11. Take the baklava out of the oven to cool and then arrange the diamond-shaped pieces on a serving dish. Top the individual pieces of baklava with ground pistachios and serve at room temperature. Note that baklava should never be stored in a refrigerator as the pastry will absorb excess moisture and become soggy.

* BeaverTails Pastry *

OTTAWA, ONTARIO, CANADA

What's more Canadian than a beaver? A BeaverTail! Not the back end of the furry mammal, BeaverTails pastries are doughy snacks first fried up in Ontario and now found across Canada.

What is It?

Taking their name and distinctive shape from the oblong tail of Canada's official animal, these pastries start with balls of whole-wheat dough that are flattened and stretched until they resemble their namesake. They're quickly fried and served sizzling hot, sprinkled with a blend of cinnamon and sugar and – if you like – a squeeze of lemon.

Origin

Grant Hooker, who founded the BeaverTails company with his wife, Pam, says that his grandmother used to make a similar doughy treat – a yeasted, cracked-wheat pastry that both Canadian and American farm families commonly prepared. The Hookers opened their first BeaverTails shop in Ottawa's ByWard Market neighbourhood in 1980, and later trademarked the name.

Tasting

A comforting cross between a doughnut and buttery cinnamon-sugar toast, BeaverTails pastries mix savoury dough with sweet toppings. Many countries have similar fried-dough snacks, but what distinguishes these is the wheaty pastry; it's more substantial than a fried bread made from white flour. And seeing as they are always cooked to order, you can eat them while they're hot and slightly crisp. The best way to sample one is while ice skating along Ottawa's Rideau Canal, a 7.8km (4.8 mile) waterway that freezes in winter to become the world's longest skating rink. The tasty snack not only fuels you up for skating or other outdoor activities during the freezing winters, it also warms up your hands as you balance the warm pastry on your napkin.

Finding It

There are stands in Ottawa's ByWard Market and, in winter, along the Rideau Canal Skateway. The pastries cost from C$3.25 to C$5 (US$3.25 to US$5) each.

* VARIATIONS * You can slather your BeaverTails pastry with all sorts of sugary toppings, from chocolate hazelnut spread to maple butter to crumbled Oreo cookies, or pretend to make them more like a meal by adding bananas (with chocolate) or apples (drizzled with caramel), but purists stick with the traditional cinnamon-sugar mix. Just be careful not to get too much sugar on your mittens!

* By Carolyn B Heller *

Recipe Our Version of a BeaverTails Pastry

The original recipe remains a closely guarded secret by the company but this version comes pretty close to the real thing, especially when served straight from the fryer and doused with cinnamon sugar.

YOU'LL NEED

2 tsp dried yeast powder

¼ cup lukewarm water

1 tsp sugar

150g (5oz) plain (all-purpose) flour

150g (5oz) whole wheat flour

1 tsp salt

¼ cup warm milk

45g (1½oz) butter, melted

1 egg

vegetable or canola oil for deep-frying

cinnamon sugar for serving

METHOD

1. Mix the yeast with the water and sugar in a small bowl and let stand for five minutes.

2. In a mixing bowl, sift both flours with the salt.

3. Make a well in the centre of the flour and add in the yeast mixture, milk, butter and egg. Mix well.

4. Tip out the dough on to a floured surface and knead for about 10 minutes until the dough becomes soft and elastic.

5. Leave the dough aside in a lightly oiled bowl to rise until it is almost double in size.

6. 'Knock back' the dough by punching the air out of it and kneading it a few times.

7. Divide and roll the dough into two balls, and continue until there are eight balls.

8. With a rolling pin, flatten a ball into an oblong, beaver-tail shape. Repeat with the remaining balls.

9. Heat the oil in a deep-fryer (or a saucepan filled with enough oil for deep-frying).

10. Fry the dough pieces, a few at a time, for a few minutes on each side until golden.

11. Using a slotted spoon, take out the pastries, sprinkle with cinnamon sugar and serve immediately.

* Bliny *

RUSSIA

A steaming-hot wafer-thin pancake, filled with anything from cherries and cream to salmon and caviar, the blin is Russia's two-fingered fast-food salute to the McMeal and a quick-fire way to the heart of the country's street life.

What is It?

Bliny differ from crepes or pancakes in that they are made of buckwheat flour and yeast and, technically, should only be fried by a Russian grandmother. In the unfortunate event that a grandmother is not available, you can find them on street corners across the nation, via ubiquitous street stalls and pop-in chain restaurants. Bliny are eaten at any time of the day, from breakfast up to the late-night post-vodka stumble home, with the fillings flipping from savoury to sweet according to mood.

Origin

Given the length and severity of the average Russian winter, it's not surprising that the first sight of the springtime sun has long been a time of festivity. Bliny, being round, yellow and hot, emerged in ancient Slav pagan culture as a symbol of the sun's return. They then shifted their meaning after the emergence of the Orthodox Church to become a central presence in the celebration of Maslenitsa, the Russian version of Holy Week. The fact that the blin eaten today is still similar to the one eaten in pagan times, managing to survive the history-wiping ravages of both the Church and Communism, is testament to its deeply embedded position in the Russian popular consciousness, not to mention its irresistible priest- and Soviet-defying tastiness.

Tasting

At the height of the Russian winter, stepping out of the cold and into a warm bliny shop is like getting a great big hug from an old friend. A queue of people stand in front of a counter of servers clutching frying pans, taking their time to choose their fillings. The bliny are then fried to order – when they finally arrive, that first bite of the piping hot, paper-thin pancake folded in a triangle, with the filling oozing out and demanding to be licked off sticky fingers, is the very definition of comfort food. But more than that, it is the social aspects of the bliny ritual that make it really stand out. Every walk of Russian life is here, popping in to shelter from the cold, watch the world trundle past and tuck into a snack they've been eating for centuries.

Finding It

Red-and-white Teremok stalls are a ubiquitous presence on the main streets of Russian cities, and despite their fast-food feel, they remain the place where most Russians pick up their on-the-go bliny. The window seats at the Teremok walk-in restaurant halfway along St Petersburg's Nevsky Prospekt have some of the best views over what is still quite possibly the grandest boulevard in the world. Expect to pay upwards of 45 rubles (US$1.60).

* TIPS * Make sure to order a mug of *kvass* with your bliny. A traditional, mildly alcoholic (less than 2%) drink made of black or rye bread and flavoured with fruit or mint, *kvass* has experienced a revival in recent years.

Recipe Bliny

YOU'LL NEED

heaping ¼ cup buckwheat flour

heaping ¼ cup plain (all-purpose) flour

⅓ tsp baking powder

¾ cup milk

⅓ tsp dried yeast powder

1 egg, separated

125g (4.4oz) butter

METHOD

1. Mix and sift the buckwheat flour, plain flour and baking powder.

2. Mix the milk and yeast together, then beat in the egg yolk.

3. Add the liquid mixture to the flour and whisk into a smooth paste.

4. Whisk the egg white until it is in smooth peaks, then fold into the flour and yeast mixture.

5. Heat the butter in a frying pan, then add the batter a tablespoon at a time, until the pan is thinly covered. Fry until the surface begins to bubble, then flip and cook the other side.

6. Serve with filling of your choice – try salmon and cream cheese or cherries and cream.

* Chimney Cake *

HUNGARY

Chimney cake *(kürtöskalács)* is a cylindrical sugary roll made of baked dough covered with walnuts, coconut and countless other toppings. It peels off in a spiral, making it great to eat with family or friends.

What is It?

This long strip of light yeast dough is wrapped around a tapered wooden spool, doused with butter and sugar, then slowly turned by hand over an open fire until the sugar caramelises. When fully baked, the ribbons form a crunchy, sugary outside crust – something akin to a hot pretzel – with a soft doughy inside. Before the pastry cools, further toppings are added: cinnamon, pecans, cocoa, vanilla – pretty much anything sweet under the sun.

Origin

Traditionally made in the hills of Transylvania, this treat originally showed up at special occasions such as weddings and christenings. As it grew in popularity and spread to market towns in the 19th century, peasants would substitute pieces of dried corn cob for wooden pins to wrap the pastry. The name comes from the cylindrical shape: originally smoke from the wood fires would escape through the top of the pastry, resembling a chimney. Today they are eaten at outdoor fairs all over the country – they're the Hungarian equivalent of the funnel cake or corn dog – and renowned as Hungary's oldest and most beloved pastry.

Finding It

Try the stalls at Budapest's August Festival of Folk Arts, where the cakes sell for around 300 forints (US$1.50).

Tasting

Eating the chimney cake is always a very social activity, and not just because it's regularly found at festival stalls everywhere. The cake's shape and consistency simply lends itself to sharing, making it easy for everyone in a group to reach their hand in and tear off a piece from a single roll – it's extremely popular with kids. Break off a piece of the chimney cake at one of the edges to watch it open and unravel like a spiral. The sugar has caramelised on the outside surface, beckoning your sweet tooth, while the soft underside might remind you of homemade sticky buns. It tastes akin to a cinnamon roll, but it's much more fun to eat.

* **TIPS** * For an interesting variation, try the cake with raisins spread about on the inside or poppy seeds on the outside. A chimney cake tastes best with coffee in the morning or with a cup of tea at night.

* By Roger Norum *

Recipe Chimney Cake

YOU'LL NEED

Dough

1¾ cups plain (all-purpose) flour

2¼ tsp dried yeast powder

2 tbs sugar

⅛ tsp salt

3 tbs butter, melted

2 egg yolks (room temperature)

½ cup milk (room temperature)

For Grilling

vegetable oil

melted butter

sugar

Topping

1 cup walnuts, ground

½ cup sugar

2 tsp cinnamon

METHOD

1. Begin by preparing the dough. Mix the dry ingredients together in a large bowl. Then whisk the liquid ingredients together, and add them slowly to the dry ingredients. Stir the mixture until it congeals to form a light dough.

2. Knead for five to six minutes. Set aside and allow the dough to rise for 40 minutes.

3. Roll out the dough and use a pizza cutter to slice the flattened dough into a long ribbon.

4. Brush a wooden spit with the vegetable oil. Starting from one end, wrap the dough around the spit, making sure to tuck in the end so that the dough does not unwind. Be sure the dough is kept fairly thin (under 6cm or 2.4in) as you stretch and wind it. Roll the entire spit on the counter in order to flatten it.

5. Brush the dough with the melted butter, then bake over an open flame for six minutes. Gradually sprinkle sugar on top until it changes to a darkish golden colour.

6. Mix the walnuts with the sugar and cinnamon. Paint another round of butter onto the dough, then roll the completed pastry in the walnut mixture.

7. Knock the mould on a table to release the cake, then stand upright to cool for several minutes. Serve warm.

* Churro *

SPAIN

What if you had a sugar-sprinkled, deep-fried pastry dipped into hot chocolate for breakfast every morning? Getting out of bed sure would be a whole lot easier.

What is It?

The Spanish take on a doughnut, the *churro* is a long, star-shaped tube (the dough is piped through a star-shaped nozzle) that's deep-fried until golden, then dunked into thick hot chocolate. Sold in *churrerías* and from stalls in the street, this is an Iberian breakfast to beat them all.

Tasting

It's the hangover to end them all, the sort that renders normal conversation impossible. Even thinking hurts. But then you catch the scent of sweet, frying dough. You stop, look around and spot the stall. A great vat is filled with boiling oil, and the fresh dough, pushed through a star-shaped nozzle, is plopped in. There is a delectable sizzle; no more than a minute passes before the crisp, piping-hot tubes are hauled out, drained and sprinkled with sugar. The first bite is red-hot but deeply addictive – a crunch then blissful softness. A few more and it's gone. The second *churro* disappears in record time. By the time the hot chocolate arrives, you're coming back to life, the grimace replaced by sugared grin. Chocolate and *churros*…a truly heavenly match.

Origins

The 'churro' sheep was a breed known for the quality of its wool. The shepherds who looked after them were, like most shepherds, only able to carry the basics, which in Spain was fried bread: simple and easy to cook on the go. Sugar was later sprinkled on top and the shape evolved into the star-shaped form, meaning the outside can crisp up while the centre stays soft.

Finding It

The Chocolateria San Ginés in Madrid serves some of the finest *churros* in the country. Expect to pay from €2 to €4 (US$2.70 to US$5.45).

* VARIATIONS * You'll find them sprinkled with cinnamon, dipped in *café con leche* (coffee with milk) and in a variety of forms (straight, curled and twisted). Down south, they tend to be thicker, and in the rest of the country they're known as *porra*. In Argentina, Peru, Mexico and Chile, you'll find them filled with chocolate or caramelised milk, known as *dulce de leche* or *cajeta*.

* By Tom Parker Bowles *

Recipe Churros Con Chocolate

YOU'LL NEED

1 cup water

½ cup unsalted butter

1 cup plain flour

¼ tsp salt

3 eggs, lightly beaten

vegetable oil (for deep-frying)

½ cup icing sugar, sifted

1 cup milk

200g (7oz) good-quality dark chocolate, coarsely chopped

METHOD

1. Put water and butter in a medium saucepan and bring to the boil, stirring until the butter melts.

2. While the liquid is still boiling, add the flour and salt and stir it swiftly with a wooden spoon until a dough forms. Continue to cook the dough for another minute then remove from the heat and transfer to an electric mixer bowl.

3. When the dough has cooled, add the lightly beaten eggs one at a time, making sure each one is fully incorporated before adding the next. Keep mixing until dough appears smooth and not wet.

4. Spoon the dough into a piping bag fitted with a large (2cm or 1in), star-shaped nozzle.

5. In a deep saucepan, pour in vegetable oil to a depth of about 6cm (2in) and heat to 180°C (350°F). (If you're not sure how hot that is, test the oil by dropping a small chunk of bread in. It should bubble to a golden brown in about 15 seconds.) Pipe lengths of dough (about 10cm or 4in is good) into the oil, cutting the dough off at the nozzle with a sharp knife.

6. Fry them until they're golden brown and crispy – they only take a minute or two – then remove them with a slotted spoon and place them on paper towel to drain. Dust with icing sugar.

7. To make the chocolate dipping sauce, simply combine milk and chocolate in a medium saucepan over a medium heat and stir until the chocolate has melted and the sauce is smooth with a satin sheen.

SERVES 8

* Crepe *

FRANCE

A venerable French icon that ranks right up there with the baguette and Mont St-Michel, these paper-thin pancakes can be sprinkled with icing (powdered) sugar, stuffed with fresh fruit or crammed with savoury fillings. On the street they're served hot, folded to fit in your hand.

What is It?

Crepes are a staple of Gallic cuisine, eaten year-round throughout the country. The batter is made of milk, flour, eggs and sugar or salt, and cooked in a thin layer on a hot, round griddle called a *billig* (or *pillig* in Breton). The versatility of their fillings and the unbridled imagination of the food-obsessed French may leave you with some very tough decisions.

Origin

Crepes evolved from simple flatbreads and get their name from the Latin word for curled, *crispus*. They originated in Brittany and Normandy, and up until the 19th century were prepared with the cheaper buckwheat flour produced in the area. This variety is still popular and is now commonly referred to as a *galette*. In sit-down creperies, *galettes* are always the main course (with a savoury filling), while crepes follow for dessert. Street stands only use crepe batter, regardless of whether the filling is savoury or sweet. On Candlemas, many families traditionally flip a crepe while holding a coin in the left hand, which is said to bring prosperity and a good harvest.

Tasting

Waiting in line on a bustling Paris street corner, you'll smell the carnival-sweet steam rising from the griddle as the crepe batter sizzles in a thin layer of melted butter. When you reach the window, you'll see the cook spread the batter with a few quick turns and a flick of the wrist, using a wooden spatula called a *rozell*. It's hard to resist biting into your fresh crepe as soon as it's handed to you in a white paper bag, folded in six. Nutella is one of the most popular fillings, but crepes go with just about anything, from lemon and sugar to ham and cheese; the textures are as variable as the choice of garnish. Sweet crepes are a gooey, dessert-like treat. In savoury crepes, the layers of sweet pancake create a mouth-watering contrast with the salty richness of the filling.

Finding It

In Paris, head to the Gare Montparnasse, around which the first immigrants from Brittany set up shop long ago. Expect to pay €3 to €5 (US$5 to US$7) for a takeaway crepe.

* TIPS * The *crêpe bretonne* or *galette* (called *krampouezh* in Breton) is the buckwheat variety, which you will almost assuredly have a chance to sample if you eat in a sit-down creperie. You'll find these crepes – which are more challenging to make than their sweeter cousins – stuffed with everything from ham, cheese and egg to *crème fraîche* and goat's cheese to potatoes and bacon. Most French prefer to wash down their *galettes* with Breton cider, which is served in small bowls. In Brittany, you'll know you've found the real deal if buttermilk is also served.

* By Meredith Snyder *

Recipe Crepes

YOU'LL NEED

1 cup milk

½ tsp vanilla extract

¾ cup flour

⅛ tsp salt

2 tbs sugar

2 eggs

3 tbs unsalted butter, melted and cooled

melted butter for coating pan

METHOD

1. In a small bowl, combine the milk and vanilla.

2. Sift flour, salt and sugar together in a medium-sized bowl.

3. In the centre of the flour mixture, make a well. Add eggs and one-third of the milk mixture to the well and whisk to gradually incorporate the dry ingredients.

4. When this is smooth, whisk in the remaining milk and melted butter.

5. Leave the batter to rest at room temperature for 30 minutes. It should be as thick as heavy cream.

6. Heat a small flat-bottomed frying pan or crepe pan (first-timers should make sure to use a nonstick pan) over medium heat and brush it with a bit of melted butter, which should sizzle but not brown.

7. Pour a small amount of batter into the pan and tilt it to allow the batter to thinly cover the bottom.

8. When the bottom of the crepe is golden brown, flip it to cook the other side. Rebutter the pan only if the crepes begin to stick.

9. Sprinkle your crepes with icing (powdered) sugar, spread them with jam or stuff them with your favourite seasonal fruit.

* Daulat ki Chaat *

DELHI, INDIA

Comprised of milk, saffron and sugar and topped with pistachios, this sweet, delightful treat is as light as air and as heavenly as moonlight. It's a popular Old Delhi street snack in winter.

What is It?

A speciality of Delhi, this distinctive winter snack is made from sweetened, whisked milk. It's then decorated with saffron, giving it an appealing orange-and-white tint. Onto this is sometimes added a layer of the edible silver leaf called *varq*. Although it's little more than an insubstantial froth, it has a particularly unique taste.

Origin

The origin of *daulat ki chaat* is lost in the mists of time. However, as it's a speciality closely associated with Old Delhi, it's possible that the Mughal emperors were among the first to savour this ephemeral treat.

Tasting

Daulat ki chaat is one of those dishes with a flavour and texture that are difficult to describe. The first taste imparts a hint of butter, then the tongue detects the subtle flavour of saffron followed by the pistachios, unrefined sugar and dried condensed milk sprinkled on top. The initial impression soon fades to leave behind a hint of creamy sweetness, prompting you to take another mouthful in order to recapture the heavenly sensation. It's a touch of the divine, a contrast with the noisy bustle of the bazaars where it's usually found. If you're a romantic type, you might detect a hint of moonlight in the mix. Because *daulat ki chaat* would collapse in high temperatures, it's only prepared in the cooler months. Its creators also claim that the dish should stand overnight beneath the moonlight for best results, and that the morning dew is essential to set it correctly.

Finding It

Daulat ki chaat stands can be elusive, but there's usually one or two vendors in the Kinari Bazaar near the Chandni Chowk metro station. A serving is ₹10 (US$0.20).

* **VARIATIONS** * Although *daulat ki chaat* is a Delhi dish, there are variants to be found elsewhere in India. Look for *malaai makkhan* or *nimish* in the neighbouring state of Uttar Pradesh.

· By Tim Richards ·

Recipe Daulat ki Chaat

YOU'LL NEED

2¼ cups cream

8 cups milk

1 tsp cream of tartar

1 tsp rose water

1 cup caster sugar

25g (0.9oz) chopped pistachio nuts

saffron (optional)

varq (optional)

METHOD

1. Blend the cream, milk and cream of tartar and then refrigerate overnight.

2. The next day add the rose water and 4 tsp of the caster sugar to the mixture, then whisk well (by hand or with an electric mixer).

3. Scoop the resulting foam in layers to serving bowls, adding caster sugar between each layer. Beat the remnant milk to continue creating foam, until all the milk is used up.

4. Chill, then serve with the pistachio pieces, saffron and *varq* sprinkled on top.

* Douhua *

CHINA, SINGAPORE & TAIWAN

If you thought tofu was for savoury dishes only – served up swimming in a sea of explosively hot chillies and pain-killing peppercorns, or fried up home-style in some tiny corner eatery – think again. *Douhua* brings out the sweet, loving caress of one of China's most underappreciated desserts.

What is It?

Douhua is a classic Chinese pudding available in many forms across Asia. Special extra-soft tofu is topped with a variety of sweet delights, like ginger-spiked syrup, peanuts, black sesame paste, coconut milk or red beans. It's usually served cold, but you can also find hot versions.

Origin

Tofu is believed to have originated sometime during the Han dynasty (206 BC–AD 220). As Buddhism spread across East Asia in later dynasties, tofu, a key staple for vegetarian monks and nuns, followed. It's incredible versatility was surely no secret, and today *douhua*, just one of its many derivatives, can be found everywhere from China to Malaysia and the Philippines to Indonesia.

Finding It

Taipei's night markets are the best place to sample great Taiwanese cuisine. Try the Shida Night Market and look for the *douhua* stall with the longest queue. Prices will vary widely depending on how many toppings you have, but average around 25 Taiwan dollars (US$0.85).

Tasting

This is all about that soft, silken, almost liquid texture. It melts in the mouth a bit like panna cotta or a delicate flan – you won't appreciate just how refreshing it tastes until you try it at the end of a long, hot summer day. *Douhua* used to be sold fresh from bikes, with wooden buckets attached to the back. This is less common today, but you'll still come across it everywhere, in stalls and restaurants alike.

* VARIATIONS *

Known as *tow huay* in Malaysia and Singapore, it comes drizzled with sweet sugar syrup. In the Philippines, it's known as *tahom* and served warm with sago balls and sugar syrup; in Indonesia it's called *wedang tahu* and comes with a ginger syrup. Taiwan has the most elaborate version, with up to a dozen different toppings. But even if it's a dessert, it doesn't have to be sweet. In the north of China you'll find it served with soy sauce, and in Sichuan, they add chillies, Sichuan peppercorns and soy sauce.

* By Tom Parker Bowles *

Recipe Douhua

YOU'LL NEED

310g (11oz) soybeans

water for soaking beans

8 cups water

1 tbs cornflour

1 tsp edible terra alba (ie food-grade gypsum or food-grade calcium sulfate, available from Chinese grocery stores)

280g (10oz) brown or white sugar

2 tbs finely sliced ginger or pandan leaves for flavouring (optional)

2 slices lemon or a dash of vinegar

METHOD

1. Rinse the soybeans to clean them, then put into a pot, adding enough water to cover the beans three times over. Soak beans until they expand to roughly twice their original size (may take eight hours).

2. Drain the beans, then add 6 cups of fresh water. Process the soybean/water mixture thoroughly with a blender.

3. Use a cheesecloth to squeeze out the liquid (soy milk) into a pot. Discard the pulp left in the cloth.

4. Add ½ cup water to the soy milk in the pot and cook on low heat, stirring and scraping the bottom of the pot continuously, until it begins to boil and foam. Remove from the heat source, then filter out the scum with a small sieve or cheesecloth.

5. Mix ½ cup water with the cornflour and terra alba.

6. Return the soy milk to the boil, then very quickly stir in the terra alba mixture.

7. Turn off the heat, being careful not to move the pot as this will disturb the setting. Cover and allow to sit for 30 minutes.

8. Meanwhile make the syrup by boiling the sugar in 1 cup water (with the ginger or pandan leaves if desired) for two to three minutes. Add the lemon or vinegar and allow to cool.

9. Drain any scum off the set *douhua*. Add the syrup and serve.

NOTE You can spice things up with ground peanuts, sesame seeds, chocolate, or a smidgen of fresh ginger sprinkled on top.

* Egg Waffle *

HONG KONG, CHINA

These puffs of golden, sweet-smelling cakey goodness are distinguished in the world of waffles by their bite-size proportions: each circular waffle is made up of 30 egg-shaped puffs, held together by a thin layer of crispy batter.

What is It?

While it might sound simple, this concoction of egg, evaporated milk, flour and sugar – known as *gai daan tsai* in Cantonese – relies on a distinctive custom-made waffle iron to ensure maximum enjoyment. Three minutes on one side, swivel, and repeat for a tear-apart snack anytime between 11am and midnight.

Origin

Just the aroma, or even the mere thought, of *gai daan tsai* (little eggs) causes older Hong Kongers to reminisce nostalgically about childhood. The egg waffle came into being in the middle of the 20th century after the People's Republic of China was established and the ensuing rush to the colony necessitated the creative use of limited culinary resources. One story goes that the batter was devised to make use of damaged eggs. Another has it that the egg-shaped waffle-maker – an offshoot of the traditional European one – compensated for a batter that itself lacked eggs, which were a luxury ingredient at the time. Even today, not all waffles include eggs – but the best do.

Tasting

Amid the savoury steaming dumpling and congee aromas wafting around Hong Kong's busy streets and markets, the whiff of a sweet, freshly baked egg waffle will hit you like a sepia-toned memory from grandma's kitchen. Then you'll see one. Waffle sellers often have three or four skillets steaming away, ensuring that each customer experiences that heady taste of a waffle served straight out of the griddle, rolled loosely on a cooling tray and plonked in a paper bag. The perfect waffle is best eaten when it's hot: the outer 'egg shell' is still crispy and the yellow innards are soft, chewy and barely there. The taste should be sweet, but not overly so, leaving a pleasant aftertaste long after the bag has been binned. The size-to-heat maintenance ratio might make the rapid eating of 30 'eggs' slightly challenging, but the easy-to-tear-and-share proportions of an egg waffle make it one of those street snacks that is best eaten among friends.

Finding It

Get one at Hung Kee Top Quality Egg Waffles on Hong Kong Island for HK$10 (US$1.30).

* BLESSED ARE THE WAFFLE MAKERS * Hong Kong's street hawkers are a dying breed, their age-old trade increasingly threatened by property developers and pragmatic lawmakers. The latest victim in this culinary twist of fate was Tai Hang waffle maker Ah Bak, a 74-year-old whose *gai daan tsai* were the last to be made using the old coal-fired method. When Ah Bak was arrested for hawking without a licence, the community rallied to save him. Unfortunately, the court took issue with his receiving social security while earning an income and the old man has not been seen since. Tai Hang locals are all the more hungry for it.

* By Penny Watson *

Recipe Egg Waffle

For die-hard authenticity, Hong Kong egg-waffle irons can be purchased at I Love Cake on Shanghai St, Kowloon.

YOU'LL NEED

⅔ cup sugar

2 large eggs

¼ cup evaporated milk

½ cup water

1 tsp vanilla extract

2 tbs melted butter

⅔ cup plain (all-purpose) flour

3½ tbs cornflour

1 tsp baking powder

2 tbs custard powder

cooking oil spray

METHOD

1. Cream sugar and eggs in a large bowl.

2. Add evaporated milk, water, vanilla extract and melted butter and mix together.

3. Sift the dry ingredients into the bowl and stir to form a smooth batter, free of lumps.

4. Cover and place in the fridge for one to two hours.

5. Heat waffle iron until hot and spray lightly with cooking oil.

6. Pour in the batter, filling the waffle iron to about three-quarters full.

7. Close the iron and swivel to coat both sides with batter.

8. Cook for two to three minutes on each side until batter turns crispy and golden.

9. Place on a cooling rack for one minute then eat while still hot.

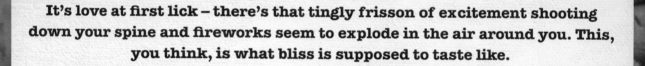

* Gelato *

ITALY

It's love at first lick — there's that tingly frisson of excitement shooting down your spine and fireworks seem to explode in the air around you. This, you think, is what bliss is supposed to taste like.

What is It?

At its most basic, gelato is a frozen egg custard, flavoured with every ingredient you can imagine, from amaretto to zabaglione, and served piled high in a long glass, crammed into cones or wedged between wafers. Italian gelato does not traditionally contain cream — it should be made with milk and either egg or cornflour — and is generally lower in fat. Although the overwhelming percentage of gelati in Italy are made from pre-made commercial mixes, you can, with a bit of perseverance, find the real homemade stuff.

Origin

Some say Marco Polo rediscovered a predecessor to the iced dessert during his travels along the Silk Road and introduced it back to Italy upon his return. Other say Catherine de Medici took her knowledge of gelato to France, when she married Henri Duc d'Orléans. Oh, and Charles I was so obsessed with the stuff he had his own 'Royal Ice Cream Maker', a man who, once retired, was paid a handsome pension to keep the secret from those greedy commoners. Wonderful stories all, but utterly without evidence to back them up.

Tasting

This is the taste of childhood that keeps on giving. But forget all those dreary modern imitators, largely 'air and fakery' in the words of Jane Grigson. For the true gelato experience, you want your custard fresh, flavoured with fruit purees made in the early hours of that morning. A proper gelateria delights the eyes as much as it does the taste buds. Like an edible artist's palate, dozens of narrow steel containers vie for your attention. There's chocolate of the darkest hue, a bright green pistachio that dances across the tongue. You go for a scoop of delicate strawberry, and then another of almond and finally cassata Siciliana. The texture is delicate and beautifully balanced, the flavours exploding around the mouth. It's neither over sweet or crushingly heavy. Just frozen delight, right down to the final lick.

Finding It

Gelateria Alberto Pico, on Via della Seggiola in Rome, is the real thing. The custard is made fresh each day and the flavours are all natural — gelato as it used to be. It costs between €1 and €3 per scoop (US$1.35 and US$3).

* VARIATIONS * Down south, especially in Sicily, you'll find all manner of granitas, which are similar to sorbet except that the ice crystals are larger and flow more freely. Around Sorrento, don't miss the ones made with the local lemons, while a coffee granita stuffed into a rich brioche bun is the most beguiling of Sicilian breakfasts.

* By Tom Parker Bowles *

Recipe Gelato

This is your basic custard-cream gelato recipe, from which you can create your own delicious flavours – think seasonal fruit, nuts, chocolate, coffee... You will get smoother results if you have an ice-cream maker, but making it by hand is just as good.

YOU'LL NEED

12 egg yolks, beaten

1½ cups sugar

6 cups milk

1 tbs grated orange or lemon peel

METHOD

Place egg yolks, sugar and 3 cups of milk in a large saucepan and whisk over a low heat, making sure not to cook the egg yolks. The mixture is ready when it sticks to the whisk. Take it off the heat, whisk through the rest of the milk and the peel. Cover and chill overnight before transferring to your ice-cream maker to do the rest of the work.

If you don't have an ice-cream maker, place a deep, durable baking dish in your freezer. When you've taken the mix off the heat and stirred through the remaining milk and peel, chill the mix over an ice bath before transferring to the chilled baking dish and into the freezer. Check the mixture every 30 minutes – when it starts to freeze around the edges, stir the frozen parts into the rest. Continue this process over the next two to three hours. The key is to avoid icy crystals so whisking it at regular intervals will ensure you get a smooth, and not frosty, result.

* Hotteok *

SOUTH KOREA

Hotteok is a soft, chewy pancake with a nutty filling that's packed with sugar, cinnamon and crunchy goodness. Hot off the griddle, it's served in a paper cup.

What is It?

Hotteok begins as a yeast-risen glutinous-rice-and-wheat-flour dough ball filled with brown sugar and cinnamon. It's then dropped on a grill, where the dough sizzles in a shallow pool of margarine before being flattened with a spatula. After cooking, one edge is cut open and stuffed with sesame seeds, sunflower seeds and nuts.

Origin

Long-time vendors say *hotteok* was an instant hit with children when it first appeared in the 1960s. Sweet, warm and inexpensive, it was prized among kids more accustomed to adversity as the country agonised through rapid industrialisation and autocratic governments. That duality of despair and delight, hunger and satisfaction, etched into the national psyche and transformed a simple pancake into a cultural icon enjoyed by people of all ages.

Tasting

There's a contagious excitement about *hotteok* that begins with the sticky, lingering aroma. Patrons jostle for position to admire the handiwork of the grandmothers who are churning out *hotteok* with factory-like precision. Once you've got one in your hand, the temptation to satisfy your craving and take a huge bite is almost overwhelming. Fight that urge – the molten sugar will burn a hole in your tongue. It's safer to start nibbling the top edge, which is where you'll find the *hotteok*'s sweet spot: the tender bread, caramelised sugar, and seeds and nuts combine to yield an earthy sweetness reminiscent of a crème brûlée. And as that sensation registers on your taste buds, you'll experience the moment of truth. *Hotteok* isn't just a street snack, it's 50 years of wistful memories rolled into a pancake.

Finding It

Try Busan's PIFF Square, a busy downtown area with several carts serving 'well-being' *hotteok* for about 900 won ($0.85USD).

* TIPS * Craving *hotteok* but can't find the ingredients? Buy the kit. If there is a Korean store in your community, chances are good it'll carry this product. The kit comes with pre-mixed flour, yeast and sweet filling. Put it all together and you'll be nibbling on Korea's iconic street food in about one hour.

· By Rob Whyte ·

Recipe Hotteok

YOU'LL NEED

Dough

¼ cup warm water

1 tsp dried yeast powder

2 tbs brown sugar

1 cup whole wheat flour

¾ cup glutinous rice flour (sometimes called sweet rice flour)

½ tsp salt

½ cup room temperature milk

3 tbs vegetable oil

Filling

¼ cup brown sugar

½ tsp cinnamon powder

2 tbs chopped peanuts, walnuts or almonds

1 tbs lightly crushed sesame seeds

1 tbs lightly crushed sunflower seeds

METHOD

1. Combine water, yeast and 1 tbs sugar in a small bowl. Stir until dissolved. Set aside for 10 minutes.

2. Combine wheat flour, rice flour, salt and 1 tbs sugar in a large bowl.

3. Add the yeast mixture to the dry ingredients. Gradually add milk while mixing.

4. Use your hands to form a ball of dough.

5. Knead the dough for three minutes and then place it in a bowl and cover. Set aside in a warm spot and allow to rise for one to three hours or until the dough doubles in volume.

6. To make the filling, combine the sugar, cinnamon, nuts and seeds.

7. Punch down the dough and knead it again for one minute. Divide it into six equal pieces.

8. Use your hands to stretch out each piece of dough and make a flat circle about the size of a CD.

9. Make a small pocket in the centre and add 1 tbs of filling.

10. Fold the outside edges of the dough into the centre and form a ball.

11. Heat the oil in a frying pan over medium-high heat.

12. Put a dough ball into the hot pan and flatten it with a spatula or large wooden spoon.

13. Cook until golden brown, roughly two minutes on each side.

14. Once cooked, place the pancakes on paper towels to remove the excess grease.

15. Serve hot.

MAKES 6 PANCAKES

* Ice Kacang *

SINGAPORE & MALAYSIA

Singapore's best-loved pudding resembles an alien moonscape – rainbow colours, surreal shapes and other-worldly textures. Welcome to shaved ice, Malay Straits style!

What is It?

The building block of ice kacang (also known as *ais kacang*, *air batu campur* or ABC) is shaved ice, but this is no mere snow cone or granita. Vendors take this pimped-up pudding and add a kaleidoscope of coloured fruit syrups, evaporated milk, red beans, sweetened corn, agar jelly, seaweed jelly and palm seeds, plus anything else the vendor can think of, all topped off with nuts or sprinkles. This isn't a dessert, it's a candy mountain!

Origin

Lots of people claim to have invented shaved ice. Hawaii has its snow cones, Sicily its granitas, the Philippines has *halo-halo*, Japan has *kakigori*. But for our money, the Singapore/Malay version takes the shaved-ice concept to a whole new level. Ice kacang translates to 'red bean ice', and sweet red beans have been joined by a dazzling array of ingredients that reflect the plantation culture of the Malay Straits – palm seeds, agar, peanuts, sweetcorn and *cendol* (rice jelly). Aficionados claim the dessert was originally concocted in Singapore, then part of the Straits Settlements, when the first ice machines were installed in the 1930s.

Tasting

Tasting ice kacang is only part of the pleasure (it tastes, as you might expect, like an explosion in a sweet shop). Watching the ritual of preparation – the blending of ingredients, a scoop of this, a pinch of that, the witches' brew of syrups, the final dusting of sprinkles – is half the fun. It's like the sundae that you were only allowed to have on your birthday when growing up, but in Malaysia and Singapore you can have it every day for pennies. When you finally sink your spoon into this fantasy creation, the first thing you notice is not the cold – well-prepared ice kacang should melt on the tongue like fresh snow – but rather the sweetness of the syrup, fruit and milk. Then the mining expedition begins. Textures and flavours pass like geological strata as you dig for the elusive treasure of the sweet, gelatinous palm seeds at the bottom of the bowl. *Sedap* (delicious)!

Finding It

Most hawker centres and food courts have an ice kacang maestro – locals rave about Annie's Peanut Ice in the Tanjong Pagar Food Center in Singapore, where you can enjoy one for between S$0.60 and S$1 (US$0.50 and US$0.80).

* TIPS * There's only one place to sample this queen of desserts – in the street. Hawker stalls sell the bona fide version, and every vendor has his or her own secret recipe and mystery ingredients. If hygiene is a concern, the permanent food courts in big cities like Singapore and Kuala Lumpur use safe, factory-made ice.

* By Joe Bindloss *

Recipe Ice Kacang

YOU'LL NEED

1 cup dried adzuki beans (red beans)

½ cup granulated sugar

¼ tsp salt

2 cups ice per person

agar jelly, available from Asian super-markets (or regular fruit jelly as a substitute)

attap chee (palm seeds) in syrup, available from Asian supermarkets

cendol (grass jelly), available from Asian supermarkets

canned creamed sweetcorn

sliced banana

rose syrup

evaporated or condensed milk

crushed peanuts

METHOD

1. Begin by preparing the beans. Soak one cup of dry adzuki beans overnight, then boil for 10 minutes.

2. Discard the first batch of liquid and add enough fresh water to cover the beans, along with granulated sugar and a quarter teaspoon of salt. Simmer until the beans are soft, then drain and chill. Alternatively, you can find sweetened red beans in cans in many Asian supermarkets.

3a. To prepare the shaved ice, you can either go the easy route or the hard one. The easy way is to add the ice one cup at a time to a blender and blend at low speed until the crushed ice has an even texture. This creates a crunchier mix than classic ice kacang.

3b. Alternatively, you can wash out an empty cardboard milk or juice carton, then fill it with water and freeze. When the entire carton is frozen solid, peel off the cardboard, and shave the ice manually using a cheese grater that catches the shavings inter-nally. Use a rapid back-and-forth motion and empty the ice shav-ings regularly into a pre-chilled bowl. Store your shaved ice in the freezer until the other ingredients are ready.

4. Prepare the agar jelly in advance and cut into small cubes.

5. Place a handful of preserved palm seeds at the bottom of each bowl, then cover with layers of ice shavings, jelly, red beans, cen-dol, sweetcorn and banana.

6. Finish with a final flourish of ice shavings, then pour rose syrup and evaporated (or condensed) milk over the creation. Top with crushed peanuts and serve.

* Jalebi *

INDIA

Visually and texturally tantalising, luscious *jalebis* – with their crunchy circular shells that ooze thick, gooey syrup – are the ultimate sugar fix and one of India's most loved sweet treats.

What is It?

Jalebis are typically orange-coloured coils of deep-fried batter, prepared from *maida* (all-purpose flour), which are dunked in an intensely sweet sugar syrup. Saffron and rosewater lend a delightfully delicate undertone to this otherwise robust Indian fritter which is a popular year-round sweet snack and especially prolific during festive occasions. Sizzled in ghee (clarified butter) or vegetable oil, *jalebis* are customarily eaten piping hot from the *kadai* (wok-like vessel).

Origin

Jalebis are believed to trace their origins to ancient Persia (where they were known as *zoolbia*), with the earliest literary record of their existence discovered in 13th-century manuscripts. Historically, during the holy Islamic month of Ramadan, *zoolbia* was one of several sweets that were traditionally distributed among the poor. Documentation suggests the sweet first came to the Indian subcontinent at least 500 years ago with the Mughals (who reigned over vast swaths of the region). Local variations to the recipe have made *jalebis* a standout among India's wildly colourful medley of *mithai* (sweets).

Tasting

Biting into a squiggly *jalebi* can be described as nothing short of, well, orgasmic. The arousing interplay of textural experiences – from the crispy yet playfully chewy outer shell to the warm, sweet syrup that slowly seeps out from within – is tempered with flirtatious hints of fragrant rosewater or possibly *kewra* (derived from flowers of the *Pandanus fascicularis* shrub). After spending energy haggling in India's frenetic, people-packed bazaars, nothing is quite as revivifying as the sugar hit of a *garam garam* (hot hot) *jalebi*. Half the fun is watching a street-side *jalebi-wallah* (*jalebi* vendor) swirl the smooth batter and masterfully flip the frying sweets until both sides have turned honey brown. Then, with another flick of the wrist, the *jalebis* are plunged into a vessel of thick sugar syrup before being popped onto a plate and handed to the hungry customer.

Finding It

The legendary Jalebiwala in Old Delhi sells scrummy *jalebis* for about ₹250 per kilo (US$5.50).

* TIPS * *Jalebis* are best eaten hot from the *kadai* so don't be sweet-talked by a vendor into buying leftovers from a batch made earlier – they're likely to lack the crunchy goodness of freshly sizzled ones. These squiggly delights – traditionally eaten by hand – are frightfully sticky, making it a good idea to carry wet wipes.

* By Sarina Singh *

Recipe Jalebis

A piping bag or a plastic bottle with a pointed nozzle is a neat and easy way of making the signature *jalebi* squiggle.

YOU'LL NEED

85g (3oz) plain (all-purpose) flour

1 tsp gram flour

½ tsp dried yeast powder

½ tsp sugar

½ tsp vegetable oil

100mL (3.4 fl oz) lukewarm water

vegetable or canola oil, for frying

Sugar Syrup

120g (4¼oz) sugar

½ cup water

pinch of cardamom powder

pinch of saffron

1 tsp lemon juice

METHOD

1. Put the plain and gram flours in a mixing bowl and add the yeast and sugar. Make a hole in the centre.

2. Pour the oil and water into the centre and mix thoroughly until there are no lumps. The texture should be slightly runny like pancake batter. Add more water if necessary. Pour the mixture into a plastic bottle or piping bag and set aside.

3. Put all syrup ingredients into a pot and bring to a rolling boil until the sugar melts and the mixture has thickened slightly. Turn the heat to the lowest setting while frying the *jalebis*.

4. Heat 3.5cm (1.5in) of oil in a frying pan. The oil is ready if a tiny amount of batter, dropped into the oil, sizzles and resurfaces without changing colour. If the batter colours straight away, the pan is too hot, so remove it from the heat for a few seconds.

5. Squeeze the *jalebi* batter into the oil in a pretzel shape approximately 5cm (2in) in diameter. Repeat two or three times, depending on the size of your frying pan, but do not crowd the pan.

6. Fry the *jalebis* until they are a golden honey colour on both sides.

7. Transfer the fried *jalebis* into the warm syrup and let soak for a few minutes.

8. Take out the *jalebis* and serve immediately.

Makes 12–15 pieces

* Martabak Manis *

INDONESIA

Although this folded pancake is celebrated across the Middle East and Southeast Asia, it's Indonesia where *martabaks* have reached their most chocolatey, cheesy pinnacle.

What is It?

Martabak manis are thick pancakes commonly consumed in the evening, with a coconut milk-and-yeast combination that gives them a certain frothiness. They're lathered in butter and stuffed with condensed milk, chocolate, crushed nuts and cheese. It's this filling that makes them stand out from the normally savoury versions found elsewhere.

Finding It

In Jakarta, there are plenty of vendors on the street Jalan Pecenongan. Expect to pay 10,000 rupiah (US$1.20) for one.

Tasting

Martabak manis are usually made before your eyes. First, out comes the pancake: its own preparation requiring an art to keep the edges brown but not burnt, the centre of the batter cooked, still fluffy and none too heavy and whole thing easily taken from the pan. For the most fulfilling experience, order the special chocolate-and-cheese flavour. Slatherings of butter and condensed milk get dark chocolate sprinkles, chopped peanuts and seeds added on one half and cheese on the other. Because the pancake this happens on is still hot, fillings have time to gel in a gluttonous goo before the *martabak manis* are folded and devoured.

Origins

Supposedly, *martabaks* (spelled *murtabak* outside Indonesia) originated in India in the Middle Ages but thanks to the trade routes, they'd soon spread to Saudi Arabia, Yemen, Malaysia, Thailand and Indonesia. *Muttabaq* is Arabic for 'folded', however, so plenty of people champion the *martabak* as a food that spread eastward from the Middle East. It was possibly Indonesia's role as the world's third-largest cocoa producer that led to the chocolate version of the *martabak* becoming indispensable here.

* MARTABAKS AROUND THE WORLD * For a snack that is essentially a pancake, it would be wrong to give Indonesians sole credit. In fact, even within Indonesia there is *martabak* division. Jakarta dubs its fat, sweet pancakes *martabak manis* but elsewhere in the country the same food is called *martabak bangka* and *terrang bulan*. Malaysia has *murtabaks* with minced mutton, egg, onion and garlic while India's version comes with boiled beef, lamb or goat meat.

· By Luke Waterson ·

Recipe Martabak Manis

YOU'LL NEED

Dough

1½ cups coconut milk

1 tsp dried yeast powder

¾ cup sugar

2 cups plain (all-purpose) flour

2 eggs, beaten

150g (5oz) granulated sugar

¼ tsp bicarb soda (baking soda)

vanilla extract

butter

olive oil

Filling

salted butter at room temperature
(must be soft and spread easily)

condensed milk

dark chocolate sprinkles

granulated sugar

peanuts, chopped fine

sesame seeds

grated mild cheese

METHOD

1. Warm up the coconut milk over low-medium heat until bubbling.

2. Let it cool off some, then mix in the yeast. Stir well until mixture has a frothy appearance. Set aside for 5 to 10 minutes.

3. Mix the sugar and flour in a separate bowl. Create a well in the centre and pour in the beaten eggs.

4. Mix until smooth, then add the frothy coconut milk and mix again. Add the granulated sugar, bicarb soda and a few drops of vanilla extract and set aside for 15 minutes.

5. Meanwhile, prepare the filling ingredients so that they are easily accessible.

6. Heat a wide cast-iron pan with butter and a little olive oil to make the grease go further.

7. When the oil is hot, turn down the heat and add one-fifth of the mixture. Ideally, you should have a pancake that is 2cm to 3cm (0.8in to 1.2in) thick.

8. Wait for the surface to dry and the outer edge to brown, then remove from the heat and place on a board (don't flip the pancake).

9. Cut the pancake in half. Spread salted butter on both sides, then add the condensed milk.

10. To make a chocolate *martabak*, add the chocolate sprinkles, a dash of granulated sugar, the chopped peanuts and sesame seeds to one half.

11. For a cheese *martabak*, add the grated cheese to the other half. Fold each half before serving and smear with a glaze of butter and condensed milk.

* Masala Chai *

INDIA

Warm, spiced milky tea is the perfect 5pm boost. The locally grown tea and spices are boiled to strong, sweet perfection at the chai-*wallah* stall (often lit with fairy lights).

What is It?

Stronger than Western-style leaf tea, Assam or CTC (cut, tear, curl) tea is boiled in water and milk – often rich buffalo milk – along with sugar and freshly chopped or ground spices. *Adrak* (ginger), cardamom and *dalchini* (cassia, or Indian cinnamon) are the most common; lemongrass, black pepper and clove are also delish.

Finding It

In Mumbai's suburb of Santa Cruz West, across from Poddar High School, an exquisite masala chai costs ₹7 (US$0.15).

Tasting

Rush hour for chai-*wallahs* (chai vendors) is twilight. People on their way home from work or the vegetable market pause for tea, people-watching and maybe a smoke. The chai-*wallah*'s elaborate counter has multiple gas stoves, lots of ancient-looking brass and stainless-steel vessels about and lights strung in the tree overhead. An image of the goddess Laxmi, with a smudge of sandalwood on her forehead, hangs from the trunk, watching over things. The tea is steeped with sugar, spices and milk in a large pot, filling the air with its sweet scent, and then poured through an old-fashioned cotton strainer into surprisingly dainty glasses (which tough rickshaw-*wallahs* incongruously hold with pinkies aloft). The *dalchini* gives the strong tea body, the cardamom provides the perfume and the *adrak* gives it bite – which the rich milk and sugar soften. The evening seems to soften, too, and one more cup puts the day gently to rest, and makes the night look a little sweeter.

Origin

For thousands of years, milk was heated with various spices and jaggery in traditional ayurvedic healing formulas. At the same time, tea, also considered a herbal remedy, was being drunk in pockets of what is now India. But it wasn't until the British East India Tea Company created vast tea plantations in the 19th century and marketed the product domestically that what we now know as masala chai was born.

* TIPS * Masala chai is often sipped with salty snacks, like *vada pao* – a fried lentil-and-potato dumpling with spicy sauce and chutney on a tiny bun. It's heavenly with chai. In Mumbai, if a full cup is too much for you, ask for 'cutting' – a half-cup at half-price.

* By Amy Karafin *

Recipe Masala Chai

YOU'LL NEED

½ cup water

2.5cm (1in) piece of ginger, crushed or chopped

3–4 cardamom pods, ground

2.5cm (1in) stick *dalchini*, crushed

2 leaves lemongrass, chopped (optional)

dash of black pepper (optional)

1 whole clove (optional)

1 heaping tsp Assam (CTC) tea

½ cup milk

METHOD

1. Add water, spices and tea to a pot and bring to a boil. The milk must not be added at this point: the ginger will cause it to curdle.

2. Once boiling, add the milk and allow to heat or boil; turn off heat immediately. Let sit for a minute or two if you like a stronger brew.

3. Some families only add the tea after turning off the heat; they then allow it to steep for a few minutes. Boiling the tea makes the taste stronger but supposedly increases the caffeine content while diminishing its beneficial antioxidant properties.

* Mithaa Paan *

INDIA

Everyone looks a little bewildered when they first taste *mithaa paan* (sweet paan), a betel leaf filled with powders, pastes, seeds, fruit and mystery. The taste is intense, with dozens of flavours happening all at once.

What is It?

Each paan-*wallah* (paan vendor) has his own style of preparation, but *mithaa paan* usually includes *choona* (slaked lime) and *kattha* (acacia-bark extract) pastes. It'll also have a little saffron if you're lucky, coconut flakes, candy-coated fennel, spices like cardamom and clove, *gulkand* (rose-petal jam), dried fruit and a maraschino cherry – all wrapped up in a betel leaf. It's eaten after meals.

Origin

Paan goes back almost 5000 years, when kings and queens had special paan attendants. The combination of *supari* (areca nut, often referred to as betel nut) and betel leaf was thought to have healing, digestive and relaxant properties. Over time it absorbed more and more ingredients – from spices to sweets to precious metals (like silver). The sweet version – *mithaa paan* – mostly lost the *supari* (which is thought to be carcinogenic); plain paan, meanwhile, picked up chewing tobacco, now the most popular form, as the red spit stains all over India's streets will attest.

Tasting

You'll see them all over India by the side of the road, near restaurants and lunch spots: paan-*wallahs*, sitting cross-legged amid stacks of shiny betel leaves and a hundred stainless-steel containers, jars, tins and boxes. They work like fast scientists, taking a scoop, a swipe, a sprinkle or a pinch of each ingredient, working quickly and in order, stopping only to ask for your preferences. The finished product is a giant wad that fills the mouth and quickly begins its symphony of textures and exotic flavours – the smooth leaf, the spicy clove and fennel, the gooey dates and *gulkand*, the sweet coconut, the crunchy sugar-coated seeds and (if you choose) the hard *supari*. Eating it is an event and the perfect ending to a meal.

Finding It

Paan is most popular in northern India, but 'Bombay paan' is special. Try the *mithaa paan* on Nawroji F Road in the Colaba district of Mumbai; it'll only set you back ₹10 (US$0.25).

* TIPS * Paan is made to order. Skip the cherry, load up on the *gulkand* or – though it's bad for you – choose which *supari* you like (the flakes are chewier than the chunks). Set aside a few minutes when you won't need to talk and pop the whole thing in your mouth. You can eat everything in *mithaa paan*, but you might want to spit out the *supari* – preferably in the trash – after savouring.

* By Amy Karafin *

Recipe Mithaa Paan

Try your local Indian grocery store for these ingredients. 'Star'-brand powder is a feature of almost every paan-*wallah's* spice collection. It might be tricky to find, but if you luck upon it, your *mithaa paan* will take you to the streets of Mumbai in a flash!

YOU'LL NEED

slaked-lime paste

kattha paste

1 betel leaf (kept moist)

preserved dates

sugar-coated fennel seeds (or normal fennel seeds if not available)

toasted coconut flakes

cardamom powder or cardamom pod

'Star'-brand powder, if available (a special blend of sweet, aromatic flavours)

gulkand

1 maraschino cherry

1 whole clove (optional)

METHOD

1. Place a dribble of the lime and *kattha* pastes on the betel leaf; spread around the leaf and blend. (In a pinch, substitute with honey.)

2. Add the preserved dates and sprinkle with sugar-coated fennel seeds, toasted coconut, cardamom powder or pod, and Star powder.

3. Spoon on a smidge of *gulkand*, and top with maraschino cherry.

4. Fold the betel leaf into a triangle, covering the mixture with three flaps of leaf. Bind together with the clove or a toothpick. *Mithaa paan* can be refrigerated for a few hours if necessary but tastes best fresh.

* Pastel de Belém *

BELÉM, LISBON, PORTUGAL

The Pastel de Belém is heaven in a tart and Portugal's sweet gift to the world. The best – from Antigua Confeitaria de Belém – is made to a secret recipe.

What is It?

The Pastel de Belém is a small baked tart with a flaky pastry shell filled with a sweet, creamy egg-based custard and sometimes sprinkled with cinnamon.

Finding It

At the Confeitaria de Belém in Lisbon, one tart costs a mere €1 (US$1.36).

Tasting

While you can sample the custard tarts in the plethora of *pastelerias* (cake shops) in Portugal and around the world, where they are known by the general name of *pasteis de nata*, the most sublime – and 'original' – *pastel* is from Antigua Confeitaria de Belém, in the Belém district of Lisbon. You can queue with the hordes to buy takeaways, which are served in a quaint cardboard tube (an incredible 19,000 tarts are sold daily), or grab a table in the historic bustling cafe, a maze of rooms decorated with blue and white Portuguese tiles. While munching on these heavenly delights, watch the masters rolling out the dough (but don't get any ideas: only three people are privy to the top-secret recipe and preparation is done behind closed doors). Breathe in the aroma of sugar and cinnamon, bite into the crunchy pastry and let your tongue linger on the luscious custard. Sinfully sweet.

Origin

The first reference to a similar 'milk tart' is in a historic Portuguese cookbook, *Infanta Dona Maria* (1538–77). Centuries later, after the closure of monasteries during the liberal revolution in the 1800s, an enterprising employee of Belém's Mosteiro dos Jerónimos offered sweet pastries to a general store (conveniently, this was attached to a sugar refinery). The pastries rapidly became renowned as Pastéis de Belém. In 1837 baking of the *pastéis* began from the same premises, now the Antigua Confeitaria de Belém, using the same monastery recipe.

* TIPS * *Pastéis* are best enjoyed with a *bica*, Lisbon's name for an espresso coffee. Sunday brunches are a fun, if busy, time to head to the cafe, when bustling waiters serve up piles of the steaming tarts.

• By Kate Armstrong •

Recipe Pastel de Belém

These days, only three people are privy to the recipe in Antiga Confiteria de Belém. Although versions of the Portuguese custard tart – known as *pastel de nata* – are reproduced throughout Portugal and even the world, the secret ingredients of the Pastel de Belém set it apart from the others. The following – we hope – is the nearest thing to the sublime, original recipe. If you want a less sinful – but less luscious – experience, substitute the cream with milk. You'll need a 12-cup muffin pan.

YOU'LL NEED

1 cup milk

¼ cup cream

5 egg yolks

3 tbs sugar

pinch of salt

2 tbs plain (all-purpose) flour

2 strips lemon peel

½ tsp pure vanilla extract or a de-seeded vanilla bean

1 cinnamon stick

500g (1lb) ready-to-use puff pastry

cinnamon

icing (powdered) sugar

METHOD

1. Preheat oven to 150°C (300°F).

2. In a large bowl, whisk milk, cream, egg yolks, sugar and salt. Carefully whisk in the flour to avoid lumps. When the batter is smooth, add the lemon peel, vanilla (or de-seeded vanilla bean) and the cinnamon stick.

3. Transfer the batter to a saucepan and use a whisk to stir constantly over low heat. It is important to heat the milk slowly to ensure that the egg yolks do not cook or 'scramble'.

4. Continue to stir until the mixture resembles thick custard. Beware of the mixture thickening around the edges of the pot; try to maintain a smooth consistency.

5. Allow to cool, then gently spoon off the milk skin from the top. Remove the lemon peel, cinnamon stick and vanilla bean (if used).

6. Roll out the puff pastry with a rolling pin on a lightly floured surface, until it's 25mm (0.1in) thick. Dust off the excess flour and roll the dough like a cigar, starting from the shorter end. With the roll lengthwise, cut the dough into 4cm (1.5in) lengths.

7. With each piece, use your thumb and/or fingers to push down the roll centre and gently press the dough to create a cup shape, working in a circular pattern. Add flour if dough becomes moist.

8. Press and shape dough gently into muffin cups; extend the dough over cup lips slightly to ensure that it won't over-shrink when baking. Shells should be around 25mm (0.1in) thick. Spoon custard mixture into each cup until three-quarter full (this leaves about 1cm or 0.4in of pastry showing).

9. Place the tray in the oven. Bake for 15 minutes or until the pastry turns golden brown. The top should be partially brown, if possible. Note: depending on oven, the tops can burn before the dough is cooked through (cover with aluminium foil to help avoid this).

10. Set aside to cool and garnish with a sprinkle of cinnamon and icing sugar.

* Sfenj *

MOROCCO

As croissants are to the French, so are *sfenj* to Moroccans. Eaten hot and sometimes sprinkled with sugar, they're essentially fried doughnuts gone pro.

What is It?

Sfenj are Moroccan-style beignets: uniquely spongy, deep-fried pastry rings made of unsweetened, very sticky (almost batter-like) yeast dough with no milk or butter added. Customarily noshed first as a morning treat and then again in the late afternoon between 5pm and 7pm, *sfenj* know no seasonal limitations, meeting hungry needs throughout the year.

Origin

Believed to have been imported by Arabs in the 18th century, Moroccan *sfenj* were originally available from stands alongside those where roasted lamb's head (a breakfast complement) was prepared in the weekly souks of major population centres. Today, as one of Morocco's prime street-food staples, *sfenj* are found at most hours of every day throughout the country.

Tasting

Morocco's labyrinthine medinas see brisk business, the constricted byways a haphazard jumble atumble with goods and food. Amid the eye-popping and energy-sapping commotion, *sfenj* are a perfect quick boost. They should always be ordered fresh, both because they're best that way and because you'll be able to witness their preparation. While not difficult to cook, *sfenj* can be very hard to get right. There's much to be learned from deft handlers – always men – including shaping the wet dough, getting it into the oil intact and fishing the fried results out with long skewers. The eating, though, is gratifyingly easy: when sweetly garnished, *sfenj* are light confections of which just one is rarely enough.

Finding It

The best *sfenj* are prepared in *hanout* (closet-sized booths) in the medinas of Morocco's biggest cities, where they sell for 1 dirham (US$0.12) each or 23 dirham (US$2.90) a kilogram.

* TIPS * While *sfenj* are scrumptious unadorned, they also come with time-honoured toppings: a dusting of sugar, a drizzle of honey or a shroud of egg. *Sfenj* are best hot – having breathed for only a moment after removal from the oil – with a glass of mint tea in the morning or a milk coffee in the afternoon.

* By Ethan Gelber *

Recipe Sfenj

YOU'LL NEED

1½ tsp dried yeast powder

½ cup lukewarm water

2½ cups plain (all-purpose) flour

1 tsp salt

vegetable oil

toppings of your choice – sugar and honey for example

METHOD

1. Add the yeast to ¼ cup of lukewarm water. Set aside for a few minutes.

2. In a large mixing bowl, combine the sifted flour, salt and yeast water and then stir in another ¼ cup water.

3. Knead the mix (being careful not to add too much more flour) until the dough is sticky and stretchy. Place in a cloth-covered bowl and set aside in a warm spot for two to four hours.

4. When the dough is light, bubbly and has doubled in size, heat the vegetable oil in a frying pan.

5. Keeping your hands wet, lightly knead the sticky dough (keeping as many of the air pockets as possible) and divide into 12 pieces. Using your palms, roll each piece into a ball and then, with your thumb, make a hole in the middle. Stretch the dough a bit to make a ring.

6. When the oil is hot, slip the rings into it, but don't overcrowd. Fry each ring for two to four minutes per side or until golden brown.

7. Remove from the oil and drain on a paper towel. Serve hot.

* Sopaipilla *

CHILE

On rainy winter afternoons, Santiagans long for *sopaipillas*. These deep-fried discs of pumpkin dough, paired with sweet *chancaca* sauce, have been a cold-weather comfort food for generations of Chileans.

What is It?

Sopaipilla dough is made with fresh *zapallo*, a South American version of the pumpkin. The dough is shaped into small circles, then quickly fried in hot oil. Though the *sopaipilla* is served with savoury condiments in many Latin American countries, most Chileans dip their pastries in *chancaca*, a molasses-like syrup made of brown sugar, orange zest, honey and cinnamon. Traditionally, *sopaipilla* is a late-afternoon snack enjoyed with a cup of tea.

Origin

Several cultures claim that *sopaipillas* were their own invention. That's because variations on the *sopaipilla* are found in many Latin American countries – particularly Argentina, Peru and Uruguay – as well as the American southwest. Linguistically, the *sopaipilla* has roots further afield: the word *xopaipa* (from the Mozarabic language spoken in the Muslim regions of the Iberian peninsula during the late Middle Ages) means 'bread soaked in oil'. It's evident that early versions of the *sopaipilla* appeared in Spain centuries ago; historical records show that Chileans were eating them (and adding their own touch, the sweet *chancaca* sauce) as early as 1726.

Tasting

On a rainy afternoon in Santiago, the city parks are deserted. But the lights stay on inside a small kiosk where a local woman is mixing dough and shaping it into round, flat circles. She'll see plenty of business today – the chilly, wet winter weather always brings a steady stream of Chileans under colourful umbrellas for their favourite nostalgic treat, *sopaipillas con chancaca*. As the vendor plunges her discs of pumpkin dough into a bubbling vat of hot oil, the rich aroma of frying dough mixes with the smell of rain on cement. Step up to the window for your *sopaipillas*, piping hot and palm-sized, grab a handful of napkins (you'll need them) and help yourself to a side of sticky-sweet *chancaca*. Dip the edge of one pastry into the syrup, then get ready to sink your teeth in. The crisp, buttery surface gives way to a lighter, almost fluffy centre; the *chancaca*'s brown sugar and citrus flavour sets off the subtler taste of pumpkin.

Finding It

On weekends you'll find dozens of *sopaipilla* vendors at the Costanera along Santiago's Mapocho River; each pastry costs around 100 to 200 pesos (US$0.20 to US$0.40).

* VARIATIONS * A *sopaipilla* consumed with sweet *chancaca*, also known as the *sopaipilla pasada*, is traditional in wintertime in central Chile. But in the south of Chile and in warmer weather, the *sopaipilla* is often served with the caramel-like *manjar*, ketchup and mustard, or with a savoury Chilean-style salsa called *pebre*.

* By Bridget Gleeson ·

Recipe Sopaipilla

YOU'LL NEED

1 *zapallo* squash (or 1 small pumpkin)

8 tbs butter, melted

5 cups plain (all-purpose) flour

¾ tsp bicarb soda (baking soda)

¼ tsp baking powder

1 tsp salt

1–2 cups vegetable oil

1¼ cups brown sugar

1 cup water

3–4 cinnamon sticks

2 tbs honey

2 tsp cloves (optional)

1–2 oranges

METHOD

1. Fill a saucepan with several cups of water and place on the stovetop over medium heat.

2. Halve the *zapallo* (or pumpkin) and remove the rind and seeds.

3. Chop it into large chunks and then add the chunks to the heating water in the saucepan.

4. Bring the water to a boil, then reduce heat slightly, stirring the *zapallo* occasionally until it's softened.

5. The *zapallo* is ready for the next step when you can slice it easily with a toothpick or knife.

6. Remove the chunks from the water and allow to cool on a plate. Then combine the zapallo with the melted butter and mash with a fork.

7. In a separate bowl, mix together the flour, bicarb soda, baking powder and salt.

8. Add the flour mixture to the *zapallo* mixture, one cup at a time. (You may not need all five cups, depending on the amount of *zapallo* you have. The dough shouldn't be overly thick or dry.) Add a tablespoon of water if needed.

9. Place the dough on a floured surface and knead gently. Let it rest for a few minutes, then roll it flat until it's roughly 1.25cm (0.5in) thick.

10. Cut out circles of dough about 10cm (4in) in diameter. Stab each dough circle a few times with the prongs of a fork.

11. Meanwhile, coat the bottom of a skillet or deep frying pan with approximately 5cm (2in) of vegetable oil. Heat the oil over medium-high heat. Drop a few dough rounds into the oil (don't crowd them) and fry for a few minutes, until the dough is slightly browned along the surface. Using tongs, pull the fried dough out of the oil and lay out to cool on a rack lined with paper towels. Repeat in batches.

12. While waiting for the batches of dough to fry, make a version of *chancaca* syrup in a separate saucepan. Combine the brown sugar, water, cinnamon sticks, honey and cloves, stirring frequently over low to medium heat. Squeeze the oranges into the mixture.

13. Strain and serve warm with the hot *sopaipillas*.

* Glossary *

açai Açai is the grape-like fruit from a palm native to Central and South America. The pulp is made by removing the flesh from the seed, freezing then mashing it.

adobo seasoning Adobo seasoning is a mix of spices and herbs used for marinating meat. The mix varies considerably from region to region throughout the Americas.

adzuki bean This is a legume common in east Asia and India (where it's known as *chori*). It's usually eaten in sweet dishes.

agar jelly Agar jelly is made from agar, an algae or seaweed extract – it's basically a vegetarian equivalent to gelatin.

aji limo This is a medium-hot Peruvian chilli.

ajvar Ajvar is a Croatian/Serbian red capsicum (pepper) relish.

amba Iraqi-style mango chutne

amchur Amchur is a powder used as a souring agent in Indian cooking. It's made from dried, ground green mangoes. You can replace it with lemon/lime juice or tamarind water if you need to.

aonori An edible seaweed, often used as a seasoning.

arborio rice Arborio is a short-grain rice with a high starch content, often used in risottos. Similar types of rice include Carnaroli and Vialone Nano.

Assam (CTC) tea A machine-processed Assam tea, usually best consumed with milk and other flavourings and sweeteners.

atta Atta flour is a hard-wheat flour. Doughs made with this flour can be rolled thin yet retain their integrity. Substitute with plain (all-purpose) flour if need be.

attap chee Immature fruit of the attap palm. Lychee could replace it.

baladi An heirloom eggplant, but can also refer to a dish prepared with them

banana leaves The leaves of the banana tree, often used to wrap food while cooking. Available frozen if not fresh in Asian and Hispanic grocery stores. Use aluminium foil for wrapping the food otherwise.

bee hoon noodles Rice vermicelli noodles.

belacan Shrimp paste – pungent and salty. Use anchovies mashed with a little water as a replacement.

betel leaf A vine leaf, common to much of Asia.

bijao leaf A leaf used for wrapping foods while cooking. Use banana leaves or aluminium foil in its place.

bird's eye chilli A small chilli, technically medium in heat, but more than hot enough for most people.

buckwheat flour As the name suggests, flour made from buckwheat (which isn't wheat at all). It's a distinctly grey flour but, colour aside, can be replaced by plain (all-purpose) flour.

caciocavallo A cheese made in the fashion of mozzarella, but aged into a hard cheese. Substitute with provolone.

candlenuts A nut used to thicken Asian soups and curries. Try almonds, cashews or macadamias as replacements. If you find candlenuts (Asian grocery stores stock them), they must be cooked before eating them.

cendol An Asian sweet drink/desert, usually made with coconut cream, shaved ice and green, gelatinous threads made from rice flour.

cha lua A pressed meat, made from finely ground pork, not unlike baloney or devon in appearance. Commonly available in Vietnamese grocery stores.

chana dhal Split, dried chick.peas (garbanzo beans).

Chinese chives Also known as garlic chives. Use chives as a mild substitute.

Chinese sausage A sweet, dried pork sausage. Not easily replaced, but a very mild, aged salami could offer a similar consistency if not the taste.

chorizos A Portuguese or Spanish pork sausage, varieties ranging from mild to spicy. It is dry-cured, like a salami, and can be eaten uncooked. Substitue with pepperoni.

clam juice The stock produced from cooking clams. Available tinned. Substitute with fish stock.

cremini mushrooms Similar to a Swiss brown or portobello, both of which could be used as a substitute.

daikon A large, tubular, white radish, mild in flavour. Substitute with jicama or red radish (which is more pungent).

dalchini Cassia bark – a cinnamon-like spice. Use cinnamon in its place.

dendê oil Palm oil, though distinct from most cooking oils in its deep red colour. Use peanut oil in place of it (but you'll lose the red hue the oil imparts).

dried corn husks Used for wrapping foods, especially tamales. Substitute with banana leaves or aluminium foil.

dried flat rice noodles Also known as flat rice stick noodles. Easy to find in an Asian grocery store. Other rice noodles could be used as a substitute.

galangal A rhizome, similar in appearance to ginger, though darker. Ginger can be used in its place, but it is much milder than galangal.

garam masala A 'sweet' blend of spices – cardamom, cloves, cumin, pepper, among others.

gari A mildly sour-tasting flour made from fermented, roasted cassava. Difficult to substitute for taste, but plain cassava flour is an option.

ghee Clarified butter.

glutinous rice flour Ground glutinous rice used in Asian deserts and as a thickener. Tapioca flour can be used as a substitute.

gram flour Ground chickpeas (garbanzo beans), also known as besan flour.

green mango Unripened mango.

green papaya Unripened papaya.

guarana syrup An extract of guarana mixed with sugar syrup.

guizador Peruvian term for stewed turmeric. See turmeric.

gulkand Rose-petal jam from northern India and Pakistan.

habañero chilli A hot chilli, in the range of bird's eye chillies though somewhat hotter.

hoisin sauce A sweet, thick, dark sauce predominantly used in savoury cooking.

holy basil A pungent Asian herb with notes of anise, pepper and mint. Substitute with Thai basil or sweet basil along with some mint.

jaggery A caked sugar made from dehydrated sugar cane juice. Palm sugar is darker but can be used as a substitute. Dark brown sugar is a further alternative.

jicama A vaguely potato-looking tuber, especially when peeled. Eaten raw, it's crunchy and strangely juicy.

katsuobushi Dried, fermented and smoked tuna, often in flakes. Also known as bonito flakes, it's used as a condiment.

kattha An astringent paste extracted from an acacia tree. A common ingredient in paan.

kimchi Pickled, fermented cabbage – a Korean staple.

laksa leaves A weirdly metallic tasting mint, with strong pepper notes. Use mint and coriander as a substitute. Also known as Vietnamese mint.

Maldive fish flakes Dried and smoked bonito tuna, more splinters than flakes. Substitute with Japanese bonito flakes (*katsuobushi*).

masa harina A flour made from hominy (hulled corn kernels).

Mexican-style vinegar-based hot sauce Many brands (eg Valentina, El Yucateco), but Tabasco is perhaps the most widely known.

New Mexico green chillies Mild green chillies.

palm sugar Sugar made from the sap of the palm tree. Use dark brown sugar in its place.

pandan leaves Long leaves from the pandan plant, used as a colouring and flavouring in Southeast Asian cuisine.

plantains Related and similar in appearance to the banana, but needs to be cooked – often used in savoury dihes.

poblano chillies A ubiquitous Mexican chilli, it's mild (usually) and used in a variety of ways. Also known as ancho chilli in its dried form.

pomegranate molasses A thick, dark, tart sauce made from reduced pomegranate juice. Use pomegranate or cranberry juice as a substitute.

provola A small-sized variant of provolone cheese, which is a semi-hard, cow's milk cheese. You can use fontina or asiago in place of it.

puffed rice Rice grains that have been heated under pressure. Kind of like Rice Bubbles/Krispies, but unsweetened.

queso anejo An aged goat or cow's milk cheese. Use romano or perhaps a mild goat's milk cheese in its place.

red Asian shallots A small red/pink onion, mild and somewhat sweet. Shallots are a fine substitute.

red curry paste A blend of dried red chillies, galangal, lemongrass, coriander root, garlic, shrimp paste, among other spices. A Thai staple. Available pre-made in Asian grocery stores.

rose syrup Rose syrup is a sweetened rose water, which itself is by-produced during the extraction of rose oil from rose petals. Use rose essence or rose water in its place.

salted radish Salted and preserved daikon radish. Available in Asian grocery stores.

sambal belacan A chilli paste made by blending together chillies, shrimp paste, lime and sugar. It's pungent and spicy. If you don't have shrimp paste, you could use anchovies to make it yourself. Or buy it ready-made from an Asian grocery store.

Sarawak laksa paste Quite different to the more common laksa pastes, this paste features sambal belacan, tamarind, garlic, galangal and lemongrass. Asam (aka Penang) laksa paste could be used in its place.

sawtooth coriander leaves A long leafed herb, serrated as the name suggests. It can be replaced with coriander.

scotch bonnet chillies A hot chilli common in the Carribbean. It can be replaced with habanero.

semolina flour A 'hard' wheat flour made from durum wheat. It is higher in gluten than plain (all-purpose) flour, but you could use thise in its place (the result will be different though).

sev A crispy, noodle-like, Indian snack.

shiitake mushrooms Also known as Chinese mushrooms, these are commonly available dried in Asian grocery stores – soak them in hot water for half an hour before using them.

shiso leaves A mint-family herb used throughout Asia. Mint can be used as a substitute.

shito A Ghanian sauce made from dried fish, oil, chilli, garlic, tomato and a variety of spices.

shrimp paste Also known as *belacan*, this is a pungent and salty paste used as a base for curries and other sauces. Use anchovies mashed with a little water as a replacement.

slaked-lime paste Calcium oxide mixed with water. You must use food-grade calcium oxide (also known as lime – like what you find in whitewash).

snake beans The pod of a climbing vine, the snake bean is unrelated to the common bean, but green beans can replace them. You'll need about four green/string beans for every snake bean.

star anise A star-shaped spice readily available in Asian grocery stores. Anise seed can be used as a substitute.

'Star'-brand powder 'Star'-brand powder is a feature of the spice collection of almost every paan-*wallah*. Difficult to replace, but if you find it, your *mithaa paan* will take you to the streets of Mumbai in a flash!

sticky rice Also known as glutinous rice. It's a short-grained Asian rice that becomes quite sticky when cooked. Try arborio rice or some other risotto rice as a replacement.

strong white flour Also known as bread-making flour, it has a higher gluten content than plain (all-purpose) flour.

sumac A generally ground spice made from the dried fruit of the sumac shrub.

supari Areca nut, chewed with betel for its stimulant effects. It can have a variety of negative physiological and neurological effects.

tahini paste Sesame seed paste.

tamarind concentrate Also known as tamarind paste, this is the pulp of the tamarind pod deseeded and ready to use. It's sour and only slightly sweet. Use lemon juice for a souring effect in its place.

tamarind paste see *tamarind concentrate*

tamarind pulp The pulp of the tamarind pod, usually available in blocks from Asian grocery stores. It will have the stony black seeds as well, which would need to be removed (usually after soaking the pulp in hot water for a while).

tamarind water The watered-down, deseeded pulp from the tamarind pod.

tapioca starch Tapioca flour, a common thickening agent. Use glutinous rice flour in its place.

terra alba Food-grade gypsum for setting soy-milk into tofu.

Thai basil Milder than holy basil, more pungent than basil – but basil can be used as a substitute.

turmeric A rhizome like ginger, usually smaller, and beneath the dull orange peel, you'll find brilliant gold. Available fresh in Asian grocery stores, and as a ground spice almost everywhere.

twarog cheese Also known as quark, this is a soft, unaged cheese. It's generally a cooking cheese. If you can't find it, try cottage cheese in a pinch.

Vegemite A spread made from yeast extract. It's sharp and pungent, deep black and smooth. It's an Australian staple. Irreplaceable (but use Marmite if you must).

Vietnamese mint A weirdly metallic tasting mint, with strong pepper notes. Use mint and coriander as a substitute. Also known as laksa leaf.

zapallo squash An enormous type of pumpkin/squash. Replace with any available pumpkin/squash.

zomi Ghanian word for palm oil.

* Authors *

Tom Parker Bowles

Tom Parker Bowles is a food writer with an ever-expanding gut. He has a weekly column in *The Mail on Sunday*, as well as being Food Editor of *Esquire*. He is also a Contributing Editor to *Departures* magazine. His first book, *E is for Eating: An Alphabet of Greed* (2004) was an opinionated romp through the world of food. His next, *The Year of Eating Dangerously* (2006) explored the more weird and exotic delicacies of the world. And his third, *Full English: A Journey Through the British and Their Food* was published in 2009 and won the Guild of Food Writers 2010 award for best work on British food. The forthcoming *Let's Eat* (2012), is a collection of his favourite recipes, gathered from around the world and recreated in his own kitchen. Tom is also known for co-presenting *Market Kitchen* on Good Food Channel from 2007 to 2010. To counteract all that eating, he once joined a gym, but sadly, it disagreed with his delicate constitution.

* Contributing Authors *

Abigail Hole Writer on four editions of Lonely Planet *India*, and enthusiastic researcher of the sumptuous, tangled flavours of *Dilli ki chaat* (Delhi street food).

Amy Karafin Lonely Planet *India* co-author, former resident of Dakar, Accra and Bombay, and master scout of dirt-cheap, vegetarian food the world over.

Austin Bush Writer of Thai food blog www.austinbushphotography.com, food writer for guidebooks and magazines including *Saveur, Travel + Leisure Southeast Asia, Chile Pepper*, and *DestinAsian*.

Brett Atkinson Lead restaurant reviewer for www.viewauckland.co.nz, habitual street-food explorer, and cookery-class attendee in Vietnam, Laos, Turkey, Malaysia and New Zealand.

Bridget Gleeson *Time Out* restaurant reviewer and author of food articles for *Budget Travel, Delta Sky* and *Luxury Latin America* magazines.

Carolyn B Heller Writes the WanderFood blog at www.WanderlustandLipstick.com, contributes restaurant chapters to numerous guidebooks, and has eaten her way across five continents.

Celeste Brash Contributor to *The World as a Kitchen*, writer of food sections for Lonely Planet guidebooks and lonelyplanet.com and erstwhile professional cook.

Daniel Savery Raz Tel Aviv-based author who devoured Europe for *A Place in the Sun* magazine and often hunts for hummus. See www.danscribe.com.

Daniel Robinson Author of food reviews – and Lonely Planet guides – to culinary hot-spots such as France, Malaysia, Tunisia, Cambodia and Israel.

Duncan Garwood A dedicated fan of southern Italian food who has written for BBC's *Olive* magazine and co-authored Lonely Planet's *Sicily* guide.

Emily Matchar Culture and food writer for magazines and newspapers, and co-author of more than a dozen Lonely Planet guides.

Ethan Gelber Contributor to various Lonely Planet publications, editor-in-chief of www.thetravelword.com and passionate food lover.

Gregor Clark Co-author of many Lonely Planet guidebooks including *Brazil, South America on a Shoestring* (Uruguay) and *Italy*.

Jessica Lee Guidebook author and tour leader in the Middle East and North Africa, and avid Levantine cuisine foodie, still searching for the perfect hummus.

Joe Bindloss Former food critic for *Time Out*'s restaurant guides, specialising in food from Southeast Asia, China, Korea and the Indian subcontinent, and current Lonely Planet commissioning editor.

Johanna Uy Food writer and blogger at www.thehappydiner.wordpress.com.

Joshua Samuel Brown Co-author of nine Lonely Planet guides; restaurant reviewer for magazines and newspapers around Asia and maintains Taiwanese travel blog Snarky Tofu.

Kate Armstrong Author of food chapter for Lonely Planet *Portugal*, enthusiastic writer of articles on street food, and pastel de nata 'aficionado'.

Luke Waterson Food and drink editor for *Real Travel* magazine, long-time Latin American traveller, author for Lonely Planet's *Peru, Mexico* and *Cuba*, salteña addict, Andes obsessive.

Matt Bolton Senior staff writer at *Lonely Planet Magazine* UK, and a sucker for anything hot, flat and fried.

Meredith Snyder Spent her childhood helping out in the kitchen and sampling street food in Paris; her travel writing has appeared on the web at BBC Travel and Vagabondish.com.

Michael Kohn Author or co-author on more than 15 Lonely Planet titles, freelance correspondent for BBC, and fan of spicy snacks from Central Asian bazaars.

Paul Clammer Regular visitor to Morocco since 1994 – first as traveller, then as tour guide and currently as guidebook author.

Penny Watson Contributor to The Age *Cheap Eats* guide, Sydney Morning Herald *Good Food*, South China Morning Post *Food & Wine*, and full-time glutton.

Rob Whyte Co-author of Lonely Planet's *Korea*, South Korea resident and *hotteok* enthusiast.

Roger Norum and Strouchan Martins Food and travel writers for various magazines including *Olive*.

Sarah Baxter Associate editor of *Wanderlust* travel magazine, contributor to Lonely Planet books and national newspapers, and Cornish pasty lover.

Sarina Singh Contributor to Lonely Planet's *Out to Eat* series and prolific travel writer with a soft spot for all things spicy.

Tim Richards Travel writer who has written about foreign food delights for many publications (see iwriter.com.au); and amateur dukkah connoisseur.

Will Gourlay Inveterate commissioning editor, traveller to Turkey, the Balkans and the Middle East, and customer at streetside charcoal grills.

Zora O'Neill Co-author of *Forking Fantastic! Put the Party back in Dinner Party* and blogging at Roving Gastronome (rovinggastronome.com).

Recipes supplied by Abigail Hole, Amy Karafin, Brett Atkinson, Bridget Gleeson, Celeste Brash, Daniel Savery Raz, Daniel Robinson, Duncan Garwood, Emily Matchar, Ethan Gelber, Jane Ormond, Jessica Lee, Joe Bindloss, Johanna Uy, Joshua Samuel Brown, Kate Armstrong, Luke Waterson, Matt Bolton, Meredith Snyder, Michael Kohn, Paul Clammer, Penny Watson, Rob Whyte, Roger Norum, Sarah Baxter, Tim Richards, Will Gourlay, Zora O'Neill

* Index *

··

Type of Dish

Cover images
All supplied by Lonely Planet Images

Front cover, clockwise from top left:
Ice cream cart, Brazil (Holger Leue); Takoyaki stall, Japan (Rachel Lewis); Churros, USA (Ray Laskowitz); Teahouse, Myanmar (Peter Stuckings); Pretzels, USA (Lee Foster); Kuaytiaw, Thailand (Austin Bush); Food stalls at Djemaa el-Fna, Morocco (Chris Mellor); Street stalls, Canada (Richard l'Anson); Sfenj, Morocco (Steven Greaves); Crab with green peppercorns, Cambodia (Austin Bush)

Front flap:
Food stall on Djemaa el-Fna, Morocco (Doug McKinlay)

Back cover, clockwise from top left:
Night market, Thailand (Austin Bush); Bowl of pho, Vietnam (Austin Bush); Making dumplings, China (Ray Laskowitz); Biscuits cooking, South Korea (Martin Robinson)

Back flap:
Pouring tea in Bagan teahouse, Myanmar (Peter Stuckings)

Background images
Corbis
p186 Desgrieux

Getty Images
p38, Jay B Sauceda; p40, Stok-Yard Studio; p176, Tim White; multiple pages: Brand X Pictures; Simon Watson; Aaron Chambers; Lumina Imaging; Ray Laskowitz

iStockphoto
p14 Amanda Rohde; p40 Vladimir Popovic; p60 Ruud de Man; p72 Temmuz Can Arsiray; p180 Claudio Baldini; p194 Jose Ruiz; multiple pages: Hudiemm; Tjasam; Enviromantic; Kristen Johansen; Tanuki Photography; Stephen Blose

Lonely Planet Images
p44, 102 Greg Elms

The World's Best Street Food

March 2012
Published by Lonely Planet Publications Pty Ltd
ABN 36 005 607 983
90 Maribyrnong St, Footscray,
Victoria, 3011, Australia
www.lonelyplanet.com
10 9 8 7 6 5 4 3 2 1

Printed in China
Lonely Planet's preferred image source is
Lonely Planet Images
www.lonelyplanetimages.com

ISBN 978 1 74220 593 9
© Lonely Planet 2012
© Photographers as indicated 2012

Publisher Piers Pickard
Associate Publisher Ben Handicott
Commissioning Editor Bridget Blair
Designer Mark Adams
Image Researcher Rebecca Dandens
Layout Designer Margaret Jung
Editors Paul Harding, Kim Hutchins, Charlotte Orr,
Christopher Pitts
Pre-Press Production Ryan Evans
Print Production Yvonne Kirk
Thanks to Hugh Ford, Nic Lehman, Kylie
McLaughlin

Lonely Planet Offices
Australia
Locked Bag 1, Footscray, Victoria, 3011
Phone 03 8379 8000 Fax 03 8379 8111
Email talk2us@lonelyplanet.com.au

USA
150 Linden St, Oakland, CA 94607
Phone 510 250 6400 Toll free 800 275 8555 Fax 510
893 8572
Email info@lonelyplanet.com

Europe
UK 2nd Floor, 186 City Rd, London,
EC1V 2NT
Phone 020 7106 2100 Fax 020 7106 2101
Email go@lonelyplanet.co.uk

Paper in this book is certified against the
Forest Stewardship Council™ standards.
FSC™ promotes environmentally responsible,
socially beneficial and economically viable
management of the world's forests.

MIX
Paper from
responsible sources
FSC™ C021741
FSC
www.fsc.org

1

Leopard skin is the mark of a Zulu chief (**1**), and, by tradition, any leopard killed by a clansman is the property of his chief and may be worn only by him. Exceptions to the rule are diviners who are acknowledged for their special skills, and a chief's councillor who as a 'badge' of office may wear leopard skin, but only a narrow band around his head.

Headdresses of Zulu women often identify their clan or area of residence; for example, the matron (**2**) is a woman of the Cunu clan. Her wooden earplugs are also a

3

4

6

characteristic adornment, still often worn by her people in the Tugela Ferry area. Today, headpieces like hers are mostly removable, but, in times past, many were made by weaving coarse knitting wool into the hair to form a permanent fixture, closed on top. The inside is packed with dry herbs, and women have been known to hide small personal treasures in their headdresses. The arrangement is usually stained with ochre or a chemical dye and often smeared with fat or oil. The headdress shown in (3) is a style from the Eshowe district; that in (4) belongs to a woman of the actual Zulu clan living in the Mhlatuzi Valley. In (5) the women are of the Ntombela clan – the porcupine quills suggest Swazi influence – while in (6) the headdresses are representative of the Gwala clan, near Eshowe.

3

Dress and regalia at times may signify not only an indivdual's clan, but also his or her age-group and status. The two girls here (1) are of the Ntombela clan; their bare breasts show that they are unmarried, but the large, woman's-style headdress combined with the rest of her outfit, indicates that the girl on the right is betrothed. The splendid beadwork (2) is of the Mabaso clan near Tugela Ferry. Zulu womenfolk are renowned for their intricate beadwork, and spend many hours at this occupation making items of decoration for themselves and all the members of their family. The two young men in their impressive ceremonial regalia (3) were photographed at the Shakaland tourist centre near Eshowe, where aspects of Zulu traditional life can still be seen. A cheeky fringe of cloth (4) is usually worn by little girls, but their older sisters, too, are seen similarly adorned in certain areas.

These two children (5) are of the Cele clan and were dressed in the ceremonial finery of

1

3

2

4

4

4

their older sister (6) especially for the photograph. The men gathered in front of a hut (7) are also of the Cele clan; their 'warrior' garb, too, is reserved for special occasions such as weddings and is no longer everyday dress. These Zulu-speaking people live in a part of KwaZulu bordering on the Transkei, and their mud-plastered huts, in contrast to the beehive structures usually associated with the Zulu, show the influence of the Pondo, their Xhosa-speaking neighbours to the south. This matron (8) – her status is denoted by her headdress and covered torso – comes from near Isandlwana, the scene of a great battle in 1879, when the Zulu impis of Cetshwayo, the last of the warrior kings, decimated the British troops and threatened to overrun the whole of Natal.

In subsequent encounters, however, the redcoats defeated the Zulu, imprisoned Cetshwayo, and destroyed the once all but omnipotent military empire founded by Shaka some 60 years earlier.

5

7

8

5

1

2

3

LIFE AROUND THE HOME

The tending of the fields and the preparation of food is very much woman's work in the rural Zulu household. Three-legged, cast-iron pots are used for cooking over open fires (**1** and **4**). The wooden stamping block (**2**) is an indispensable utensil for crushing maize – which is boiled with dried beans. On the grinding stone, meal from both maize and sorghum is milled. Equally important around the home are clay pots for water and beer. Zulu women are adept at pottery, but the younger children play their part, too – this group (**3**) has been sent out to collect dried aloe leaves which are used as fuel to fire pots (see page 15).

The Zulu are a patriarchal society and, when sons of the family head marry, they bring their brides back to their father's home which is constantly enlarged with additional huts. Since polygamy is widely practised

4

and each wife is entitled to her own hut, the household may grow considerably — as many as 20 huts is not unknown. The arrangement of huts is far from haphazard and, with the cattle byre at the focus, each is placed strictly according to the status of its occupant. This homestead (5) shows the symmetrical layout of a medium-sized family in the remote Mhlatuzi Valley. This area is of great significance in Zulu history as it was at the confluence of the Mhlatuzi and Mvuzana rivers (6) that the young Shaka led his warriors to victory over King Zwide's Ndwandwe army under General Soshangane, thus becoming supreme head, King of all the clans of Zululand, and founder of the Zulu nation. The battle took place in 1819 and by coincidence within a kilometre or two of Shaka's birthplace — "Bull's Run" — about three-quarter-way into the centre of the photograph.

Courtship and marriage amongst the rural Zulu, as it is in all traditional black societies, is governed by strict procedures and protocol, but there are some aspects which are probably unique to the Zulu. For example, the two girls on the left of this photograph (1) are wearing men's clothes and are acting out part of a ceremony in which girls dress in their brother's regalia and set out to woo a chosen girl on his behalf. The other photographs depict common scenes around a Zulu home: an egg in a grass nest especially fashioned and placed in the cattle byre fence (2); a storage hut for dry maize on the cob (3), and a sorghum threshing floor (4).

3

1

2   4

This little boy (5) in the remote Keat's Drift area had probably not seen many white people in his short life and was not at all happy about the camera. The stone hut wall behind him is an interesting departure in construction method from the usual beehive which is thatched to the ground. The reason is purely practical and is quite common in areas where termites are a problem. The other, more confident fellow (6) is taking his father's flock out to browse after it has spent the night in the byre, protected from predators. Tending the livestock in the veld is very much the chore of the youngsters of the homestead.

In many rural Zulu communities there is a noticeable lack of grown men. This is a result of economic necessity: work opportunities are few and far between in country areas and adult men are frequently left with little choice but to leave the countryside to seek employment in the towns, cities and on the mines.

A girl places an *inkhata*, a circle of grass, on her friend's head (7) to help her carry a beer pot more comfortably. The pot shown would normally be used for drinking as those for carrying have a lip or flange around the top to prevent splashing.

1

2

It took a fair walk to reach this family settlement (**1**). I knew from previous experience that the white flag indicated that a man in the home had become engaged, but the red one puzzled me. A local Zulu said: '. . . yes, the white flag shows that he *is* engaged, but the red flag says that, even so, he has rich red blood and is looking for another girl as well'. I have not come across this anywhere else in my travels but rural traditions are so unique and localized at times that I would hesitate to contradict the accuracy of this interpretation.

A cow quietly chews her cud outside the byre of one of the remotest homes I have

3

5

6

visited (**2**), yet it was scarcely 20 kilometres from the town of Eshowe. The owner said: 'Yes, there *are* pythons here. . . and black mamba . . . and sometimes, even a leopard'.

The Zulu's abiding love of domestic animals is evident even in early childhood (**3**).

Natural materials are used almost exclusively in building Zulu 'beehive' huts. The framework of saplings tied with rushes is built by the men (**5**), while the thatching is done by women. The end result (**4**) is a sturdy and neatly constructed dwelling.

Sleeping mats (**6**) are made by the womenfolk using dried river rushes.

DANCING AND MUSIC

Long, long ago the Zulu people learned the recreational value of dancing and singing and to this day need little prompting to exercise their considerable talent. They put their all into it (**1** and **3**) and physical fitness

1

2

gives them amazing endurance. Although to the uninitiated these routines may seem spontaneous, many are highly structured. The complex steps and songs with their intricate harmonies often embody the traditions and lore of the clans handed down through generations. Not all music is a test of the muscles: this girl (**2**) pays close attention to every variation of tone as she taps away at the single string of *makweyena* in a serenade to her boyfriend.

3

Men's dancing (**4, 5** and **6**) invariably tends towards stylized battle movements. Small shields and good stout sticks (traditionally assegais) are part of the ceremonial regalia. With vigorous leaps, thrusts and parries they show off their prowess. Day or night is dancing time – whenever opportunity offers.

4

5

6

1

2

CRAFTS

Nimble fingers and sensitive hands mould and shape the many items necessary for daily living. In these scenes (**1** and **2**) a woman makes a beer strainer from a special type of grass. Beer strainers are also made from strips of lala palm leaves; a few of these lie against the hut in **2**. Though the process is not shown here, wine is made from the sap of the lala palm. (*Lala* is the Zulu word for sleep, referring no doubt to the soporific effects of the beverage.)

Zulu women are renowned as potters and the following sequence gives a glimpse of their technique. First the clay is prepared by kneading on a stone slab (**3**) and the base is fashioned and placed in a circle of grass, or *inkhata*, to steady the construction as the

3

4

6

7

5

8

sides are painstakingly built up and rounded (**5** and **4**). The completed pot is then patterned with a shaped piece of dry gourd, and polished with a smooth stone. Patterns are sometimes engraved while the clay is still soft with a strong plastic hair comb (**6**). The pot is fired in strong, hot flames fueled by the resinous leaves of the aloe (**7**) – it emerges brown or red and is then enclosed in a heap of dry grass and blackened in a fast-burning, smokey fire (**8**).

In his *Zulu-English Dictionary* Dr A.T. Bryant says of Zulu pottery: 'The African pottery of today is often in shape and pattern strongly similar to vessels made in the East, and the simple earthen pots nowadays common in every Zulu kraal are almost identical with those in Egypt at a period 6 000 years ago'.

Spears and drums are synonymous with Zulu life. The young man here (1) pares a stick for a spear shaft down to his chosen 'feel'. At the beginning of the 1800s – when Shaka Zulu moulded the Zulu nation – the people already had primitive foundries where they smelted iron ore and made their own spearheads. A grisly legend has it that they used human blood in the forging process to improve the quality of the steel.

1

Zulu country is sub-tropical and drums need regular attention: the hot, humid weather slackens the tension of the cowhide drums, which then have to be tightened by drying them out beside a fire (2).

2

The origins of beadwork are uncertain but it is a craft at which the Zulu women excel, rivalled only by their Nguni kinsfolk – the Ndebele farther to the north in the Transvaal, and the Xhosa to the south in the Transkei, Ciskei and Cape Province. Here a young girl patiently picks up tiny glass beads on a needle (3). Today, the fashion is to use cotton from the nearest trader's store for threading beadwork, but traditionally, oxgut was used. Gut is still regarded as the best material, but not all families still know how to prepare it. Examples of fine beadwork include this beer pot lid of beaded grasswork (4) and two different types of belts for women (5 and 8). Zulu men are accomplished carvers of wood, as evidenced by these antiques – a milking pail (6) and a meat tray (7).

4

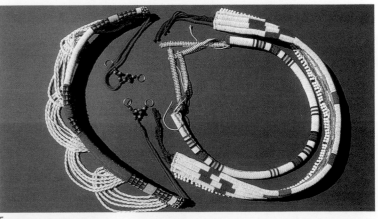

5

6

7

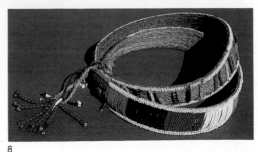

8

3

CEREMONIES AND RELIGION

The man blowing the horn (1) announces to the neighbourhood that he or a man of the family has become engaged. He may blow it every evening at dusk for a week. Then his girlfriend secludes herself in some quiet area and waits for visitors to come and 'see her beauty'. A girl's 'coming out' ceremony (2) is a most important event as it announces her availability for marriage. The drape over her chest and shoulders is fat from a newly killed ox. The bank notes in her hair were pinned there by male admirers.

The youngest of six wives (3) of a prosperous man of the Cele clan.

1

2

3

Beer drinking is an integral part of any gathering or festival and here a man (4) offers beer in customary fashion. Sacrifice, too, is very much part of the traditional way of life and is done to placate and please the ancestral spirits. For this purpose a goat is sometimes killed by stabbing an assegai down through the neck to the heart (5).

4

5

6

8

7

Traditional Zulu religion is ancestor worship, but Christianity has gained considerable ground. A popular cult is that founded by a Zulu prophet named Shembe. Unlike many missionaries of old who insisted that national dress be discarded on becoming a Christian, Shembe encouraged it. Meetings on ceremonial dates, with dancing and singing, drums and trumpets, are indeed awe-inspiring occasions (**6**, **7** and **8**).

DIVINERS

1

2

3

4

Sangomas, or diviners, are people of considerable power in traditional Zulu society and even in the relatively westernized black urban communities they wield a great deal of influence. The *sangomas'* power derives from the belief that they alone are able to mediate between people and their ancestral spirits. The following photographs depict aspects of a *sangoma's* world and, because they were taken in different areas, show different forms of regalia. The subjects range from an old grandmother in deep discussion with her grandson, who is already a *sangoma* at fourteen (1); a tutor leading her pupils in their graduation dance (2); two girl *twasas*, or initiates (3); two men setting their problems before their *sangoma* (4) and a vigorous old practitioner performing a ritual dance in her sanctum (5).

Sangomas have many functions, and they wage a never-ending battle against witches and people with evil intent. This old and experienced diviner at Shakaland (1) instructs her *twasa* how to sprinkle medicine around the home to protect it against witches and (2) she burns incense in a potsherd to clear the air and call up her ancestral spirits. She may also froth up medicine in a clay pot for the purpose. When the spirits arrive, they 'sit' in the beaded loops beside her head and speak into her ear. But only *she* can tune into them and hear their 'voices'. A further study of this colourful old character is given on page 24.

1

2

Headdresses differ among *sangomas* but most contain gall bladders of sacrificed animals and here the skin of a red fowl has been added (**3**). The fresh warm skin was put on the *sangoma's* head and allowed to dry there, assuming the shape of her head.

When I first met Nyamakaheesh (**4**), he had never been photographed. He had consistently refused 'because. . .' (he said) '. . .with the possession of my image, another can bewitch me'. Once I had come to know him well I photographed him many times at *his* request 'because. . .' (he said again) '. . .you must not waste film on just *anyone.*'

5

In the Zulu home cattle horns are displayed with pride above the door to the hut (**5**) as they are from animals offered up to the ancestral spirits and show everyone that the family has not forgotten its forefathers.